CLEAR BLUE WATER?

The Conservative Party and the welfare state since 1940

Robert M. Page

First published in Great Britain in 2015 by

Policy Press
University of Bristol
1-9 Old Park Hill
Bristol
BS2 8BB
UK
t: +44 (0)117 954 5940
pp-info@bristol.ac.uk
www.policypress.co.uk

North America office:
Policy Press
c/o The University of Chicago Press
1427 East 60th Street
Chicago, IL 60637, USA
t: +1 773 702 7700
f: +1 773-702-9756
sales@press.uchicago.edu
www.press.uchicago.edu

British Library Cataloguing in Publication Data
A catalogue record for this book is available from the British Library

Library of Congress Cataloging-in-Publication Data
A catalog record for this book has been requested

ISBN 978 1 84742 986 5 hardcover

Cover design by Policy Press from an original idea by Robert M. Page
Front cover image kindly supplied by London Transport Museum Ltd
Printed and bound in Great Britain by by CPI Group (UK) Ltd, Croydon, CR0 4YY
Policy Press uses environmentally responsible print partners

Dedicated to the University of Kent
on its 50th anniversary

Contents

About the author

Robert M. Page is currently Reader in Democratic Socialism and Social Policy at the University of Birmingham. He was formerly a Lecturer in Social Policy at St David's University College, Lampeter (1980-88), Lecturer in Social Policy and Administration at the University of Nottingham (1988-98), and Senior Lecturer and then Reader in Social Policy at the University of Leicester (1998-99). He has written on a wide range of social policy topics particularly the British welfare state since 1940.

Other books by Robert M. Page include:

Stigma, London: Routledge and Kegan Paul, 1984.

Modern thinkers on welfare, Hemel Hempstead: Harvester-Wheatsheaf/ Prentice-Hall, 1995, (Edited with Vic George).

Altruism and the British welfare state, Aldershot: Avebury, 1996.

British social welfare in the 20th Century, London: Macmillan, 1999, (Edited with Richard Silburn)

Understanding social problems, Oxford: Blackwell, 2001, (Edited with Edward Brunsdon and Margaret May).

Global social problems, Cambridge: Polity, 2004, (Edited with Vic George).

Revisiting the welfare state, Maidenhead: McGraw-Hill/Open University Press, 2007.

Acknowledgements

The University of Kent at Canterbury celebrates its 50th anniversary in 2015.[1] It seems appropriate therefore to acknowledge the part that 'UKC', as it was formerly known, has played in my own career. I was fortunate to have been both an undergraduate and postgraduate student during what can be described as a golden era from 1973 to 1979. I came into contact with a wide range of sparkling and erudite scholars not just in my chosen undergraduate degree programme in social policy and administration but also in allied subjects such as economics, law, politics, sociology and social anthropology. Vic George then encouraged me to study for a higher degree. My PhD thesis entitled 'Felt stigma and the unmarried mother: a social policy and administration approach', formed the basis of my first book, *Stigma*, which was published in 1984. By happy coincidence, a new edition of this book will also be published this year.

I am greatly indebted to Jane Wilton for all her love, support and encouragement during the long gestation period of this book. I am particularly grateful to her for reading and commenting so perceptively on successive drafts of this volume when I am sure she would have much rather spent her 'spare' time playing tennis.

I would also like to record my thanks to all those at Policy Press who have been so supportive at every stage of this project, in particular Alison Shaw, Emily Watt, Laura Greaves, Laura Vickers and Susannah Emery.

Preface

A number of authoritative texts have been published charting the development of the British welfare state. Some of these books cover developments as far back as the Elizabethan age,[1] while others have focused on narrower time frames.[2] Texts devoted to the ideology and policies of a specific political party have been far fewer in number.[3]

The idea of a pervasive welfare consensus or settlement is one of the factors that helps to explain the preponderance of cross-party accounts of welfare developments since the Second World War. From this perspective it is argued that, during the period between 1945 and 1979,[4] both Conservative and Labour governments came to accept the case for a mixed economy, for the need for economic interventionism to secure growth and full employment, and for a protective welfare state. Although there has been a lively debate as to whether such accords were more akin to a pragmatic accommodation (settlement) than some form of deep 'ideological' fusion (consensus),[5] the most common viewpoint is that there were more points of agreement than difference between the major parties. The dominance of what can be termed the 'social administration' approach to social policy[6] also helps to explain why there have been relatively few party political accounts of social policy developments since the war. From a social administration perspective, social policy has come to be seen as more of a technical endeavour that is best left in the hands of independent, empirically sophisticated, 'boffins',[7] who will devise solutions for those social problems deemed to require ameliorative action.

One of the other factors that helps explain the paucity of Conservative accounts of the post-war welfare state is the party's lukewarm or even hostile disposition to this type of collective arrangement. For many traditional Conservatives, Labour's post-war construction of the welfare state was a further example of the kind of 'enterprising' endeavour that politicians and governments should studiously avoid on the grounds that it will disturb the organic equilibrium that has evolved gradually and peacefully over time.

There are, however, some compelling interrelated reasons as to why the Conservative approach to the welfare state is worthy of study in its own right. First, the Conservative Party has been in power for considerable periods of time since the Second World War. As such, it has actively shaped the development of the welfare state and, as a consequence, has had a significant impact on the life chances and opportunities of millions of British citizens. Even if one were to accept that the Conservatives only govern on the basis of pragmatism or common sense, an exploration of their policy and practice is likely to prove illuminating. The fact, however, that many commentators have identified the Conservatives as an ideological party provides a second reason as to why a study of the party's approach to the welfare state may be of value. Exploring the ideological positioning of the Conservative Party over time enables one to understand more clearly why it has not only resisted specific welfare initiatives emanating from its political opponents but also pursued strategies that are more likely to fulfil some of its long-term ambitions such as the creation of a property-owning democracy. Third, an in-depth study of the party's approach to the welfare state also alerts one to the additional possibility that there might not be one overarching Conservative approach to the welfare state but rather a number of competitive visions. In the same way that observation of the ebb and flow of a river at different times of the day or year will reveal subtle differences in the colouration of the water, so an in-depth study of Conservative thinking and practice can reveal different hues of 'blue'.

This book identifies four distinctive post-war Conservative approaches to the welfare state. While each draws from the family of Conservative values and beliefs outlined in Chapter One, significant differences of emphasis and approach can be identified. One Nation Conservatives (Chapters Two and Three), for example, believe that the state has a positive 'welfare' function to perform. They are also more favourably disposed towards working-age adults who are unfortunate enough to require financial assistance from public funds, believing that this is more likely to result from ill fortune rather than laziness or some other undesirable personal attribute. While the modern technocratic Conservatives discussed in Chapter Four also draw on a broad range of traditional Conservative themes, they regard themselves as decidedly un-ideological, preferring to rely instead on an eclectic mix of Conservative ideas that they believe will enable the nation to advance both economically and socially. Neo-liberal Conservatives (Chapter Five) have expressed concerns about the 'pale blue' approach to the welfare state adopted by both One Nation and modern technocratic Conservatives. They sought to establish a more authentically 'blue' approach to the welfare state that focused on the harm that this institution had caused to British society and the consequent need to introduce a more radical form of change based on individualism, freedom and choice. More recently, the progressive neo-liberal Conservatives (Chapter Six) have distanced themselves from their older neo-liberal sibling by adopting a more emollient tone towards social minorities and by developing a positive, rather than negative, narrative when making the case for welfare reform.

The title of this volume, *Clear blue water?*, is not intended to convey the impression that the book will identify and then analyse key differences between Conservative and Labour Party approaches to the welfare state, though these will certainly be alluded to. Rather, the term is used to refer to an attempt to discover if there is a distinct Conservative approach to the welfare state. In this endeavour it will often be necessary to refer to economic and industrial policy during the period under review in order to provide some necessary context for the social policy developments that occurred in a particular epoch.

Finally, this book will not attempt to provide a comprehensive evaluation of the merits and demerits of Conservative social policy in the post-war era. The aim is to explore Conservative ideas and the ways in which they have been articulated by leading political actors in order to gain a better understanding of the party's approach to the welfare state since the Second World War.

Robert M. Page
Selly Park, Birmingham
January 2015

ONE

Conservatism, the 'modern' Conservative Party and the welfare state

In this chapter, an attempt will be made to explore some of the values and ideas that have come to define conservatism.[1] The discussion will have an Anglo-centric focus, although many of these themes will have broader applicability.[2] This will be followed by a review of the influential strands of conservatism that have been embraced by the modern Conservative Party and their impact on thinking about the welfare state. The chapter concludes with a short contextual overview of the party's approach to state welfare in the early decades of the 20th century.

Conservatism

In his book on conservatism, Roger Scruton (2001) captures the elusive nature of this doctrine, arguing that it rarely announces

> itself in maxims, formulae or aims. Its essence is inarticulate, and its expression, when compelled, sceptical. But it is capable of expression, and in times of crisis, forced either by political necessity, or by the clamour for doctrine, conservatism does its best, though not always with any confidence that the words it finds will match the instinct that required them. (p 1)

At root, the notion of conservatism is most closely associated with a desire to protect or preserve an established or familiar way of living. While this represents a useful starting position, it begs the question of what is to be protected and for what purpose? As Heywood (2007) notes, 'if conservatism were to consist of no more than a knee-jerk defence of the *status quo*, it would be merely a political attitude rather than an ideology. In fact, many people or groups can be considered "conservative" in the sense that they resist change, but certainly cannot be said to subscribe to a conservative political creed' (p 68).

It is important to note that many self-professed conservatives, including those who are members or supporters of the Conservative Party, would regard themselves as having non-ideological inclinations and dispositions that develop slowly and are 'honed by maturity and experience of life' (Ball, 2013, p 2). Their attitudes towards economic and social issues are formed on the basis of common sense and pragmatism rather than a premeditated ideological stance.[3] From this perspective, then, conservatism is portrayed as pragmatic, moderate, and protective of an existing social order that has stood the test of time.[4] This emphasis on the non-ideological nature of conservatism owes much to a desire on the part of those who subscribe to this creed to distinguish themselves from what they regard as the 'ideological' doctrines of liberalism and socialism based on 'grand schemes of social engineering' (Eccleshall et al, 1984, p 80).[5] For conservatives, it is always preferable to keep to 'the broad road of pragmatism' than leave it 'for the dense thickets of principle' (Charmley, 2008, p 2).

While conservatism may be difficult to define precisely, this should not automatically preclude it from being regarded as an ideology.[6] As Heywood (2007) argues, 'conservatism is neither simple pragmatism nor mere opportunism. It is founded on a particular set of political beliefs about human beings, the societies they live in, and the importance of a distinctive set of political values. As such like liberalism and socialism, it should rightly be described as an ideology' (p 68). In a similar vein, Green (2002) contends that conservatives must have 'an ideological map of the world' of some kind if they are to be in a position to 'identify objects of approval and disapproval, friend and foe' (p 3).

What then are the distinguishing features of this ideological perspective? Five interrelated aspects of conservatism that have informed Conservative Party thinking can be identified.

1. Human nature and aptitudes, 'perfectibility' and inequality

Those of a conservative disposition have tended to adopt what they would describe as 'realistic' or 'common sense' views of human nature in which instinct and desire are accorded greater weight than logic and rationality. While conservatives acknowledge that human beings can be reflective and rational and on occasions selfless, they contend that such virtues coexist with much stronger baser impulses, which can give rise to selfish and antisocial forms of conduct. Given the depth of human frailty, conservatives believe it is vital to control for the possibility of harmful acts through the rule of law and the threat of punishment.

Unlike many liberals and socialists, conservatives reject the idea that it might prove possible to 'improve' individuals or the wider society through reasoned argument. As Gray (2009) notes, 'British Tories have not swallowed the canard that human life is open to indefinite improvement by judicious use of critical reason. For them, human reason is a weak reed, on which they must rely in daily life and in the formation of policies, but in which it is folly to have faith' (p 136).

Conservatives also subscribe to the view that there are significant differences in human characteristics, qualities and capabilities. As Willetts (1992) explains, there are naturally occurring 'inequalities in looks, in intelligence, in talents and prudence. We are not equally good singers or runners. We have different aptitudes' (p 111). While such differences are likely to result in a wide diversity of life experiences and the emergence of a class-based society, this is not seen as justifying 'artificial' government interventions designed to improve the prospects of those not fortunate enough to have secured a winning ticket in life's lottery. While conservatives will seek to counter serious forms of inhumanity within society, they are extremely reluctant to take action to prevent outcomes that reflect the impact of natural inequalities. As Dorey (2011) notes, 'if human nature is such that individuals are naturally both unequal in their attributes, and motivated primarily by self-interest or acquisitiveness, then it logically follows that there can be no moving inevitably towards a better model of society, or even the creation of a new society' (p 10). Non-interference of this kind is also supported by more religiously minded conservatives who believe that secular interventionism runs counter to divine or transcendent intent. From this perspective, prevailing economic and social hierarchies reflect the will of God and the resultant inequalities should therefore be accepted rather than challenged. The compensation for those who lose out in this process is the prospect 'of a better afterlife by virtue of working hard and displaying due deference and respect to their apparent superiors ... in this world' (Dorey, 2011, pp 12-13). Secular attempts to iron out economic and social inequalities that arise from natural differences are deemed to be futile. It is argued that once these artificial impediments are withdrawn, inequality will quickly take hold once again. As Braine (1948) contends, 'Some men will be rich, some will be poor. Some will be masters, some will be servants. A few will lead, the rest will follow. In a free society material inequality is natural and fundamental' (p 67). Conservatives maintain that a 'levellers' strategy, though deemed ethically superior by some of their opponents, is both impractical and unrealisable.

Inequality is also defended by conservatives on the grounds that it brings mutual benefits to both rich and poor. Allowing the 'talented' to rise to the top is seen as the best means of ensuring economic prosperity and forms of governance that will benefit all members of society. Attempts to stifle the talented on the basis of envy or 'social justice' benefits no one.[7] A number of conservatives have also raised concerns about the illegitimate means that would have to be employed by any government that is determined to create a more egalitarian society. In *The middle way*, Harold Macmillan (1938) warns against the threat to personal freedom such interference would bring. 'I do not see how Britain with all its rich diversity and vitality, could be turned into an egalitarian society without, as we have seen in Eastern Europe, a gigantic exercise in despotism' (p xviii).

2. Tradition, hierarchy, order and social change

Conservatives place great store on tradition, seeing it as 'the aggregated wisdom of generations' (O'Hara, 2011, p 26). Institutions, such as the common law and parliamentary conventions, which have stood the test of time are seen as being beneficial for contemporary citizens as well as for future generations.[8] Although some of these 'traditions' might have a more contemporary provenance than is commonly recognised,[9] it is still deemed preferable to rely on them rather than opt for rational, expert formulated, alternatives. Crucially, the continued vitality of any tradition is deemed to depend on active adherence to social conventions and common courtesies, not on vague theoretical commitments.[10]

Conservatives are committed to the maintenance of hierarchy in society. According to Edmund Burke, the 18th-century 'Whig' political philosopher (who many regard as the father of modern Conservative thought),[11] the ruling aristocracy was regarded as having an inalienable and inherent right to rule on account of both its natural social 'superiority' as well as its long-standing practical experience of exercising leadership within society. Burke favoured, for example, the retention of a hereditary second chamber within the British parliamentary system on the grounds that it was populated by those whose concerns 'were not the short-term interests of a living human being, but the long-term interests of a family. And first among such interests is a deep-seated desire for social and political continuity' (Scruton, 2001, p 49). While some conservatives have been willing to accept the need to replenish the upper echelons of society on the basis of merit, they have tended to favour a more gradual form of social mobility than their liberal counterparts. Indeed, Peregrine Worsthorne

(1978) reminds conservatives of the need to take all necessary steps to 'prevent tomorrow's aspirants to power pushing themselves upwards so fast that nobody can rule in an orderly and civilized fashion' (p 141). As he pointedly remarks, conservatism 'is about resisting over-speedy renewal of the ruling class, to the point where evolution descends into revolution' (p 141).

Conservatives attach great importance to the maintenance of social order, based on the rule of law, within society, as this is seen as a prerequisite for the exercise of personal freedom. In contrast to liberals, who believe that the exercise of authority should be a matter of negotiation between free individuals, conservatives prefer to rely on tried and tested methods in which authority is vested in those adjudged best able, on grounds of well-established status, to exercise such power. In short, there is a natural demarcation between those who enforce the rules and those who are expected to abide by them.[12] As Heywood (2007) notes, 'In schools authority should be exercised by the teacher, in the workplace, by the employer, and in society at large, by government. Conservatives believe that authority is necessary and beneficial as everyone needs the guidance, support and security of knowing "where they stand" and what is expected of them' (p 77). Importantly, those whose role it is to follow the rules are deemed to gain as much benefit from this process as those enforcing them.

In turning to the issue of social change, one might assume that conservatives would be implacably opposed to change. Indeed, the conservative voice is usually at its most vocal during periods of rapid change or transition such as when Burke counselled against the harmful consequences of the French revolution. However, although conservatives are wary of change, not least when it is has an ideological basis, they recognise that society is not static and that legitimate 'adjustments' can be sanctioned as long as they are slow and measured and the perceived capacity for harm is adjudged minimal.[13] As Gray (2009) makes clear, for conservatives 'the costs and advantages of reform need always to be weighed in detail, radical reform should go with the grain of the national character and tradition rather than against it, and conservatives should view with the deepest suspicion proposals for radical reform that are inspired by hubristic ideology rather than by evident necessity' (p 136). Importantly, although conservatives may lament the loss of some traditions as a result of social 'evolution', this does not mean that they will then seek to restore a 'lost' past as soon as the opportunity presents itself. As Gray (2009) contends, 'the sound conservative policy cannot be nostalgic in inspiration: once the cake of custom is broken, we must do our best with what is left. It cannot be baked anew' (pp 137–8).

3. The individual and the wider society

Conservatives believe in the freedom of the individual and have always opposed attempts by collectivists to impose unnecessary constraints on the ability of citizens to make meaningful choices or to follow a particular life course provided their actions are legal and do not harm others. However, it is recognised that individuals value association with others within the family, at work and in leisure pursuits.[14] Accordingly, conservatives believe that any meaningful understanding of individualism must be linked to existing social contexts rather than to abstract theory. Individuals are seen to exercise personal freedom within an existing social order based on tradition and custom and a complex system of rights and responsibilities. From this perspective, it is not possible for individuals to be detached from the norms and mores of a pre-existing community. It is within these varied communities and through the operation of long-standing intermediary institutions that 'individuals are formed and which for the most part their lives find meaning' (Gray, 2009, p 141).

Conservatives have been highly supportive of the notion of society, believing that it amounts to something more than the statistical aggregation of the individuals within it. Society is seen as a delicate, evolving organism in which all individuals have a unique and vital role to play. As Heywood (2007) explains, 'organisms are not simply a collection of individual parts that can be arranged and, indeed, rearranged at will. Within an organism, the whole is more than a collection of its individual parts; the whole is sustained by a fragile set of relationships between and amongst its parts, which, once damaged, can result in the organism's death' (p 74). It is not surprising, therefore, that when conservatives question the existence of an organic society of this kind, such as when Margaret Thatcher declared (in an interview with *Woman's Own* in September 1987) that 'there is no such thing' as society, it is always likely to cause consternation among traditionalists.[15] While conservatives concede that this social organism will evolve and adapt over time, assisted where needed by judicious forms of government intervention, they believe that radical forms of surgery should always be resisted.

4. Private property and the market

For conservatives, the ability to own and dispose of property is seen as a natural human instinct that is socially valuable. According to Quentin Hogg (1947), the author of the influential post-war text *The case for Conservatism*, there are four 'interconnected reasons' as to why conservatives support the notion of private property (pp 99-102). First, 'property' has come to be seen as an integral part of an individual's 'character' (on which conservatives place such great store[16]) or 'personality'. Possessions in the form of the ownership of a home or a particular make of car come to define and 'locate' the individual. Second, private property can bolster the family: '[P]rivate property is the natural right and safeguard of the family, which is itself the natural unit of society and is and ought to be the foundation of the whole fabric of civilized society' (Hogg, 1947, p 100). Third, the existence of private property benefits the wider community by providing individuals with a legitimate incentive to work hard and become financially secure. Fourth, private property ensures that wealth is not concentrated in the hands of an oppressive government or state. As Norton (1996) argues, it 'imparts a necessary bulwark against the over-mighty state. To vest all property in the state would leave the citizen naked in confronting tyranny' (p 75). During the post-1945 period, Conservative leaders such as Eden and Thatcher promoted the expansion of home ownership on all of these grounds.[17]

For conservatives, the distribution of property, like income, reflects 'natural' disparities in talent, ability and endeavour. As such, they oppose any attempt by government to redistribute property on egalitarian grounds, not least because they believe that such remedies would create more harm than good. They do, however, contend that property ownership does entail certain obligations and responsibilities. For example, those who inherit an historic family estate are seen as having a duty to maintain the property and protect precious heirlooms, such as works of art, in order that they can be enjoyed by subsequent generations. Property owners are also expected to ensure that the enjoyment they gain from the ownership of property does not come at the expense of the well-being of their neighbours or of the wider community. Scruton (2001) even goes so far to suggest that conservatives should be willing to accept 'a law of forfeiture' in cases where it can clearly be demonstrated that this would bolster 'the order and equilibrium of society' (pp 97-8).

Conservatives have also been highly supportive of the free market, believing that it represents the best means for generating wealth and prosperity. Markets are seen as being able to respond quickly and impartially to changes in consumer preferences through the price mechanism, a device that also alerts producers to the need to adapt if they are to secure increased profits or stem losses. The fact that market activity and the resultant outcomes are seen to result from mutually beneficial forms of voluntary, spontaneous activity, rather than forcible forms of collective planning, is seen as having other beneficial social consequences. Free markets ensure that workers do not press for unrealistic wage increases that will lead to unemployment, while producers are mindful of the potentially adverse consequences to their livelihood if they decide to increase their prices above those of their main competitors.

Conservative support for the free market is, however, contingent rather than absolute. Conservatives recognise that market activity needs to be regulated, controlled and sometimes overridden to ensure that it does not have detrimental effects on other fundamental aspects of social life. Moreover, as Gray (2009) makes clear, market activity only represents one aspect of human life.

> Vital as the market is as an expression of individual freedom, it is only one dimension of society in which individuals make choices and exercise responsibility. People also live in families and belong to churches and other voluntary associations in which market exchange is inappropriate or peripheral. (p 156)

5. Democracy, the state and the role of government

Given their belief in hierarchy, order and tradition, conservatives have tended to be cautious in lending their support to increased forms of democracy. According to Scruton (2001), unmoderated forms of democracy that privilege 'the living and their immediate interests over past and future generations' (p 47) can undermine the longer-term 'needs' of the community and the nation. In addition, the conservative assumption that wisdom and knowledge are unequally distributed in society has led its advocates to oppose any deepening of democracy that might transfer power from a 'responsible' elite to an 'uneducated' and ill-informed 'mass'. Calls to extend democracy to the 'ordinary' citizen in previous eras have often been resisted because of fears that those newly enfranchised might attempt to redistribute wealth from rich to poor. In periods of economic and social unrest, democracy might even prompt an 'unsophisticated' electorate to turn to an authoritarian leader, who might pose a threat to long-standing freedoms and the rule of law.

However, conservatives have also come to recognise that increased forms of representative democracy can have positive effects. Extending the franchise was seen as one way of forestalling social unrest and preventing revolutionary forms of change. The fact that 'patriotic' members of the working class were reluctant to support the General Strike called by the TUC in 1926 persuaded many Conservatives that an increased electorate would not give rise to disruptive challenges to the established order. Moreover, by giving an electoral voice to the working class, the Conservatives would be able to demonstrate that they were genuinely interested in ameliorating the harsh economic and social conditions endured by those subsisting on modest incomes. It should also be noted that working-class electoral support has proved invaluable in securing the long-term electoral success of the Conservative Party.[18]

The conservative approach to the state and the role of government is, like its advocates' view of democracy, also highly nuanced. On the one hand, the state is seen as the embodiment of institutions and traditions that have stood the test of time and as a consequence is regarded as being a legitimate source of authority by all members of society. As Lord Cecil (1912) claimed, 'as long as State action does not involve what is unjust or oppressive, it cannot be said that the principles of Conservatism are hostile to it' (cited in White, 1950, p 88). What, then, constitutes an appropriate role for government? According to Gray (2009), Conservative governments have a wide range of legitimate duties. They have 'a responsibility to tend fragile and precious traditions, to protect and shelter the vulnerable and defenceless, to enhance and enlarge opportunities for the disadvantaged, to promote the conservation and renewal of the natural and human environment and to assist in the renewal of civic society and the reproduction of the common culture without which pluralism and diversity become enmity and division' (p 138).

Although the state may often perform its legitimate functions in a highly effective and responsive fashion, conservatives are always alert to the possibility of the emergence of an overly authoritarian state that might run rough shod over ancient liberties or might over-extend itself in ways that threaten social stability. In the case of the former, conservatives have expressed concern about the threat of socialist ideas. The prospect of 'a nation herded into community centres, served by municipal shops and ale houses, restricted, confined and supervised by hordes of unloving officials' (Braine, 1948, p 5) fills them with dread. In terms of the latter, Willetts (1992) argues that 'conservatives have learned through painful experience that big government does not embody a sense of community but threatens it. If our benign and co-operative relations with our fellow citizens become instead functions of the state, then we are indeed reduced to merely atomistic individuals pursuing our own self-interest' (p 74). For conservatives, the encroachment of the central state is seen as being particularly threatening to civil society, localism and the tradition of mutualism.[19] Accordingly, as a rule of thumb, state intervention should be avoided when civil society in all its manifestations is deemed to be working effectively. It is only when it malfunctions and is incapable of self-correction that the state should step in.

While all of these five interrelated themes can be said to form part of the British Conservative tradition, those who subscribe to this political 'ideology' are unlikely to agree on the relative weight that should be placed on any particular element. Indeed, the emphasis on pragmatism within conservative thought often results in certain elements coming to prominence at different points in time. Moreover, it is entirely possible for members of the Conservative Party to hold a heady mix of libertarian, authoritarian and paternalistic views on social and economic issues simultaneously.[20]

In the next part of this chapter, attention will focus on the relationship between conservative ideas and the British Conservative Party in the 'modern' era. What form or strands of conservatism have held sway within the party during this period?

Conservatism, the 'modern' Conservative Party and the welfare state since 1940

Since its 'formation' in the 1830s, the Conservative Party has, like other major political parties, been home to a broad range of opinions and traditions. Over time, it has experienced its share of internal strife and controversy over issues such as free trade and tariff reform, the Irish 'question', imperialism and fledgling forms of state welfare.[21] The diverse response of Conservative politicians to questions of this kind makes it extremely difficult to argue that a distinctive form of conservatism has taken firm root within the party. It is more the case that a particular variant of conservatism has dominated at a particular point of time.

A number of authors have attempted to identify the particular strand of Conservatism that has held sway in specific eras. In a typology of the Conservative tradition from the 1830s to the 1930s, Leach (2009), for example, distinguishes between Peelite Conservatism in the 1830s and '40s (pragmatism, gradualism, acceptance of parliamentary reform, repeal of the Corn Laws), Disraelian Conservatism in the 1860s and '70s ('One Nation', paternalism, patriotism and imperialism, 'Tory democracy') and Unionism from the mid-1880s to the 1930s (preservation of the union with Ireland, imperial preference, protection, social reform). Hickson (2005), in a review of the post-1945 period, identifies four distinctive Conservative 'ideological' perspectives: traditional Toryism, New Right, centrist and One Nation. Those who subscribe to the tenets of traditional Toryism remain strongly attached to the nation, the maintenance of social order and the need to uphold the authority of the state. Those of a New Right persuasion share many of the core values of the traditional Tories, but can be distinguished by their embrace of economic liberalism. They believe that the development of state involvement in both the economic and social spheres has curtailed economic freedom and resulted in the growth of undesirable forms of welfare dependency. As the name implies, centrists are to be found in the middle of a shifting left-right spectrum. They favour 'pragmatic' as opposed to 'ideological' policymaking. As Garnett and Hickson (2009) contend, 'Centrists are concerned primarily with party unity and loyalty to the party leadership in order to best win elections' (p 4). They are associated closely with the notion of 'statecraft' – the art of winning elections and securing a reputation for governing competence in areas of major importance such as foreign affairs and economic policy.[22] As Hickson (2005) notes, from this perspective, the 'aim of the Conservative Party should be to win elections, maintain control of "high" politics and leave "low" politics to others. The central state would retain power over key areas of decision-making and the authority of the state could be maintained by not getting embroiled in "low" politics, thus minimising the number of policy areas it would be responsible for and the number of controversies in which it would become embroiled and thereby allowing a greater chance for the Conservative Party to maintain power' (p 181).

The roots of the One Nation tradition can be traced back to Disraeli's stark observation about the two 'strangers' (the rich and the poor) in British society whose only common reference point was their 'inhabiting' of the same terrain. It places great emphasis on the need to maintain social unity within an economically unequal society. The pursuit of this goal has led One Nation Conservatives to accept the case for economic interventionism and state welfare.

Another 'contemporary' classification scheme has been provided by Peter Dorey (2011) in his study of British Conservatism and inequality. Dorey distinguishes between One Nation Conservatism, neo-liberal

Conservatism and post-Thatcherite Conservatism. In terms of the second of these categories, Dorey equates 'neo-liberalism' with 'those Conservatives (both in the party itself and among their intellectual acolytes among what became known, during the 1970s, as the New Right) who were free market fundamentalists'. They believed that the 'market and individual or private endeavour were the only viable or feasible means of wealth creation and resource allocation, and were therefore inclined to attribute most economic problems not to "market failure" but to governmental refusal to allow "the market" to operate naturally free from political interference' (p 111). The 'new' Conservatism that has emerged in the post-Thatcher era is seen as having a stronger civic element. According to Dorey (2011), 'the new Conservative narrative depicts Thatcherism as over-relying on "the market" to tackle social problems, while (New) Labour looks first and foremost to the state for solutions. The New Conservatism, though, purports to look to society itself, as constituted by a multiplicity of families, communities, voluntary bodies, charities and social enterprises, to tackle societal problems and thereby re-establish One Nation' (p 166).

In this volume, which covers the period from 1940 to the present day, an adapted version of Dorey's typology will be followed. Four strands of modern Conservatism will be examined: One Nation Conservatism (1950-64), modern technocratic Conservatism (1965-74), neo-liberal Conservatism (1974-97) and progressive neo-liberal Conservatism (2005-15). As will be discussed in Chapters Two and Three, the insights of One Nation Conservatism were particularly influential in relation to the party's approach to the welfare state in the period from the late 1940s to the mid-1960s. Following a brief interregnum in the period from 1965-74 in which a modern technocratic Conservatism held sway (Chapter Three), neo-liberal Conservatism came to prominence, though its influence on Conservative debates about the welfare state has deeper historic roots. The seeds of the final 'tradition', progressive neo-liberal Conservatism (PNLC), were sown during the party's years in opposition from 1997 to 2010 but only came to fruition after David Cameron was elected as party leader in 2005. Although drawing on the insights of both progressive One Nation and neo-liberal Conservatism, the PNLC approach can lay claim to being a distinctive hybrid in Conservative political thought.

The identification of these four strands of Conservatism should not be taken as conclusive evidence that there were seismic shifts in the party's thinking about the welfare state in the post-1940 era. However, while some common blue threads can be detected, it remains the case that the Conservative approach to the welfare state is best understood as a battle between competing strands of thought.

Before exploring the development of Conservative approaches to the welfare state since 1940 in subsequent chapters, it is useful to venture upstream and explore some earlier 20th-century developments in Conservative thinking and practice in this sphere.

The Conservative Party and state welfare in the early 20th century

Since its formation in the early 19th century, the modern Conservative Party has been supportive of those forms of state action that help to enhance the economic and social well-being of the nation and minimise any negative impacts arising from this organic form of change. The Conservative case for government intervention was pursued more vigorously in the early decades of the 20th century as the party came to terms with the growth of a working-class electorate, New Liberalism, the emergence of a reform-minded Labour Party, and the need for a collective response to pressing social issues such as unemployment. Within Conservative circles, debate centered on the type and scale of ameliorative state activity. While some Conservatives were willing to countenance increased intervention as a form of pragmatic adaptation to new economic and social conditions, others feared that the growth of state initiated reforms might involve a betrayal of core party values.

Those who favoured intervention tended to do so on the basis of traditional Conservative thinking relating to the ineffectiveness of 'civil' remedies with regard to pressing social problems. As Green (2002) explains,

> if agencies of civil society have been seen to be fulfilling a valuable and effective social role, then the Conservative predisposition has been to keep the State from intervening in their sphere of activity; but if they have been seen as failing, then Conservatives have supported State intervention either to support or supplant them. Similarly, if the State has been seen to be intervening to the point where valuable agencies of civil association and action have been unnecessarily undermined, then demands for the State's withdrawal have been made. (p 279)

Given underlying tensions about the appropriateness of state action, It is not surprising that there were significant differences of opinion about particular forms of economic and social intervention in the early decades of the 20th century. In terms of economic policy, the debate centred around the question of whether the Conservative Party should promote a stronger role for government 'intervention', albeit of a kind that stopped short of public ownership or direct control, in order to ensure that British industry became more efficient and therefore better able to withstand the pressures of international competition.

Progressive-minded Conservative interventionists such as Steel-Maitland, Macmillan and Boothby[23] believed that Britain's economic performance would deteriorate rapidly, with a concomitant rise in unemployment, unless industry were modernised and made more competitive. For these progressive politicians, the state was seen as having a vital enabling role to play in the economic sphere. Its central task was to encourage, and where necessary cajole, the industrial and banking sectors to update their operations 'through rationalization, amalgamation, and the adoption of the most up-to-date techniques of production and marketing' (Green, 2002, p 263) to meet the challenges of a new economic era. Interventionist-inclined Conservatives were particularly supportive of state efforts to encourage employers and employees to work in partnership,[24] which was seen as a way of enhancing the status and self-esteem of workers, leading to improved productivity that would boost the British economy. Broader acceptance of the case for economic intervention was reflected in the establishment of public corporations such as the British Overseas Airline Services (1939), the setting up of specialist government agencies such as the Milk Marketing Board (1933) and the provision of low-interest government loans to industry.

During the inter-war period, economic intervention was, however, strongly opposed by those Conservative MPs who remained committed to 'traditional' economic orthodoxies in the form of balanced budgets, the maintenance of the value of the currency and prudent forms of public expenditure. Such Conservatives were concerned that even modest forms of state intervention would distort the operation of the free market – an approach that provided protection to inefficient producers who were unwilling to adapt to new economic circumstances. Accordingly, at times of economic turbulence, this group of economic liberals prioritised cuts in social expenditure,[25] which contributed to the perception that the party was in thrall to the 'hard-faced men' who had entered parliament in 1918 with an explicit commitment to roll back the state (Francis, 1996, p 59).

Divisions were also apparent among Conservatives in relation to social policy. Economic liberals such as the publisher and former Liberal 'collectivist' Ernest Benn believed that the embryonic welfare state promoted by New Liberals and socialists in the early part of the 20th century would have adverse economic and social consequences.[26] The spiraling cost of state provision was seen, for example, as having a deleterious effect on enterprising and industrious citizens, who would eventually decide to pare back their entrepreneurial activity because of a growing resentment that their hard earned rewards were being frittered away on the indolent and undeserving by overly generous Poor Law guardians. These economically liberal Conservatives were also concerned that the growth of state welfare would undermine the willingness of adults to take responsibility for their families and crowd out valuable forms of voluntary action. Over time it was feared that the principle of self-help would be undermined and the character of the poor irreparably damaged.

Although 'progressive' Conservatives shared the concerns of economic liberals about the need to control the cost of state welfare in the decades preceding the Second World War, they believed that judicious forms of social expenditure could not only fulfil the Disraelian objective of 'elevating' the condition of the people, but also bolster the capitalist economy. Financially prudent, well-designed state welfare initiatives in areas such as education and healthcare were seen as a way of helping citizens to become self-reliant and prosperous. The formation of the Unionist Social Reform Committee (USRC) in 1910 was one early attempt to provide the public with a clearer understanding of what progressive Conservative social policy was seeking to achieve in an era of more 'programmatic' politics. According to one leading USRC acolyte, F.E. Smith,[27] it was necessary for Conservatives to ensure that their remedial solutions to contemporary social problems were 'crystallised and laid before the electorate with the least possible delay' (cited in Ramsden, 1980, p 16). Subsequently, interventionists such as Macmillan, who had been an active member of Clifford Allen's progressive, 'cross-party' Next Five Years Group (1934–38), made valiant efforts to persuade his own party to pursue more imaginative forms of social policy. In his influential text, *The middle way*, Macmillan (1938) contended that the dividends from the economic reforms he had proposed should be used to ensure that citizens were granted shorter working hours, paid holidays, 'extended education' and 'earlier retirement on more generous pensions' (p 370).

In contrast to the economic liberal wing of the party, these progressive Conservatives believed that state welfare was an effective way of *neutralising* rather than *engendering* working-class support for anti-capitalist doctrines such as socialism and communism. Stanley Baldwin, who was Prime Minister of Conservative or Conservative-dominated National governments on three occasions between 1923 and 1937,[28] was initially wary of the virtues of programmatic forms of economic and social policy, preferring to rely on a low-key, tried and tested, non-enterprising, 'safety first' approach. However, following intense lobbying from trusted colleagues such as John Buchan[29] and J.C.C. Davidson,[30] he changed tack and agreed, for example, to the establishment of a Conservative Research Department in 1930.

Under Baldwin's leadership, a more progressive Conservative approach to social policy began to emerge.[31] For example, during Neville Chamberlain's tenure (1924-29) at the Ministry of Health (which at that time had responsibility for housing, old age pensions, roads and Poor Law administration), there was a striking flurry of activity on the social front. Within two weeks of his appointment as Minister of Health, Chamberlain 'had presented a provisional programme to the Cabinet outlining 25 measures covering everything from reform of pensions, housing, rent restrictions, rating, the Poor Law and local government to legislation dealing with milk hygiene, the control of therapeutic substances, smoke abatement, the regulation of maternity homes and the registration of births, marriages and deaths. By the time the second Baldwin government left office in 1929 no fewer than 21 of these proposals had been passed' (Self, 2006, p 106). Although a number of these reforms such as the *Housing Act (1923)*, the *Widows, Orphans and Old Age Contributory Pensions Act (1925)* and the *Local Government Act (1929)* were significant initiatives in the history of social policy, it is questionable whether they should be regarded as foundation stones of the post-war welfare state. Rather, they might best be regarded as pragmatic, piecemeal measures designed to ameliorate specific social problems.[32]

Although there had been a greater willingness on the part of the National government to take a more interventionist stance on social issues prior to the outbreak of the Second World War, there was no settled position within the Conservative Party about what constituted an appropriate role for the state in relation to the promotion of social welfare. As we will see in Chapter Two, the underlying tensions between economic liberals and progressives continued to be played out during the Second World War.

This chapter has explored various dimensions of conservative thinking and traced the evolution of the 'modern' Conservative Party's approach towards the state welfare in the early part of the 20th century. In the following chapters, the focus will be on developments from 1940 to the present day. Consideration will be given to the Conservatives' approach to state welfare during the period of the wartime 'coalition' government from 1940 to 1945 (Chapter Two). Attention will then turn to the emergence of the One Nation approach to the welfare state, which held sway in the period from 1945 to the mid-1960s. This will be followed by a discussion of the 'modern technocratic approach' to the welfare state, which was pursued under Edward Heath's leadership of the party from 1965 to 1974. The resurgence of neo-liberal Conservatism in the 1970s and its impact on social policy under both the Thatcher and Major governments will be the subject of Chapter Five. Finally, the 'progressive' variant of neo-liberal Conservatism that David Cameron has pursued both in opposition and government will come under the spotlight in Chapter Six.

TWO

From war to peace: the Conservatives and the welfare state in the 1940s

The Conservative Party's growing dominance in British politics was underlined at the 1935 General Election when the 'National' Conservative government was re-elected to office. The Conservatives secured 47.8% of the popular vote, returning 386 MPs to Westminster. Although Labour recovered from its disastrous showing in the 1931 General Election (when it was reduced to just 52 MPs), it only managed to win 154 seats on the basis of 38% of the popular vote.

It was acknowledged within Labour circles that there was limited prospect of the party making significant inroads into the Conservative vote by the time of the next General Election in 1939 or 1940. However, the outbreak of the Second World War disrupted the domestic political scene and proved to be a catalyst for a dramatic revival in the fortunes of the Labour Party. In this chapter, attention will be focused, first, on the impact of the Second World War on the Conservative Party's approach to social policy during the period of coalition government from September 1940 until 1945. Attention will then shift to the growing influence of progressive 'One Nation' Conservatism towards the end of the war, which was to underpin the party's peacetime thinking on the welfare state from the early 1950s to the mid-1970s.

Conservative social policy during the Second World War

Labour's decision to join the coalition government in 1940, which was conditional on Neville Chamberlain relinquishing his position as Prime Minister,[1] had a significant impact on the Conservative Party's approach to social policy for the remainder of the war and beyond. Labour's willingness to join the coalition was premised on a clear understanding that there would no longer be an exclusive focus on the military campaign. At Labour's insistence, post-war reconstruction was to be moved up the political agenda. This proved advantageous for progressive Conservatives such as Boothby and Butler, whose interventionist inclinations had already been boosted as a result of the need for extensive forms of government intervention on the home front following the outbreak of war. After the resignation and subsequent death of Neville Chamberlain (who had continued to lead the Conservative Party within the coalition and chair the Committee on Home Affairs) in the autumn of 1941, the political pendulum edged further in a progressive direction. The influence of the 'Men of Munich' such as Neville Chamberlain, Sir Samuel Hoare and Sir John Simon ebbed away following Churchill's government reshuffle, which led to preferment for 'progressives' such as Eden, Boothby and Macmillan as well as the inclusion of reform-minded Labour politicians such as Attlee and Morrison and the influential trade unionist Ernest Bevin.

It should be noted, however, that the key ministerial roles at the Home Office (John Anderson), and in the 'departments' for Education (Herwald Ramsbotham), Health (Malcolm MacDonald) and Pensions (Walter Womersley) remained in the hands of 'traditional' conservatives after this reshuffle. This reflected Churchill's cautious and pragmatic approach to social reform. While he recognised the importance of initiatives that might bolster civilian morale, he was reluctant to spearhead any campaign for uncosted forms of post-war reconstruction while the war was still to be won.[2] Moreover, the fact that Churchill regarded himself as a national statesman rather than a party politician meant that he was ambivalent about the need to formulate a distinctively Conservative form of social policy. Indeed, it was only after his preferred option of an extended period of coalition government proved untenable (following the allied victory in Europe in 1944 and Labour's subsequent decision to press for a General Election), that Churchill belatedly acknowledged the necessity of greater clarity about the Conservative's approach to economic and social policy.

A further factor hindering the development of a distinctive Conservative approach to state welfare during the war was the party's limited capacity for policymaking. At the outbreak of hostilities, the Conservative Research Department (CRD), which had been established in 1929, was closed down for the duration of the conflict (though it briefly re-opened between January and June 1940).[3] Although Churchill was receptive to research evidence and expert guidance as exemplified by his reliance on Lord Cherwell, he was not favourably disposed towards the CRD, believing that it had always 'worked with the rest of the Party to support his political opponents and to limit the effectiveness of his friends' (Fort, 2004, pp 95-6). However, other senior figures in the party such as Sir Douglas Hacking believed it was important to respond more positively to a rapidly changing economic and social environment. R.A. Butler was given the task of gauging public opinion and modifying the party's policy in the light of these broader changes. By 1941, a Post War Problems Central Committee (PWPCC) had been established. It was chaired by Butler and included figures such as David Maxwell-Fyfe and Henry Brooke. As a first step, eight sub-committees in areas such as education, industry, the constitution and electoral reform were convened. By the end of the war, the number of these sub-committees had doubled to include areas such as the social services and local government. The need to ensure a balance of party opinion on each of these sub-committees coupled with extensive scrutiny and review of the reports emanating from these bodies resulted, perhaps inevitably, in uncontroversial and 'unexciting' documents that lacked the dynamism and impact of rival publications such as the Beveridge Report.[4]

The Beveridge Report, 'reconstruction' and the 'White Paper chase'

The publication of the Beveridge Report on social insurance on 1 December 1942 (Beveridge, 1942) proved to be a turning point in the direction of the Conservative Party's approach towards state welfare for the remainder of the war. In his *Report on social insurance and allied services*, Beveridge called for the introduction of a comprehensive scheme of social insurance to provide non-time-limited financial support for contributors and their families in the event of unemployment or sickness and a pension in old age. In addition, Beveridge pressed for the introduction of family allowances for all households with dependent children, the creation of a National Health Service for all free at the point of use and a commitment to full employment. His 'reconstruction' manifesto seemed to capture the 'never again' spirit of the time. In a series of carefully planned articles and broadcasts prior to publication, Beveridge succeeded in stimulating public interest in his report.[5] Coming shortly after the allied victory at El Alamein, a large queue of prospective customers formed outside the Stationery Office in the Strand on the day of publication. Over 100,000 full and abridged copies of the report were sold by the end of the month. It was not just the practical policies of the Beveridge Report that struck a chord with a war-weary public, but also the 'rich vein of Cromwellian and Bunyanesque prose' (Timmins, 2001, p 23) used by the author with the tantalising prospect of slaying the five giants (want, idleness, squalor, disease and ignorance).

Beveridge's astute use of the media to stimulate public interest in his report prior to publication and his persistent attempts to persuade the War Cabinet to accept his proposals in full had alerted Churchill and his trusted advisers such as Bracken, Beaverbrook, Cherwell and the Chancellor, Kingsley Wood, to the possibility of public calls for the swift implementation of the report's recommendations. In a memo to Churchill two weeks prior to the publication of the report, Wood expressed major reservations about Beveridge's plan, contending that the social insurance scheme was both too costly and poorly targeted. In addition, Wood believed that many of Beveridge's other proposals, such as the abolition of the administrative role of the approved societies and 'the right of strikers to unemployment pay' (Addison, 1977, p 220), would prove to be contentious and damaging to the war effort.

Various steps were taken to ensure that the government could forestall public demands for early implementation of the report's key recommendations. On the advice of Bracken, the Minister of Information, attempts were made to muffle Beveridge by denying him an official press conference and by refusing him public funds to publicise his report. Two days before publication, however, the official line suddenly changed. Sensing that the report might have a role to play in demoralising the enemy, Bracken informed Beveridge that the government now favoured 'maximum publicity, including a press conference and a broadcast postscript' to be delivered by the author himself (Addison, 1977, p 217). On the day of publication, details of the report were broadcast by the BBC in 22 languages.

The public euphoria that greeted Beveridge's proposals led to a further revision in the coalition's response to the report. In order to dampen down 'unrealistic' popular expectations that a new social security scheme would soon be implemented, Cyril Ratcliffe (the Director-General of the Ministry of Information,) instructed the Political Warfare Office not to publicise the report, while a War Office Army Bureau of Current Affairs pamphlet containing details of the Beveridge plan was withdrawn from circulation to the armed forces just two days after its publication.[6]

Traditional Conservative unease about the report was reflected in the first Cabinet discussion of its contents in January 1943. Wood reiterated his concerns about the new scheme, not least the adverse impact that its implementation would have on other areas of government activity. Resistance also came from a secret committee of Conservative MPs set up by Churchill, under the chairmanship of Ralph Assheton, to ascertain the wider views of the party. Although the committee accepted the case for the introduction of family allowances and universal provision for old age, it favoured a less generous, time-limited (six months) unemployment insurance scheme. A less expensive and better targeted compulsory health scheme (restricted to those with incomes of less than £420 a year) was also deemed essential to protect the interests of private medicine.[7]

This tepid response from the Conservative-led coalition posed a problem for most Labour members of the government. When the report was considered by the Reconstruction Priorities Committee, chaired by Sir John Anderson, the Labour minister Herbert Morrison argued, unsuccessfully, for a more positive official response to Beveridge's proposals, believing that it would prove both affordable and popular. The Conservative members of the War Cabinet acknowledged that an unduly negative response to the report could prove damaging. The official line that eventually emerged was that the coalition would support the report in broad principle and take steps to prepare any necessary legislation. Crucially, however, implementation was to be delayed until after the war. When the coalition's stance was outlined by Anderson in a lacklustre opening speech during a three-day debate on the report in February 1943, it 'created a disastrous impression on Labour and progressive opinion' (Donoughue and Jones, 2001, p 315). Despite a spirited interpretation of the coalition's position by Morrison in his closing address for the government (in which he stressed the coalition's acceptance of 16 of Beveridge's 23 recommendations), he was unable to forestall the 'biggest rebellion against the Churchill government in the war' (Donoughue and Jones, 2001, p 315). One hundred and nineteen backbench MPs supported an amendment tabled by Labour MP James Griffiths calling for the immediate implementation of the Beveridge Report. Although the government won the vote, it was widely acknowledged that the Conservatives had reignited public fears that they remained a party opposed to major social reform.

While the majority of Conservative backbench MPs supported the official coalition line on the Beveridge Report, there were signs of discontent among some younger members, who believed that some of their older colleagues, who had been 'elected under very different circumstances in 1935', had lost touch with public opinion and consequently failed to recognise the emergence of a progressive zeitgeist (Addison, 1977, p 229). For example, Quintin Hogg, whose progressive instincts had been sharpened by wartime service, warned his 'anti-collectivist' Conservative colleagues during the parliamentary debates on the Beveridge Report that their reluctance to embrace welfare reform was a major political blunder that would sow the seeds of social revolution.[8] Progressive Conservatives also lent their support to Ernest Bevin's Catering Wages Bill in January 1943, which was designed to guarantee a minimum wage for restaurant, hotel and bar staff.[9]

The progressive voice was strengthened by the formation of the Tory Reform Committee in March 1943 by Lord Hinchingbrooke, Hugh Molson, Peter Thorneycroft and Christopher York. The group sought to encourage the Conservative leadership to disassociate itself from economically liberal influences within the party and to press ahead with social reform. The group, which eventually attracted around 40 members, produced a manifesto – *Forward by the right* (Tory Reform Committee, 1943) – as well as articles for the party's monthly journal *Onlooker*, pamphlets and short works including *Full speed ahead! Essays in Tory reform*[10] and *One year's work.*[11] The group was supportive of Keynesian demand management techniques and the pursuit of full employment. It explored a wide range of topics in its publications including 'aviation, agriculture, coal, education, housing, land use, war pensions and workmen's compensation' (Dorey, 2011, p 74). One of its greatest 'coups' was to secure a government defeat by just one vote on an amendment bought by Thelma Cazalet-Keir in March 1944, on the question of equal pay for women teachers.[12] This prompted the government to turn this issue into a vote of confidence, which led to a tactical retreat by the 'rebels' and the reversal of the original decision. According to Ball (2013), the group's 'lack of practical experience, blithe confidence, self-absorbed cliquishness, desire for the limelight, open ambition, and the loose attitude to loyalty which often seemed to accompany it, did not render them attractive to the main body of older and staider backbenchers' (p 351). Indeed, a number of those with strong free market and individualistic sentiments, such as Sir Spencer Summers, Alexander Erskine-Hill and Ralph Assheton, were so concerned by what they perceived to be the negative influence of the Tory Reform Committee that they set up a counter-organisation, the Progress Trust, in November 1943 to promote their anti-collectivist version of Conservatism. Fears of collectivist advance also led another prominent neo-liberal Conservative backbencher, Ernest Benn, to establish, with the support of industrialists such as Lord Leverhulme and Lord Perry, the cross-party Society for Individual Freedom in 1942, while MPs including Douglas Hacking, Waldron Smithers and Leonard Lyle established the National League for Freedom in April 1943.[13]

It was, however, the progressive voice that gained ground as the party 'slithered haltingly and unpersuasively towards collectivism' (Harris, 2013, p 365). Churchill acknowledged that the party had been damaged by its lukewarm response to the Beveridge Report, as evidenced by a loss of support in five of the six 'uncontested' by-elections[14] that took place around the time of the Commons debate on its contents.[15] Churchill took to the airwaves to reassure the public of his party's support for full employment and for post-war reform, including 'national compulsory insurance for all classes, for all purposes, from the cradle to the grave' (Addison, 1992, p 369. See also, Toye, 2013, pp 203-6). In this so-called 'four years' plan speech, Churchill also pledged his support for reform in areas such as housing, health and education.

Labour members of the Cabinet (Attlee, Bevin and Morrison) responded to backbench criticisms of their lack of zeal for wartime change by circulating a Cabinet paper in June 1943 entitled 'The need for decisions', which stressed the importance of immediate reforms rather than waiting for an assessment of the financial viability of any proposed changes at the end of hostilities. They pressed for legislation to be prepared in areas such as social security, education, full employment and health.[16] This led to the creation of a new Ministry of Reconstruction in November 1943, which would spearhead the coalition's reform agenda.

Education was seen as the one main policy area where the Conservatives could most comfortably demonstrate their commitment to social reform, not least because of broad cross-party support for the pre-war recommendations of both the Hadow Report (which advocated secondary education for all from the age of 11 to 15[17] – Board of Education, 1931) and the Spens Committee[18] (Board of Education, 1938), which 'recommended the abolition of fees in all state schools and a tripartite division of secondary education into grammar, secondary modern and technical schools' (Timmins, 2001, p 74). After being appointed President of the Board of Education in July 1941, R.A. Butler sought to improve educational opportunity and improve the physical condition of school buildings in ways that would not antagonise the Church (which was keen to retain denominational influence in the 50% of all schools that were under its control at the start of the war) or the leading public schools, which cherished their independence and were implacably opposed to state interference. Butler managed to secure the co-operation of the Anglican Church for the changes he sought to bring about as a result of a good personal relationship with the newly enthroned 'progressive' Archbishop of Canterbury, William Temple. Under the new arrangements, church schools could opt for either aided status, which enabled them to retain control of the governing body and the appointment of teachers as well as the religious parts of the syllabus, or controlled status, which gave the Local Education Authority greater powers in terms of governance and staff appointments but would leave churchmen with control of the religious content of the syllabus.[19]

Ably assisted by his Secretary of State, David Chuter-Ede (Labour), Butler was eventually able to secure the passage of a new Education Act (1944) that guaranteed free secondary education for all children on the basis of their aptitude and abilities from the age of 11 to 15. In order to ensure that his bill became law, Butler recognised that he needed to reassure both backbench Conservative MPs and leading churchmen that his plans posed no threat to the independence of the public schools. Accordingly, he set up a separate independent enquiry under Lord Fleming, to consider how a more fruitful relationship between the public schools and the maintained sector might be established in post-war Britain. This skilful manoeuvre ensured that this contentious issue did not derail his bill.[20]

The 'progressive turn' among Conservative members from 1943 until the end of Churchill's caretaker administration in July 1945 led to a flurry of activity, which has come to be known as the 'White Paper chase.' Responding to Beveridge's call for the establishment of a National Health Service, Ernest Brown (the National Liberal Minster of Health) and Tom Johnson (the Labour Secretary of State for Scotland), presented a health reform paper to the Reconstruction Priorities Committee in 1943. In line with ideas emerging from the Medical Planning Commission of 1942 and the Socialist Medical Association, they recommended local government take over the running of both primary (in which groups of salaried GPs would provide care in newly established health centres) and secondary healthcare.[21]

The British Medical Association expressed concern about these proposals, objecting to both the principle of local government control and the idea that doctors should become state employees rather than independent, fee-based, contractors. Henry Willink (National Conservative), who succeeded Brown in November 1943, eventually produced a 'toned down' White Paper entitled *A National Health Service* in February 1944 (Ministry of Health, 1944). Its publication date had been delayed by Churchill to enable two of his most trusted advisors, Brendan Bracken (the Minister of Information) and Max Beaverbrook (the Lord Privy Seal) to identify, and amend, any contentious recommendations.[22]

The final version of the White Paper attempted to reconcile two different party political approaches to health reform. For example, Labour's preference for the establishment of health centres staffed by salaried GPs was tempered by the suggestion that part-time clinicians working in these centres (as well as those who preferred to practice independently) would continue to receive capitation fees. Predictably, the document failed to receive a ringing endorsement from the wide range of interested parties. The British Medical Association, which had many Conservative-inclined members, was particularly agitated by the threat of state control and the prospect of a wholly salaried profession, while the voluntary hospitals feared that their autonomy would be undermined. Such was the virulence of this response that Willink made a concerted effort to placate Conservative and clinical protestors by modifying his proposals, much to the annoyance of the Socialist Medical Association and many Labour MPs.[23]

In terms of employment, a White Paper was published in May 1944 following lengthy discussions involving the economic section of the War Cabinet and the Reconstruction Priorities Committee. It was broadly supported by frontbenchers (although many backbenchers remained sceptical). The White Paper had been rushed out in order to ensure that it would not be upstaged by Beveridge's own 'independent' report on the same topic.[24] According to Lowe (2005), the White Paper was 'both contradictory and vague', failing as it did to resolve underlying 'theoretical, administrative and political disagreements', not least over Keynesian ideas on the causes and remedies for unemployment (p 116). Nevertheless, all members of the coalition were now in agreement that a key role for any post-war administration would be to ensure the maintenance of a high and stable level of employment.[25]

In the light of the Commons rebellion over Beveridge and the subsequent reservations about the viability of the scheme (particularly in relation to family allowances, full employment and subsistence benefits) contained in the internal government review conducted by Sir Thomas Phillips (a long-term adversary of Beveridge),[26] Sir Thomas Sheepshanks was asked to conduct a further review into social security reform. His committee accepted the case for reform and supported Beveridge's proposal for a universal, tripartite (employers, employers and the state) funded social insurance scheme that would offer protection against major risks such as unemployment, sickness and old age. However, like the Phillips Committee, the Sheepshank Committee remained opposed to the idea of subsistence benefits thereby helping 'to ensure that means-tested benefits would continue to play a major part in the development of anti-poverty policy throughout the post-war period' (Harris, 2004, p 292). A White Paper entitled *Social insurance* was eventually published in September 1944,[27] and included the recommendation for a separate Ministry of National Insurance (which was established on 8 October 1944 under the direction of the Labour Minister Sir William Jowitt). In the event, only one sphere of social security was the subject of legislative change before the end of the war, namely, Family Allowances.[28] Given that the inter-war governments had been opposed to the demands of the family endowment movement spearheaded by Eleanor Rathbone, this was a major accomplishment. Demands for the introduction of family allowances intensified throughout the war. A memorandum on the subject was delivered to Chancellor Kingsley Wood by an all-party group of MPs in June 1941. This led to the publication of a White Paper, *Family Allowances*, in May 1942 setting out the case for, as well as some of the potential pitfalls of, such a benefit.[29] Following Beveridge's call for a 'workable' Family Allowance scheme (weekly payments of eight shillings for second and subsequent children) in his report of 1942, Sir John Anderson, who had succeeded Wood as Chancellor, announced that the coalition would legislate in this area, though the 'non-subsistence' payments would be restricted to five shillings per week payable for each eligible second and subsequent child. The legislation received Royal Ascent during Churchill's caretaker administration on 15 June 1945.

The coalition also responded to Beveridge's call to end the evil of squalor by publishing a White Paper on housing in March 1945[30] (Ministry of Reconstruction, 1945), which accepted that every family should have the right to a separate, affordable dwelling. The White Paper recommended that between three and four million homes be built in the decade or so after the end of the war. Significant party differences remained, though, over the role of the state in relation to planning, rebuilding and land control.[31]

Fissures within the coalition became more apparent in relation to reconstruction as it became clear that an allied wartime victory was in sight[32] (Jefferys, 1991). Although Churchill harboured hopes that the wartime coalition government might continue at least until victory had been secured in the Pacific (hopes that were shared by Labour ministers such as Morrison, Bevin and Dalton, on the grounds that a further period of coalition government would provide the best opportunity to secure the policy gains that would be 'lost' in the event of a General Election defeat), these proved to be stillborn. By early 1944, Labour's National Executive Coalition had made it clear that while it would continue to support the coalition until victory in Europe had been achieved, it would seek a General Election at the earliest possible date thereafter. This view was reaffirmed at the party conference on 21 May 1944. Two days later, the coalition government came to an end. Churchill formed a caretaker administration that governed until the General Election, which took place on 5 July 1945.

The Conservative Party was not in the best shape to fight a General Election in 1945 for a number of reasons. First, its 'honourable', 'principled' and wide-ranging interpretation of the electoral truce that the main parties had voluntarily entered into at the start of the war[33] proved disadvantageous. At the outbreak of war, Conservative Central advised its constituency associations that they should suspend their political activities and focus instead on the war effort by supporting the work of the Ministry of Information, the Air Raid Precaution service and other charitable organisations. This advice was revised, however, when it was acknowledged that 'too total a closure might give the party's opponents potentially insuperable advantages' (Thorpe, 2009, p 17). Local associations were therefore encouraged to maintain some form of local presence, even though it was recognised that this would be problematic given the temporary laying off of agents, military call-ups and the difficulties in sustaining local support networks at a time of increased population churn. In contrast, it has been argued that Labour maintained a more overtly political presence in many localities (including the active support of co-operative societies and trade unions), which reflected its narrower interpretation of the electoral truce. Support for the Labour cause was aided by the fact that many of its activists were able to continue with their political work as a result of being in reserved occupations (a point that was highlighted by Quintin Hogg, 1945, in a book entitled *The left was never right*, which drew attention to the deeper patriotism and wartime sacrifice of Conservative MPs).

Second, the Conservative Party had failed to promote a distinctive vision for society at a time when the established economic and social order was being challenged from all points of the compass. For example, a famous editorial in *The Times* penned by E.H. Carr in July 1940, called for the transformation of society, while commentators such as Thomas Balogh, Maxwell Fry and J.B. Priestley set out some radical ideas for change in post-war Britain in the January 1941 edition of the popular weekly magazine *Picture Post*. Film makers such as John Baxter (*Love on the Dole, The Common Touch, Let the People Sing*) and Humphrey Jennings (*A Diary for Timothy*) also caught the 'transformative', 'never again' spirit of the age with their broadcasts. The Church of England, under the leadership of William Temple, also promoted the case for change. In his influential Penguin book *Christianity and the social order* (1942), Temple expanded on many of the changes that the Anglican Church had debated in a special conference in 1941, including the need for paid holidays and family allowances.[34] The absence of a robust Conservative response to these developments can be explained in part by the limited resources at the disposal of both Central Office and the Conservative Research Department at this time. Complacency was also a factor. Despite opinion polling suggesting that Labour was on course for electoral victory and significant by-election reversals (the last of which occurred at the hands of Common Wealth in Chelmsford in April 1945 on a 28% swing, just weeks before the first votes in the General Election were cast[35]), the Conservatives remained confident that Churchill would be able, like Lloyd George in 1918, to reap a 'khaki' political dividend on the basis of his wartime success.

Third, the decision to focus almost exclusively on Churchill's leadership qualities rather than the party's programme proved to be a misjudgement. While there was broad agreement that Churchill was an electoral asset, there were questions over the extent to which the campaign should be built around him. Lord Woolton was among those who believed that the party should give due emphasise to its preparedness to embrace social reform, not least because this would demonstrate to a sceptical public that the Conservatives had finally distanced themselves from the hard-hearted reputation acquired as a result of their tepid response to social distress during the inter-war period.[36] In contrast, Beaverbrook believed that the party should focus on the dangers that an incoming Labour government posed for the health of the economy, personal freedom and private enterprise.

The decision to focus on the wartime leader's attributes was underlined by the title of the party's manifesto, *Mr Churchill's declaration of policy to the electors* (the word Conservative failed to make an appearance). The manifesto, which had been drawn up by Henry Brooke and David Clarke on the basis of PWPCC papers and other coalition documents, sought to reassure voters that the party would continue with the four-year reform agenda that Churchill had set out in his wireless broadcast in 1943. The manifesto reaffirmed that one of the primary aims of the next Conservative government would be to maintain 'a high and stable level of employment' (Dale, 2000, p 63). It would also give priority to the completion of 220,000 permanent homes within two years with a further 80,000 in the pipeline. A nationwide and compulsory scheme of national insurance based on the 1944 White Paper would be introduced (Dale, 2000, p 65), as would a comprehensive health service 'covering treatment from the GP to the specialist' free at the point of use. New buildings and additional teachers were to be provided to ensure the successful implementation of the 1944 Education Act.

The manifesto also highlighted Conservative fears about the direction that the nation might take if a Labour administration were to come to power. Concerns were expressed about Labour's divisive class-based politics, its attachment to the 'state machine,' its ideological commitment to nationalisation (Dale, 2000, p 60) and its desire to 'impose' on Britain 'a permanent system of bureaucratic control reeking of totalitarianism' (p 68). This latter line of attack owed much to the influence of two of Churchill's most trusted lieutenants, Ralph Assheton (who became party chairman in 1944) and Max Beaverbrook. Finding common cause with the sentiments expressed by Hayek in *The road to serfdom* (1944), Assheton drew Churchill's attention to the merits of this text and even directed that one-and-a-half tons of the party's 'precious paper assignment' for the election should be assigned to the publisher Routledge in the unrealised hope (publication had to be delayed until March 1946) that 12,000 additional abridged copies of the text could be published before the end of the campaign to aid the Conservative cause (Cockett, 1995, p 93).

The purportedly totalitarian inclinations of Labour were highlighted in the first, and most infamous, of Churchill's four General Election broadcasts on 4 June 1945. Churchill suggested that the return of a socialist government would give rise to an attack on a citizen's 'right to breathe freely without having a harsh, clumsy, tyrannical hand clasped across the mouth and nostrils'. He predicted that a Labour government would have to 'fall back on some form of Gestapo, no doubt very humanely directed in the first instance', in order to curb 'free, sharp, or violently worded expressions of public discontent' (cited in Kramnick and Sheerman, 1993, p 481).[37]

The public reaction to this broadcast was extremely negative. Mass Observation reported that many potential voters had found it disappointing and a cause of 'genuine distress' (Calder, 1971, p 667), while Gallup recorded a 69% disapproval rating.[38] In response, Churchill changed tack in his subsequent broadcast (13 June 1945), highlighting wartime improvements in health and nutrition, his party's prospective reform programme and the coalition's social insurance plans.[39] However, in his third broadcast (21 June 1945), Churchill returned to the threat that Labour posed to personal freedom, referring to the Beaverbrook press' exposé of the shadowy influence that Harold Laski and the National Executive Committee would exert over Labour's post-war policy agenda.[40]

Attlee's measured response to Churchill's 'Gestapo' broadcast helped to enhance his reputation as the prospective leader best equipped to 'win the peace'. More generally, Labour's record as highly effective, patriotic members of the coalition government and its unequivocal commitment to state-led economic and social reform appeared to have convinced a broad cross-section of the public that they could place their trust in the party of the Left to lead the nation forward after the war.

Despite favourable polling evidence, Labour insiders shared the commonly held view that the Conservatives were on course to secure an overall majority of around 30 seats in the General Election. Accordingly, they were also taken aback by the sheer scale of their electoral victory when the result was finally declared on 26 July 1945 (additional time had been allowed for the count so that the votes of those serving overseas in the armed services could be recorded). In the 1935 General Election, Labour had secured 154 seats (out of 604) on a 38% share of the vote. In the 1945 contest, it had increased the size of its vote to 48%, winning 393 of the 604 seats that could be contested. It achieved 61% support among first-time voters as well as the majority of the forces vote and even managed to convince significant numbers of suburban and rural middle-class voters to put their faith in Labour.[41]

Although the scale of this defeat (which was not as severe as that of 1906) caused consternation in Conservative circles, it did not lead to destructive forms of infighting. According to many Conservatives their election defeat was linked to Labour's supposedly unprincipled willingness to exploit wartime circumstances for party advantage and to the Tories own failure to convince wavering voters that they were no longer the party of appeasement and laissez-faire.

The need to restore the party's organisational strength was accorded key importance in the aftermath of the election defeat. Lord Woolton (who had served in the coalition government as an independent) joined the party and succeeded Ralph Assheton as party chairman on 1 July 1946. Over the next five years, Woolton presided over a dramatic expansion in the party's political activities including a highly successful membership drive.[42]

Under Woolton's chairmanship, the Conservative Research Department (with David Clarke as its Director and R.A. Butler as its chairman) was reorganised and expanded. By 1950, both its annual budget and staffing complement (50) had increased significantly.[43] The Conservative Political Centre was established in 1945 to provide policy and other relevant advice to MPs as well as to engage with local members through lectures, training courses and publications.[44]

There was, however, no immediate change of direction in relation to the party's policy agenda following the General Election defeat. Churchill, who continued to lead the party, remained opposed to detailed policy prescriptions, which he believed limited the room for manoeuvre of a prospective Conservative administration. He was also convinced that Labour's commitment to economic planning and social reconstruction would prove unworkable with the consequence that disillusioned voters would quickly switch their allegiance back to the Conservatives.

Churchill's limited interest in domestic policymaking following his party's electoral defeat (he preferred to devote his time to foreign policy and to the drafting of his lucrative war memoirs) and his consequent failure to establish anything other than a reactive Conservative policy agenda was a source of irritation for 'progressives' such as Butler, Hogg and Macmillan (who was one of several high-profile Conservative electoral casualties in the 1945 election). Labour's electoral success provided further evidence for this younger generation of MPs that the party now needed to make one of its periodic 'doctrinal' shifts in the light of 'irreversible' changes in the economic and social landscape. Change was seen as vital if the party was to have any possibility of capturing the much-needed votes of skilled workers and the growing number of trade unionists in a future election.[45]

The carrying of a resolution demanding a clearer statement of contemporary Conservative doctrine and policy at the party's first annual post-war conference at Blackpool in 1946 did, however, persuade Churchill of the need for a more constructive challenge to Labour's approach. He set up an industrial policy committee, headed by R.A. Butler, which, after a wide-ranging consultative process, led to the publication of *The Industrial Charter* (Conservative and Unionist Central Office, 1947). The charter sought to reassure party members and the wider public that the Conservatives had jettisoned its support for laissez-faire. Equally, though, it was made clear that the party's active support for targeted forms of state interventionism did not signify any dilution of the party's long-standing faith in the role of markets and entrepreneurial activity. Reassurance for neo-liberal-minded Conservatives came in the form of a pledge to cut direct taxation and the number of civil servants, to bring an end to rationing and unnecessary regulation and to reinstate key features of the *Trade Dispute Act* that the Attlee government had removed.[46] The charter also promised that the government would engage in economic interventionism to stimulate demand so that high employment levels could be maintained and workers guaranteed 'a reasonable expectation of industrial security (Conservative and Unionist Central Office, 1947, p 29). Harmonious relations between employers and employees would be fostered through profit sharing schemes and joint consultation processes. Legitimate trade union activity was to be encouraged on the grounds that it contributed to 'the national welfare' (Conservative and Unionist Central Office, 1947, p 21). According to R.A. Butler, the charter provided a clear alternative to the socialist approach to economic issues. The charter was 'viable, efficient and humane' and would 'release and reward enterprise and initiative but without abandoning social justice or reverting to mass unemployment' (Butler, 1971, pp 132-3).

The charter stimulated a great deal of interest and was warmly endorsed by members attending the party's annual conference at Brighton in 1947 following 'discreet backroom work by Eden, Butler and Macmillan' (Thorpe, 2004, p 345). Formal opposition to the charter was restricted to ardent diehards such as Sir Waldron Smithers (who was heavily involved in the freedom fighting fund[47]) and Sir Herbert Williams. According to Smithers, the charter amounted to 'milk and water socialism' and posed a threat to national sovereignty. After four delegate votes were recorded against the charter at the 1947 conference, 'the wags said it was Smithers and a friend putting up both hands – an observation made before Smithers badly damaged his wrist punching a wall in frustration at the direction the party was taking' (Thorpe, 2010, p 348, note 244).

The doctrinal 'equipoise' that had characterised *The Industrial Charter* was also to the fore in a subsequent policy review published in 1949 – *The right road for Britain* (Conservative and Unionist Central Office, 1949) – which set out to provide a 'broad and simple statement' of the 'Conservative outlook and aims' (p.5). The initial draft of this publication, written by a leading light of the progressive cause, Quintin Hogg (whose own influential book *The case for Conservatism* had been published two years earlier), was the subject of considerable internal revision in the light of some underlying tensions between the economic liberal and progressive wings of the party.[48] The compromise document contained much to reassure the economic liberals that the party would continue to champion free enterprise, individualism and home ownership ('setting the people free') and that the denationalisation of the iron and steel industries and a review of rent control regulations were firmly on the agenda. Equally, though, the publication emphasised some strong progressive themes, including the positive role that the social services could play in post-war Britain.

This document also signalled that the party was beginning to arrive at a more settled position with regard to the welfare state. Although the Conservatives had opposed parts of Labour's post-war legislative programme, particularly its proposals for the National Health Service,[49] they now accepted that the welfare state was to become a permanent feature of post-war society. One of the clearest signs of this rapprochement came in a series of speeches by Churchill in the months leading up to the appointed day for the introduction of the National

Health Service (5 July 1948), in which he emphasised the pivotal role that both he and his party had played in bringing about social reform of this kind.[50] *The right road for Britain* reaffirmed that the Conservatives were fully supportive of the new social services: 'We regard them as mainly our own handiwork. We shall endeavour to maintain the range and scope of these Services and the rates of benefit' (Conservative and Unionist Central Office, 1949, p 42). This reassurance that the welfare state would be safe in Conservative hands did not mean, however, that the party would refrain from moulding these services in ways more in keeping with its underlying values and principles. Accordingly, reference was made to the growing cost of the NHS, 'the tendency to create enormous and unwieldy multilateral schools' (Conservative and Unionist Central Office, 1949, p 44) and the 'shameful' levels of waste and extravagance to be found in the public sector (Conservative and Unionist Central Office, 1949, p 44).

Conservative support for the welfare state was reiterated in the party's General Election manifesto of 1950 – *This is the road*[51] – which asserted that the maintenance of full employment would be the first aim of a Conservative government, that a social security safety net would remain in place and that improvements in health provision would be undertaken once administrative efficiencies had been introduced. The manifesto committed the party to reducing class sizes, particularly in primary schools, and to improving the supply of housing through the reinvigoration of the private sector. Significantly, though, the Conservatives contrasted their prudent approach towards the welfare state with their 'profligate' tax and spend opponents, who believed that 'social welfare' should always be available 'from the state free, gratis and for nothing' (Dale, 2000, p 76).

By the time of the General Election on 23 February 1950, the Conservative Party had moved in a One Nation direction. Considerable efforts had been made to convince the electorate that the party would seek to improve, rather than dismantle, the welfare state. The only remaining question was whether the party had done enough to persuade the electorate to turn away from Labour.

THREE

Towards a One Nation Conservative welfare state? The Conservatives and the welfare state, 1950-64

Despite a much-improved performance, the Conservatives failed to win the 1950 General Election, securing 43.5% of the popular vote and 298 of the 620 available seats. Given the narrowness of their defeat, many within the party believed that 'one more heave' (Thorpe, 2004, p 353) would prove sufficient to overturn Labour's slender overall majority of six seats at the next General Election.

The emergence of the One Nation Group

In an effort to ensure that a distinctive, 'modern' Conservative message would be firmly in place by the time of the next General Election, a group of nine newly elected MPs (including Edward Heath, Iain Macleod, Angus Maude and Enoch Powell)[1] established the One Nation Group shortly after the party's 1950 defeat. At the first meeting, Macleod informed the group that he had been commissioned to write a pamphlet on the social services by the Conservative Political Centre and suggested that the new group be involved in its preparation.[2] According to Walsha (2000), the pamphlet was intended to 'provide a powerful case for a distinctly Conservative welfare policy' that would be able to trump 'socialist social welfare provision in both philosophy and practice' (p 191). While the contributors to the pamphlet *One Nation. A Tory approach to social problems* (Macleod and Maude, 1950) were fulsome in their praise for social reformers such as Owen, Nightingale, Dickens and Shaftesbury and fully accepted the case for increased state welfare provision, they were keen to ensure that such activity did not undermine 'competitive free enterprise', which they believed represented the best means of achieving the 'efficiency and flexibility' required to maximise the 'country's wealth' (Macleod and Maude, 1950, pp 72-3). They expressed particular concern about the adverse impact of Labour's redistributionist welfare strategy, which they believed posed a threat to 'the future well-being of even the poorest' (p 18).

As Walsha (2000) points out, the One Nation Group (ONG) had no wish to 'engineer or consolidate the case for a compromised form of Conservatism intent on meeting socialism part-way' (p 190). This was made clear in the opening paragraph of *One Nation*:

> There is a fundamental disagreement between Conservatives and socialists on the question of social policy. Socialists would give the same benefits to everyone, whether or not the help is needed, and indeed whether or not the country's resources are adequate. We believe that we must first help those in need. Socialists believe that the State should provide an average standard. We believe that it should provide a minimum standard, above which people should be free to rise as far as their industry, their thrift, their ability or their genius may take them. (Macleod and Maude, 1950, p 9)

According to the ONG, the Conservative Party needed to distance itself from Labour by prioritising economic stability over egalitarian social spending and by placing greater emphasis on selectivity rather than universalism. State welfare support should be set at a satisfactory minimum standard, not at the unaffordable optimal levels favoured by socialists.

Although the principal aim of the contributors to *One Nation* was to map out the broad parameters of a modern Conservative approach to the welfare state, some contributors were prepared to put forward more concrete policy proposals. In the case of housing, the 're-creation of a large and expanded sector for private house building' (Macleod and Maude, 1950, p 35) was seen as the key to increasing the supply of competitively priced homes for rent or purchase through such means as planning and licencing reform. Local authorities were also to be encouraged to focus on slum clearance and the 'abatement of overcrowding' rather than the needs of 'better off' tenants (Macleod and Maude, 1950, p 36). In education, priority was to be given to improved primary provision on the grounds that if the 'basic schooling given there is inadequate, or if the child's eagerness to learn is killed at the primary stage by dreary surroundings and uninspired or over-burdened teachers, money spent on secondary or further education is largely wasted' (Macleod and Maude, 1950, p 48). Improvements in the quality of technical schools and colleges were called for, as well as higher salaries for teaching staff. In the case of healthcare, the emphasis was less on service improvement and more on the rising cost of provision. More effective identification of priorities and the introduction of user charges to curb unnecessary demand were seen as two key ways of maintaining cost control within the service. In addition, 'any sentimental urge to divert, through state action, too great a proportion of the nation's resources to the old' ((Macleod and Maude, 1950, p 64) was to be resisted. The informal and voluntary sectors were to play the leading role in meeting the 'welfare' needs of older citizens.

The desire to 'blend judicious Statism with strong inflections of liberal market laissez-faire ideas' (Green, 2002, p 247) proved to be an abiding theme in subsequent One Nation publications in the 1950s. In *Change is our ally* (Powell and Maude, 1954), the recognition that 'social and political considerations should often override economic ones' was not seen as compromising 'the general principle that freely-operating competition is the most effective means of promoting economic advantage' (Powell and Maude, 1954, p 96). Similarly, in *The responsible society*, it was made clear that modern Conservatives did not favour ever-increasing degrees of state welfare provision. On the contrary, the party remained 'pre-disposed (as most socialists are not) to let the individual pay and act for himself when he can' (One Nation Group, 1959, p 35).

One Nation Conservatism

The fact that the membership of the One Nation Group has, since its inception, included politicians from across the Conservative political spectrum,[3] suggests that the term has broad applicability across the party. Indeed, it could be argued that one of the defining features of the 'modern' Conservative Party has been its desire to govern on behalf of the whole nation, to uphold long-established traditions and institutions and to avoid factionalism. From this perspective, it is no surprise, for example, to find that Margaret Thatcher declared herself to be a One Nation Conservative, albeit one of a patriotic, property-owning, rather than paternalistic, ilk.[4] In a *Sunday Times* interview in 1993, for example, she declared that 'Socialism is two nations. The rule of the privileged rulers and everyone else. It always gets to that. But what I am desperately trying to do is create one nation by having everyone being a man of property or the opportunity to be a man of property.... I'm a one nationer' (cited in Seawright, 2010, p 25). Her successor, John Major, also declared himself to be a One Nation Conservative who was unable to fulfil many of his interventionist inclinations because of adverse economic weather.[5]

According to Seawright,[6] the attempt to use the term One Nation in a narrow, paternalistic, interventionist sense can be explained by the political manoeuvrings of certain factions within the party. For example, he argues that in the 1970s and 80s, Iain Gilmour (who served in the Cabinets of both Edward Heath and Margaret Thatcher) attempted to equate the term One Nation exclusively with his own brand of paternalistic Conservatism in an effort to distinguish it from the resurgent, hard-hearted, neo-liberal variant that had come to prominence in the party at that time.[7] Seawright (2010) also suggests that a number of neo-liberal-inclined Conservatives were happy to support Gilmour's efforts in this regard on the grounds that it would allow them to promote their own doctrinal position with greater clarity.

It is, however, difficult to refute the claim that within post-1945 Conservative circles and beyond, the term One Nation has come to be associated with the progressive, interventionist, inclusive, paternalistic strand of party thinking that can be traced back through a line stretching from leaders such as Disraeli and Baldwin as well as other influential party figures such as Steel-Maitland[8] and F.E. Smith[9] (Campbell, 2013) to Macmillan[10] and Boothby.[11] From this perspective, a One Nation Conservative is characterised by paternalistic concern for the well-being of the poor, acceptance of the need to limit the level of inequality in society, support for a managed capitalism, effective industrial partnerships and the welfare state, and opposition to unbridled individualism and the doctrine of laissez-faire.[12] While such beliefs set progressive-minded One Nation Conservatives apart from those party members of a more decidedly neo-liberal persuasion, it is important not to overstate these doctrinal differences. One Nation Conservative support for increased government economic intervention and the welfare state did not mean any weakening of support for traditional Conservative concerns such as sound finance, efficiency, low taxes, thrift, self-reliance, personal freedom, voluntarism and charitable activity. For One Nation Conservatives, the task was to secure a better balance between individualism and collectivism and between the market and the state. Although, some more ardent economic liberals feared that this amounted to acquiescence with the tenets of social democracy or even communism,[13] the One Nation approach slowly began to exert more influence in terms of the direction of Conservative economic and social policy during the 1950s and beyond.[14]

One Nation Conservatism and the welfare state, 1950-55

One indication of the need for a more explicitly progressive One Nation approach to social policy came at the party's annual conference in Blackpool in October 1950 when delegates pressed the leadership to commit itself to building a minimum of 300,000 homes a year on its return to government.[15] One Nation influences could also be detected in the General Election manifesto of the Conservative and Unionist Party of 1951 (reprinted in Dale, 2000). The Conservatives once again sought to reassure the electorate that they posed no threat to the newly established welfare state. Their specific commitments were relatively modest, being restricted to increased house building, more effective spending in the areas of health and education and helping pensioners with the greatest needs. However, the central theme of the manifesto, and the accompanying poster campaign,[16] was the socialist mismanagement of the economy, which the Conservatives argued had given rise to shortages and profligate forms of social expenditure. In his manifesto address, Churchill claimed that only a Conservative administration 'not biased by privilege or interest or cramped by doctrinal prejudices or inflamed by the passions of class welfare' would be able to stimulate enterprise, increase the availability of consumer goods, 'halt the rising cost of living' and 'prune waste and extravagance' in all government departments (Dale, 2000, pp 95-9).

The party also made an explicit attempt to win the support of women voters. The party had sought to distance itself from organisations like the British Housewives League, which campaigned against the adverse effects of Labour's austerity measures on the daily lives of the ordinary 'housewife' on the grounds that it was too closely connected with the extreme right of British politics.[17] However, the Conservatives recognised that they stood to gain politically if they presented themselves as 'the champion of the female consumer by recognizing the burden borne by women under post-war austerity and promising relief in the form of decontrol, restoration of the price mechanism, and increased supplies of consumer goods' (Zweiniger-Bargielowska, 2000, p 262).

Although the party secured a marginally smaller proportionate share of the popular vote (48%) than their Labour opponents (48.2%) in the 1951 General Election, this proved sufficient to secure a 17-seat majority for the Conservatives. Their improved performance in suburban seats coupled with their ability to attract former Liberal voters (only 109 Liberal candidates stood in the 1951 General Election compared with 475 in 1950) enabled the Conservatives to win 321 out of the 617 contested seats.[18]

Restored to the premiership at the age of 77, Churchill's first Cabinet reflected his preference for reliable and experienced ministers. Butler's appointment as Chancellor gave hope to those who wanted to see a One Nation influence on domestic policy, as did Macmillan's decision to accept the challenge of meeting the party's pivotal house-building plans by agreeing to become Minister for Housing and Local Government in October 1951. Those appointed to the remaining non-Cabinet social policy posts tended, however to come from the 'right' of the party – Crookshank (health), Heathcoat-Amory (pensions), Horsbrugh (education) and Peake (National Insurance).

The new government's commitment to the welfare state was put to the test in the aftermath of its election victory. Faced with a substantial balance of payments deficit that had triggered international speculation against the pound, Butler sought to limit imports, tighten monetary policy and keep a tight grip on public expenditure.[19] The need to curb expenditure limited the policy options for the new departmental teams that had taken the reins at education, National Insurance and pensions.

In education, Horsbrugh asked local authorities to make a 5% cut in their capital spending plans for 1952/53, while the Economic Policy Committee Sub-committee on the Economic Situation, chaired by Butler, contemplated raising the entry age for compulsory schooling (and lowering the school-leaving age), while the Treasury proposed the re-imposition of school fees.[20] Although Horsbrugh was able to fend off most of these proposals, the school-building programme was delayed, which limited the possibility of cutting class sizes in the secondary sector. The improved financial outlook in 1954 did, however, give Horsbrugh's successor, David Eccles, the opportunity to press ahead with an expansion of technical education, a reduction in all age schools in rural areas and an increase in school building.

Health spending, which had grown rapidly since the inception of the NHS, was also targeted for retrenchment. Various ways of reducing expenditure and boosting revenue were explored. These included increased prescription charges, the introduction of hospital 'hotel' fees and the withdrawal of ophthalmic and dental services. After much internal deliberation, it was eventually decided to increase prescription charges by one shilling and introduce a £1 fee for standard dental treatment (both measures being incorporated in the 1952 Health Act). The appointment of Iain Macleod, a leading One Nation Conservative and supporter of the welfare state, as Minister of Health 1952 did not, however, result in any major expansion of health provision. Instead, Macleod attempted to stabilise the service and reduce the rate of increase in NHS spending. The setting up of the Guillebaud Committee in May 1953 to investigate NHS spending provided Macleod with an opportunity to foil Treasury demands for cost-cutting measures such as the suspension of the ophthalmic and dental services, charges for ambulance services and the prohibition of non-standard drug prescriptions[21] on the grounds that such decisions should be delayed pending the publication of the committee's report.

In the area of social security, incoming ministers had to deal with some of the complex consequences of the Beveridge 'settlement'. Treasury resistance to the notion of subsistence benefits and concern about a projected deficit in the National Insurance Fund had to be balanced against manifesto commitments concerning improvements in pensioner incomes, which were being eroded by inflation. Various measures were taken to deal with these problems, although they proved to be only temporary expedients. The failure to uprate pensions in line with inflation had resulted in growing numbers of pensioners being forced to supplement their National Insurance (NI) pensions through means-tested National Assistance payments, which were set at a more generous 'subsistence' rate. In an attempt to rectify this issue, NI pensions for married couples were increased in 1953. These were to be funded by increased employer and employee contributions.

A committee headed by Sir Thomas Phillips was set up in May 1953 to review the NI scheme. In its report published in 1955, the committee recommended that a new actuarial formula for NI contributions be introduced that would better reflect projected rises in longevity. The report also suggested that it might be necessary to increase the pension age to 68 for men and to 63 for women. Any move towards more generous subsistence benefits was ruled out as both undesirable and unaffordable. The impact of the report was undermined to some extent by the government's pre-emptive decision to respond to growing public disquiet about the declining value of pensioner benefits by agreeing to increase the basic pension for a couple to 40 shillings per week – the measure being incorporated in the *National Insurance Act* of 1955.

In the light of the party's much-vaunted house-building target, it is not surprising to find that the new Minister of Housing, Harold Macmillan was in a stronger position to resist Treasury demands for restraint in this area of social policy. By putting his department on a war footing and relying on the expertise of the businessman Sir Percy Mills and an energetic junior minister, Ernest Marples, rather than his permanent secretary, Thomas Sheepshanks, Macmillan was able to meet his annual target of 300,000 new homes ahead of schedule in

1953. As Bridgen and Lowe (1998) point out, Macmillan's success was based on 'uncontrolled local authority building based on a generous subsidy structure, increased encouragement of private sector building; and economy in the use of building materials through reductions in building standards and the use of experimental buildings' (p 204). Although Macmillan was the subject of criticism from constituency associations and from the party chairman, Lord Woolton, because of his over-reliance on public sector construction, he recognised that active local authority support was vital if he was to meet his projected target. It was only when he felt confident that his house-building goal could be achieved that Macmillan felt able to turn to more traditional Conservative housing concerns such as a reduction in local authority subsidies, the promotion of owner-occupation and the re-establishment of market rents in both the public and private sectors.

The Eden years, 1955-57

By the time that Churchill had finally been 'persuaded' to stand down as Prime Minister and party leader in early April 1955[22] at the age of 80, the Conservatives could claim with justification that, contrary to the predictions of their Labour opponents, their tenure in office had not led to mass unemployment or the dismantling of the welfare state. Churchill's successor, and long-term leader in waiting, Anthony Eden, called a snap General Election, which took place on 26 May 1955. In the party's manifesto, *United for peace and progress: The Conservative and Unionist Party's policy,* much was made of the ideological divide between the two main parties. Labour was portrayed as the party of nationalisation, regulation and controls and shortages, which involved 'an endless vista of filling in forms, cutting out coupons, applying for permits, waiting on housing lists and standing in queues' (see Dale, 2000, p 105). In contrast, the Conservatives were the party of freedom and opportunity, who would always be willing to 'give a lead', provide 'support and advice', 'protect the public interest' and 'restrain abuse', but would not interfere in the 'day to day running of business' or tell 'housewives how to do their shopping'. By enhancing the freedom of both producers and consumers, it was envisaged that living standards would double over the next 25 years. Eden made great play of the Conservatives' commitment to the creation of a property-owning democracy, a phrase that had first been coined by the influential inter-war Conservative thinker, Noel Skelton.[23] Skelton had been concerned that rapid working-class advancement in the spheres of politics and education had not been matched in relation to property rights. To rectify this situation Skelton had advocated greater levels of 'industrial co-partnerships and profit-sharing' (Francis, 2012, p 277).[24] Although Eden was supportive of measures of this kind, he placed greater emphasis on private home ownership, believing it to be the key way of empowering the ordinary citizen and of attracting them to the Conservative cause.

The party's welfare record was highlighted in the party's General Election campaign in 1955. Voters were reminded that under the Conservatives the social services had been 'extended and improved' (Dale, 2000, p 110) with nearly 350,000 homes being built in 1954, pensions and benefits uprated, new schools constructed and plans set in train for new hospitals. The Conservatives promised, over the course of the next parliament, to eliminate all remaining slums and modernise older properties, cut class sizes, add one million new school places, improve scientific and technical training, build many more new hospitals and give 'constant attention' to the needs of pensioners relying on state benefits.

The manifesto also provided evidence of the emergence of a distinctive non-egalitarian, One Nation Conservative approach to the welfare state:

> We denounce the Labour Party's desire to use the social services, which we all helped to create, as an instrument for levelling down. We regard social security, not as a substitute for family thrift, but as a necessary basis or supplement to it. We think of the National Health Service as a means, not of preventing anyone from paying anything for any service, but of ensuring that proper attention and treatment are denied to no-one. We believe that equality of opportunity is to be achieved, not by sending every boy or girl to exactly the same sort of school, but by seeing that every child gets the schooling most suited to his or her aptitudes. We see a sensible housing policy in terms, not of one hopeless Council waiting list, but of adequate and appropriate provision both for letting and for sale. (Dale, 2000, p 119)

On election day, the Conservatives captured 49.7% of the popular vote (on a 2% national swing), enabling them to secure a 58-seat majority. A comfortable majority of this kind provided Eden with a clear opportunity to implement a One Nation Conservative welfare programme. How was he to fare? As with so many post-1945 governments, Eden's new administration was soon put to the test.

The economy began to overheat and the balance of payments position deteriorated in the latter part of 1955. By late summer, the pound was coming under pressure and a credit squeeze had been introduced. Eden was reluctant to adopt anti-inflationary measures that might undermine his One Nation credentials. Accordingly, he rejected calls for the ending of bread subsidies, but did agree to an emergency 'pots and pans' budget[25] in October 1955, which resulted in the Chancellor being criticised, not least by his opposite number Hugh Gaitskell, for clawing back many of the concessions that had been introduced in his pre-election budget.

Butler's successor at the Treasury, Harold Macmillan, responded to the worsening economic position by curbing expenditure (including cuts to bread and milk subsidies), increasing interest rates and tightening hire purchase arrangements. In his first and only budget on 15 April 1956, Macmillan found his room for manoeuvre limited as he attempted to curb price and wage inflation (which were running at 3.5% and 4.5% respectively). He delivered a 'broadly neutral budget' that was most notable for the decision to encourage saving by the introduction of Premium Bonds.[26]

The deteriorating economic outlook was proving particularly disconcerting to existing and prospective middle-class Conservative voters who believed that they were having to bear more financial pain than their working-class compatriots, whose threats of industrial action all too often led to generous wage settlements being sanctioned by the Minister of Labour Sir Walter Monkton (who was known as the 'oil can' on account of his emollient approach when dealing with trade unionists).[27] The formation of two middle-class pressure groups in 1956 – the Middle Class Alliance and the People's League for the Defence of Freedom – coupled with disappointing by-election results in constituencies such as Torquay, Gainsborough and Tonbridge, served to confirm opinion poll evidence that support for the Eden government was fast ebbing away.[28]

Given the underlying economic 'malaise', it is not surprising that there was little appetite for developing or enhancing state welfare provision during the Eden era. Indeed, the main imperative was to curb the growth in social expenditure without giving rise to renewed voter unease about the party's commitment to the welfare state.

Persistent economic shocks since the creation of the welfare state including the convertibility crisis of 1947, the devaluation of 1949, the Korean war, the Suez canal crisis and balance of payments difficulties ensured that Treasury officials were constantly seeking to control social expenditure by means of annual reviews as well as one-off ministerial reviews such as that conducted by the Swinton Committee.[29] In response to an expenditure review in 1955 predicting that social expenditure would rise faster than GNP over the next five years, a Social Service Committee was established in 1956. This was intended to be a 'collaborative' exercise in which the Financial Secretary of the Treasury (Henry Brooke) would set out spending trends and dilemmas to minsters in areas such as education (Eccles), health (Robert Turton), National Insurance (John Boyd-Carpenter) and housing (Duncan Sandys). Treasury attempts to secure cost savings (£146 million over five years), by imposing higher NHS charges, increasing the school entry age from five to six and raising the price of school meals, were, however, successfully rebuffed by the spending ministers concerned, who relied on a 'range of historical, social, administrative and political arguments' to spike the guns of the Treasury hawks.[30]

The report of the Guillebaud Committee in 1956 also caused dismay in Treasury circles. Instead of identifying ways to control spending or making the case for the introduction of an insurance-based scheme (an option which Macmillan favoured), the committee (influenced by the forensic examination of NHS spending by Brian Abel-Smith and Richard Titmuss) reported that the modest cost increase from £374.9 million in 1948-49 to £388.6 million in 1952-53 (constant prices) resulted from inflation and a wider range of services rather than profligacy. The committee pointed out that NHS spending as a percentage of GNP had actually declined from 3.82% (1948-50) to 3.52% (1952-53). The committee's findings that the service was 'under-funded' and that hospitals were in need of urgent additional capital investment effectively scuppered Treasury hopes of securing major savings in this sphere.[31]

Although Macmillan's successor at the Department of Housing and Local Government, Duncan Sandys, refused to attend the Treasury reviews mentioned, he was prepared to make some expenditure savings. He agreed to phase out the general needs subsidy to local authorities as permitted under the Housing Subsidies Act of 1956 and to a reduction in the ability of local authorities to obtain 'cheap' funds under the Public Works Loan scheme. He was, however, less sympathetic to Treasury demands for an artificial cap on council house construction, preferring instead to allow local authorities to decide on the appropriate number of units they would provide. This was, however, subject to an agreement to fund this through rent increases (and where necessary rent rebates) that would be applied to both older and newer properties. *The Housing Subsidies Act* also provided additional financial support for councils that were prepared to countenance high-rise developments (four storeys or more). This led to a 500% increase in these so-called 'tower blocks' by 1960.

Treasury demands for economy had limited effect in the area of social security arrangements, save for minor modifications to the earnings rule for pensioners, modest enhancements in war pensions and industrial injuries benefits and an agreement to withdraw any plans for higher benefit payments.[32] The main policy objective was to resist demands for higher benefit payments.

The Education Minister David Eccles fared rather better in his dealings with the Treasury. With Eden's support he was able, for example, to secure a commitment to improve 'growth enhancing' technical education (including day release for recent school leavers). A White paper on technical education was published in February 1956 (Department of Education, 1956), which included plans for 12 new Colleges of Advanced Technology.[33]

Long-standing concerns surrounding Eden's physical and temperamental suitability for the premiership resurfaced after his temporary withdrawal from public life on grounds of ill health following the Suez debacle in 1956. Although the party had been broadly united and highly supportive of his decision to retake the Suez Canal by force following Nasser's audacious decision to 'nationalise' this vital shipping lane, murmurings of discontent came to the surface following the ignominious decision to beat a hasty retreat in the face of diplomatic pressure from the United Nations and prospective economic sanctions from the US.[34] During Eden's recuperative break in Jamaica during the height of the political storm that followed the withdrawal from Suez, Butler (1971) was left with the onerous task of 'withdrawing the troops, re-establishing the pound, salvaging ... relations with the US, and bearing the brunt of criticism from private members, constituency worthies and the general public' (p 194). On his return to England, Eden found that confidence in his ability to lead both his party and the nation had ebbed away. He eventually tendered his formal resignation on grounds of ill health in 1957, to be replaced (following 'soundings' conducted by Lord Salisbury and others) by Harold Macmillan, who had proved adroit in outmanoeuvring Butler in the succession battle.[35]

The Macmillan era (January 1957 to October 1963): towards an 'opportunity' (welfare) state?

Act One: January 1957 to October 1959

In the first and only budget presented by Macmillan's new Chancellor Peter Thornycroft in April 1957, strong export growth was used as a justification for some modest tax cuts totalling some £100 million.[36] However, Thorneycroft was concerned about rising inflation, a theme that was subsequently taken up by Macmillan in his 'never had it so good' speech at Bedford football ground in July 1957 in which he drew attention to the fragility of rising living standards in the light of inflationary pressures. The prescience of Macmillan's warning came to the fore later in the summer when sterling came under pressure amid international fears about the scale of government spending. Thorneycroft and his like-minded neo-liberal junior Treasury team (Nigel Birch and Enoch Powell) responded to this unexpected 'shock' by tightening control of the money supply (the bank rate was increased from 5% to 7% in September 1957) and by pressing for prospective expenditure levels to be held at 1957-58 levels, even if this might give rise to higher levels of unemployment. Thorneycroft opposed ministerial demands for higher spending to the tune of £153 million. Instead, he called for significant cuts including the withdrawal of Family Allowances for second children, increased NI contributions and higher charges for school milk – measures that were opposed by Macleod and Butler who thought they would re-ignite public concerns about the party's commitment to the welfare state. Following an uneasy stand-off between Thorneycroft and his Cabinet colleagues over the size of the cuts (which was exacerbated by time constraints occasioned by Macmillan's imminent departure for a tour of Africa), the Chancellor and his two Treasury ministers, Birch and Powell, resigned from the government. This incident served to underline Macmillan's progressive paternalist disposition to economic and social policy. While he remained keen to maintain a strong economy, Macmillan was unwilling to preside over a rise in unemployment (the devastating effects of which were ingrained on him as a result of his experiences as a North-East MP in the inter-war years) even if this led to higher rates of inflation.

This 'little local difficulty', as Macmillan described it, did not have any major consequences for Macmillan's government but, as Thorpe (2010) reminds us, it 'marked only a temporary end to the doctrine of economic liberalism underpinned by sound money' (p 406). Thorneycroft's successor, the 'amiable west-country squire'

Derick Heathcoat-Amory (Clarke, 1996, p 269), oversaw a significant improvement in the economy. Price inflation was brought under control not least as a result of a fall in import prices, tax cuts of £50 million were announced in the 1958 budget, and the bank interest rate was cut to 6% (20 March 1958) and subsequently to 4% (20 November 1958). In the pre-election budget of 1959, consumer confidence in the Conservatives' stewardship of the economy was boosted still further by news of a cut in the standard rate of income tax from '43.5 to 38.75 percent', a 16% cut in purchase tax, the restoration of investment allowances and a two-pence reduction in beer duty.[37]

During this first phase of Macmillan's premiership (January 1957 to October 1959), there were a number of social policy developments that illustrated some key differences between the One Nation Conservative approach to the welfare state and that of the Labour opposition. For example, the 1957 Housing Act represented a concerted attempt to counter Labour's attempts to ensure that housing, at least in the rented sector, became seen as an integral part of the welfare state. Following on from an earlier statute (the *Housing Rent and Repairs Act* of 1954, which had allowed private landlords to increase rents to cover the cost of necessary repairs), this new piece of legislation attempted to revive the private rented sector by allowing market rents to be levied, and tenant security to be gradually reduced, for all new lettings. Rents levels would also rise for existing controlled tenancies above a set rateable level. Although the passage of the Act gave rise to some fierce parliamentary exchanges between the two main parties, its initial impact was not the sharp rise in rents predicted by opposition critics (though these did occur) but, rather, increased sales, rather than re-lets, of decontrolled properties.[38]

In the area of education, the new minister, Geoffrey Lloyd, was keen to solidify the One Nation Conservative policy that had been established by his predecessor David Eccles. This meant retaining selective grammar schools and the broader tripartite system they operated within, and resisting Labour's plans for comprehensive schooling. It was recognised, however, that parental unease about the administration of the 11-plus examination and the geographical disparities in the availability of grammar school places needed to be addressed. In terms of the latter, state funds were to be allocated in ways that would ensure that between 15% and 25% of pupils in each local education authority would have access to selective schooling. In the White Paper, *Secondary education for all: A new drive* (Ministry of Education, 1958), efforts were also made to improve parental confidence in the secondary modern sector by investing more heavily in these schools and allowing more academically minded pupils to sit GCE examinations.[39]

There was also significant legislative development in social security as Boyd-Carpenter, with Macmillan's support, attempted to develop Conservative-style NI reform that would deal with public concerns about the inflation-driven fall in the value of pensions as well as with growing demands for more generous provision in retirement, which had been fuelled in part by Labour's pledge to introduce half pay pensions for all workers. Macmillan had hoped for a speedy resolution of this issue. However, protracted debate between Boyd-Carpenter and the Treasury over the new scheme, not least over the 'opting out' arrangements favoured by the Social Security Secretary, meant an uneasy compromise in the shape of the 1959 *National Insurance Act*, which was enacted shortly before the General Election.[40] Under the new arrangements, workers earning between £9 and £15 per week were to be provided with an additional state 'earnings related' pension on retirement. Employers could opt out of this new scheme if they could demonstrate that they were operating a scheme for their employees that was at least as good as the state alternative.[41]

As was noted previously, the lengthy deliberations and final report of the Guillebaud Committee served to insulate the NHS from any dramatic change in the early part of the Macmillan era up to 1959. Macmillan was keen to see a shift from a tax financed to an NI-funded NHS. In 1956-57 just 6.4% of NHS expenditure was covered by national insurance contributions. It was felt that a shift to national insurance funding would enable income tax to be reduced and ensure that both practitioners and patients took a keener interest in the cost of provision by a more transparent funding arrangement. Although the NI contribution to the NHS was increased to 14.4% in 1959-60[42] following the *National Health Contributions Act* of 1957, the idea of a fully NI-funded NHS was eventually abandoned as impractical.[43]

Butler's move to the Home Office from the Treasury in January 1957 proved to be the catalyst for the emergence of a more liberal One Nation Conservative approach to penal policy. After presiding over the *Homicide Act* of 1957, which limited the use of the death penalty to some instances of murder, Butler introduced a landmark White Paper, *Penal practice in a changing society* (Home Office, 1959), which emphasised the role that both in-house (the Home Office Research Unit had been set up in 1956) and external (the establishment of the Institute of Criminology at Cambridge University) bodies could play in understanding and combatting crime. Significant investment in prisons and borstals was recommended, as was the introduction of specialist

Attendance and Detention Centres for young people. Psychiatric, psychological and after-care services were also to be improved and expanded (see Jarvis, 2005). Butler was more cautious in his response to the Wolfenden Report on homosexual offences and prostitution in 1957. While he was willing to press ahead with reform on the laws relating to prostitution, he believed that the British public were not yet ready to support legal liberalisation in relation to homosexuality.[44]

This first phase of the Macmillan era also saw the issue of immigration move up the political agenda. 'Race' disturbances in Nottingham, Notting Hill and Dudley in 1958 fuelled anxieties within the party about the potential for social disharmony resulting from unrestricted non-white immigration from Commonwealth countries.[45] At the party's annual conference in Blackpool, delegates supported a motion calling for immigration controls despite Butler's plea that the historic rights of commonwealth citizens to come to Britain unheeded should continue to be respected.[46]

In their 1959 election manifesto (*The Conservative Party General Election manifesto 1959: The next five years*), the Conservatives drew attention to the economic progress that had occurred as a result of eight consecutive years of Conservative rule, declaring that their aim was to 'double the British standard of living' in a generation and to provide greater opportunities for citizens to 'earn more and to own more' and 'create a better life for themselves' not least through reductions in taxation. The manifesto also reflected a growing concern in party circles that the heavy emphasis on ensuring that 'the good things in life' could be 'enjoyed by families large and small' should not detract from non-materialist reasons for voting Conservative:

> Conservatism is more than successful administration. It is
> a way of life. It stands for integrity as well as for efficiency,
> for moral values as well as for material advancement, for
> service and not merely self-seeking. (Dale, 2000, p 130)

For progressive One Nation Conservatives, the provision of state social services for those in legitimate need was one way of fulfilling the party's ethical vision. Not surprisingly, therefore, the party's welfare record in developing the social services was highlighted in the manifesto. 'We have provided over two million new homes and almost two million new school places, a better health service and a modern pensions plan' (Dale, 2000, p 130). In terms of specific welfare pledges, the party promised to defend the grammar schools from 'doctrinaire socialist attack', while bringing the quality of the secondary modern sector 'up to the same high standard'. Teacher training provision would be increased, class sizes reduced and university student numbers increased by a third. In housing, priority would be given to slum clearance, the relief of overcrowding and the needs of older people. The party rejected as 'costly and bureaucratic nonsense' Labour's plan to bring three million privately rented homes under council control. The Conservatives also promised that they would oversee a big programme of hospital building and the continuation of preventative health measures such as the *Clean Air Act*. The need to ensure that older people benefited from the rise in national prosperity was also emphasised.

The degree to which the Conservatives' social, as opposed to economic, agenda was uppermost in voters' minds is, however, open to question. Certainly aspirational voters in 'newly prosperous areas like Dagenham and Coventry (where Labour lost a seat for the first time since the war) and in new working-class housing developments such as at Boreham Wood or Birmingham's outer estates' (Kynaston, 2013, p 364) appeared to respond most positively to Conservative warnings that their growing prosperity would be jeopardised by the return of a Labour government. On a 78.75% turnout, the Conservatives gained 49.4% of the popular vote in the 1959 General Election, giving them a third successive peacetime victory and an overall majority of 100 seats.

Act Two: October 1959 to October 1963

With a large parliamentary majority, the prospects for the new Conservative government appeared to be extremely favourable. However, within 18 months of his election victory, Macmillan's popularity was on the slide and the party began to recognise that it would be an uphill task to secure a fourth consecutive election victory. In particular, the government's ability to deliver continued economic prosperity was being called into question. Despite Chancellor Heathcoat-Amory's desire to take more stringent steps to dampen down an overheating economy in what proved to be his last budget in 1960, Macmillan insisted on a more neutral set of measures that left the underlying problem unresolved.

Although Heathcoat-Amory's successor, Selwyn Lloyd, was prepared to adopt a more interventionist strategy, he found it difficult to nudge the economy in a more positive direction not least because of external economic pressures. Following a 'cautious' budget in 1961 in which the surtax threshold was raised from £2,000 to £4,000, more deflationary measures were introduced in a 'mini budget' in July to offset the threat of devaluation occasioned by the revaluation of the

German mark and the adverse impact of an unofficial dock strike the previous May.[47] Credit was tightened, the bank rate was increased and cuts in expenditure were set in train. In addition, a 'pay pause' for public service workers and a subsequent 2.5% 'ceiling' in 1962, were to prove extremely unpopular. Selwyn Lloyd's second budget in April 1961 was again fiscally neutral and was widely adjudged to have done little to resolve the economic malaise. Party members were cheered by the decision to scrap the so-called 'schedule A' tax on owner-occupiers, though a future cohort of potential voters would have been less enamoured by the 'toffee tax' on sweets and ice cream.

In an effort to improve the economic outlook, Macmillan launched a 'New Approach', which, like his earlier proposal for British membership of the European Common Market, was intended to restore the Conservative's reputation as competent, forward-looking guardians of national prosperity. A corporatist National Economic Development Council ('Neddy') formed part of this New Approach, as did the National Incomes Commission ('Nicky'), which was set up to adjudicate on pay claims. It was envisaged that a formal 'independent' body of this kind would ensure that pay awards could be set at fair levels that would deliver the magic elixir of steady growth, full employment, low inflation and a stable currency. The lack of Trades Union Congress co-operation (the unions had been highly critical of the earlier surtax concessions to the rich), did not, however augur well for this new body.

How then did the welfare state fare in these more troubled economic times? Housing bore the brunt of Selwyn Lloyd's early attempts to pare back social expenditure. The Cabinet agreed to a £5 million reduction in the housing programme in 1960, followed by a further reduction in 1961/62, which reduced the number of houses built in England and Wales from a projected 115,000 to 100,000. However, at a time of household growth, increased homelessness and a spike in property prices fuelled by the growth in speculative private sector investment (which had been stimulated by measures such as the abolition of the betterment tax), the new Housing Minister, Charles Hill, with Macmillan's support sought to reverse this trend.

It was recognised that the 1957 *Rent Act* had failed to revitalise the private rented sector. Indeed, this latter initiative had become tainted by what came to be known as 'Rachmanism', a term associated with the unscrupulous methods used by Perec Rachman, the landlord of large number of rental properties in the Notting Hill area of London, to 'persuade' sitting tenants paying low controlled rents to vacate his properties so that higher market rents could be levied on new occupants. These included unannounced visits from 'wrestlers and boxers' (Sandbrook, 2005, p 313) and 'lifting the roof off one property' (Jefferys, 1997, p 143). In response to opposition taunts that the 1957 Act only served to confirm that the Conservatives always sided with the private landlord rather than powerless, hard-pressed tenants, the government developed a more interventionist public sector housing strategy culminating in the *Housing Acts* of 1961 and 1963. Both statutes highlighted the need for greater emphasis to be given to areas where the housing shortfall was particularly acute. Housing associations and co-operatives were encouraged as a way of combatting the 'failure of the private rented sector' (Bridgen and Lowe, 1998, p 225). The limited impact of these measures led Hill's successor, Keith Joseph, to secure Cabinet agreement for a more ambitious house-building target of 350,000 homes in 1963. However, as Bridgen and Lowe (1998) conclude, despite some 'innovative measures' in the 1963 *Housing Act*, such as the development of housing associations in large towns, the government's attempt 'to defuse the housing issue between 1962 and the general election in 1964' proved 'unsuccessful' (p 232).

The new, fiscally Conservative, Minister of Health, Enoch Powell, was supportive of the need to control current NHS spending. His economic liberal sympathies were confirmed shortly after his appointment when he raised NHS charges (prescription charges were doubled from 1 shilling to 2 shillings per item). As a consequence, 22% of NHS funding would in future come from NI contributions and charges compared with just 11% in the early 1950s.[48] Powell's reputation as a 'hatchet man' (the cartoonist Vicky always portrayed him with an axe in his hand)[49] appeared to be confirmed by his determination to constrain the pay of nurses[50] in accordance with Selwyn Lloyd's pay pause and to limit NHS expenditure to 2.5% per annum or less between 1961 and 1965 through efficiency savings. However, it should be noted that one of the reasons why Powell was so determined to control current expenditure was that it provided him with an opportunity to rectify chronic capital under-investment in the NHS. An ambitious ten-year hospital plan for England and Wales (Ministry of Health, 1962) was published in the early 1960s paving the way for the construction of 90 new hospitals at a cost of some £500 million. Powell's tenure at the Ministry of Health was also notable for his decision to begin the closure of long-stay mental hospitals and to encourage the growth of community-based care. The poor standard of care in many of these long-stay hospitals coupled with the development of new drugs (that enabled patients to be more easily 'cared' for in the community), convinced Powell that half of all existing Victorian asylums could be closed within 15 years. While there was undoubtedly an economic rationale for this change of policy, Powell was also persuaded that the new measures would improve the quality of care for many long-term patients.[51]

In his final stint at education, David Eccles was faced with a battle to retain sufficient funds to fulfil the school building improvements outlined in the 1958 *Education Act*, which were the key to securing a reduction in class sizes. Treasury demands for expenditure to rise by no more than 3% as opposed to the projected 4.6% rise were strongly opposed by Eccles and the budget reduction that was eventually agreed was soon the subject of further debate following a projected rise in class sizes and the consequent need for more trained teachers. Following Eccles' departure from the government, his successor Edward Boyle managed to secure an additional £7 million for teacher training and an extra £5 million for school building for 1963/64.[52]

As Raison (1990) has pointed out, although there was little significant legislative change in the education sector during this period, education remained a topical issue not least because of a number of landmark reports by Crowther (on education provision for 15- to 18-year-olds – Central Advisory Council for Education, 1959), Newsom (on provision for children aged 13 to 16 of 'average or less than average ability – Central Advisory Council for Education, 1963) and the Robbins Report on higher education (Committee on Higher Education, 1963) as well as continuing concerns about the 11-plus system. Boyle's appointment as Education Secretary marked a shift in government thinking on comprehensive schooling. This proved to be a growing source of concern for more traditionally minded Conservatives who feared egalitarian educational change.[53] While Boyle was opposed to any forcible attempts to close the grammar schools, he favoured the voluntary expansion of comprehensives, noting that some 90 local education authorities had opted for, or were proposing (either wholly or in part), to introduce educational provision of this kind.

Social security presented innumerable problems for the second Macmillan government as it sought to establish the key elements of a Conservative post-Beveridge income support system. In particular, there was continued debate on whether the party should continue with a universal as opposed to selective system, the relationship between National Insurance and National Assistance, and the adequacy or otherwise of benefit payments.[54] In practice, a 'muddling through' strategy became the default position, with changes in benefit levels being introduced in response to political pressures from both claimants and their Labour opponents. Benefit payments were increased in an ad hoc manner so that the government could not be accused of abandoning its commitment to improve the living standards of pensioners, but by the end of the Macmillan era the Conservatives had still not established a clear basis for their social security policy.[55]

As was noted earlier, immigration was becoming a more significant theme in Conservative circles following the 'race' rots of 1958, particularly in areas experiencing growing levels of non-white New Commonwealth settlement like Birmingham, where a divide was opening up between those MPs demanding tighter controls such as Gurden (Selly Oak), Lloyd (Sutton Coldfield), Lindsey (Solihull), Pitt (Edgbaston) and Cleaver (Sparkbrook), and others such as Boyle (Handsworth) and Jones (Hall Green), who were more relaxed about this development. In the spring of 1961, Conservative supporters had helped to establish the 'non-political' Birmingham Immigration Control Association. In the following July, 600 white Smethwick council tenants went on a so-called 'rent strike' to register their protest at the local authority's decision to allocate a maisonette to an immigrant from Pakistan. The growing demand for tighter immigration controls was reflected at the party's annual conference in 1961 where 39 constituency motions were submitted calling for action to stem the growth in numbers coming to the UK. In response to growing concern among its own supporters about the rise of non-white immigration, the government introduced what it attempted to portray as a 'non-racist' Immigration Bill, based on work permits, as part of the Queen's speech in October 1961. This eventually formed the basis for the *Commonwealth Immigration Act* of April 1962. However, as Brooke (1996) reminds us, the 'shape and justification for the bill were predictable. The latter rested entirely upon the question of colour and the protection of white identity, while the shape, based upon an employment voucher system, was consciously intended to mask the racial basis of the bill' (p 162).

Following an unimpressive set of by-election results, most notably in Orpington in March 1962,[56] Macmillan made a number of ministerial changes to freshen up the government in the following July. In the so-called 'night of the long knives', Macmillan axed a third of his Cabinet, including the Chancellor Selwyn Lloyd, Charles Hill (housing), David Eccles (education), Lord Kilmuir (the Lord Chancellor) and Harold Watkinson (defence), replacing them with a group of predominantly younger ministers such as Maudling, Joseph and Boyle.

The expansionist economic strategy pursued by the new Chancellor Reginald Maudling provided Macmillan with grounds for optimism that his reshuffle might restore his government's fortunes, particularly in the light of De Gaulle's decision to veto Britain's application to join the European Economic Community in January 1963. Maudling's budget of April 1963 was designed to help deliver an ambitious 4% non-inflationary annual growth rate. Tax cuts worth £260 million were announced, including increased personal allowances, which took 3,750,000 people out of tax altogether, and the abolition of Schedule A tax on home ownership.[57] However, events in the shape of Macmillan's ineffective response to the spy and sex scandal surrounding the Defence Minister John Profumo[58] quickly dashed any hopes of a permanent recovery in the government's standing. In the face of growing party disillusionment with his leadership and declining public support coupled with personal health concerns, Macmillan, albeit after some prevarication,[59] decided to stand down as Prime Minister in 1963. He was eventually succeeded by Alec Douglas-Home who, having renounced his hereditary peerage under the terms of the recent *Peerage Act* of 1963, made his way up steadily through the field to beat more fancied runners such as Hailsham (who sweated up badly in the parade ring) Maudling (who failed to quicken when asked) and Butler (who stayed on gamely but never looked a likely winner).[60]

Douglas-Home's premiership did not get off to the most auspicious start, as both Macleod and Powell refused to serve in his Cabinet. During his short period in office, Douglas-Home's attention was focused primarily on trying to secure a fourth General Election victory. The party's decision to compete with Labour over ownership of the modernisation agenda appeared to be a high-risk strategy given that Douglas-Home's aristocratic background and diffident persona ('Dull Alec') appeared to put him at a great disadvantage in comparison to his sharp ('Smart Alec'), media-savvy, 'man of the people', 'classless' Labour opponent, Harold Wilson (who had succeeded Hugh Gaitskell following the latter's premature death earlier in the year).[61]

Although the publication of the Robins Report on higher education helped, for example, to bolster the Conservative's modernisation credentials, the decision to abolish Resale Price Maintenance (under which producers were able to control the resale price of the goods they manufactured) in order to augment the party's forward-looking image was arguably less well judged, as was Edward Heath's (the new Minister of Trade and Industry) decision to drive through this measure despite opposition from the small business community that was to trigger a significant backbench revolt.[62]

By delaying the election until October 1964, Douglas-Home succeeded in clawing back the opinion poll lead that Labour had built up since the end of the Macmillan era. He emphasised the improving economic situation that had been occasioned by the expansionist policies pursued by Maudling and the steady rise in prosperity that successive Conservative governments had helped to deliver. The government's long-standing economic competence was highlighted in the party's General Election manifesto of 1964 – *Prosperity with a purpose*.[63] To emphasise this theme, the Conservatives promised to use 'the growth of wealth to expand opportunities for the young, to provide more generously for the old and the sick and the handicapped ....' (Dale, 2000, p 143). In terms of specific welfare pledges, the school-leaving age was to be raised to 16 for all new secondary school entrants in 1967 and grammar schools were to be protected from the 'Socialist plan to impose the comprehensive principle' (p 154). The social security scheme was to be reviewed with benefits targeted on those 'whose needs are greatest' (p 155). House building was to be expanded to 400,000 dwellings per year, with all slum clearance to be completed by 1973. Existing forms of rent control were to be protected. Three hundred hospitals would be built or renovated to 'ensure that every man, woman and child in the country has the access to the best treatment' (p 157) and increasing numbers of health visitors, home nurses, home helps and social workers' would be provided to support older people living at home.

In the event, Douglas-Home was unable to secure a fourth consecutive electoral term for the Conservatives as Labour secured a narrow overall majority of just four seats. Although the Conservatives had lost 1.75 million voters since 1959 and had seen their share of the national vote slip from 49.4% to 43.4%, it would be misleading to suggest that the result represented a resounding endorsement for Labour. As Sandbrook (2005) reminds us, 'if a mere nine hundred voters in eight crucial constituencies had voted for the Conservatives instead of Labour, or even abstained, then Home would have stayed in office' (p 16).

Under both Eden and Macmillan, the One Nation Conservative approach to the welfare state had taken firm root. The welfare state was now widely perceived to be safe in Conservative hands, even though the priorities and strategies differed from Labour's. Arguably, the period between 1959 and 1964 was the high point of One Nation Conservatism. By the time the Conservatives were next in government, there was renewed questioning about the role and purpose of the welfare state in Conservative circles.

FOUR

The Heath 'interregnum': modern technocratic Conservatism and the welfare state, 1965-74

The 1964 General Election

The narrowness of the Conservatives' General Election defeat in 1964 meant that there was no immediate pressure for Douglas-Home to stand down as party leader. A second contest was thought to be imminent given Labour's slender majority, which was reduced to just three following the by-election defeat of the Foreign Secretary, Patrick Gordon-Walker, at Leyton in January 1965.[1]

The possibility of an early election encouraged Douglas-Home to instigate a major policy review, which was to be directed by the new shadow Chancellor Edward Heath, who had succeeded Butler as Chairman of both the Conservative Research Department (CRD) and the Advisory Committee on Policy. Heath, a technocrat by inclination, was keen to introduce a set of policy proposals that would appeal to owner-occupiers, young married couples and Liberal 'swing' voters in time for a snap election.[2] By the spring of 1965, some 36 policy groups had been established, the majority of which were able to submit initial reports to the new CRD Director, Brendon Sewill, by the summer of that year.[3] The ideas emerging from these reports included a renewed bid for entry into the European Economic Community, trade union reform and greater emphasis on 'selectivity' in the field of social policy. These were subsequently included in a policy document entitled *Putting Britain right ahead* (Conservative Political Centre, 1965), which was launched at the party's annual conference in Brighton in October 1965, shortly after Heath (having seen off challenges from Maudling and Powell following a ballot of his fellow Conservative MPs)[4] had succeeded Douglas-Home as Conservative leader.

Although Heath was personally sympathetic to One Nation ideas, he was not wedded to this strand of Conservative thinking or, indeed, to the neo-liberal ideas that were emerging from various think tanks. For Heath and his so-called Heathmen,[5] the main imperative was to modernise and streamline existing economic and social institutions so that Britain could regain its pre-eminent position in the world. Any policy ideas that furthered this aim were to be given serious consideration. For Heath, it was not a question of the provenance of a policy idea but rather the question of whether it might help further his modernising crusade. Pragmatic, evidence-based, expert-led policy and practice rather than 'pure' ideology was the order of the day. The term modern technocratic Conservatism captures this approach.

The policy prescriptions outlined in *Putting Britain right ahead* formed the basis of the party's General Election manifesto in 1966,[6] *Action not words: The new Conservative programme*, which contained 131 specific pledges. The remodelling of the welfare state was a key element in Heath's modernising agenda. As the manifesto made clear:

> We intend to revitalise our welfare state so that those most in need get the most help and so that our money is used sensibly and fairly. We will be working to a fresh pattern of social priorities to meet new needs and help build our community on more responsible lines. We want to see more generous help for those who have special needs not yet met by the Welfare State. We want to see family life strengthened by our Conservative social policies. We intend that there should be full equality of opportunity but not that we should all be equally held back to the pace of the slowest. Our policies are designed to bring higher quality and wider choice into our lives. We reject the kind of outdated thinking which leads to cuts in university and college expansion in order to provide free drugs for all. (Dale, 2000, p 165)

Targeting support on those most in need, identifying new pockets of need, increasing opportunity, and improving quality and choice were to be the watchwords of the modern Conservative approach to social policy. In social security, the party pledged 'to concentrate better care and the biggest benefits on those most in need' (Dale, 2000, p 166). Educational opportunities were to be enhanced by 'putting the needs of the individual child before Party doctrine' (Dale, 2000, p 166). In an effort to narrow the gap between state and fee-paying schools, 'independent schools of high standing' were also to be given the 'opportunity to become direct grant schools' (Dale, 2000, p 170). More primary schools were promised and teacher training places increased. The manifesto also promised to ensure that 'the entire nation' would be 'decently housed' (Dale, 2000, p 166). Government support for home ownership was to be achieved by means of helping with deposits or with interest payments. An annual house-building target of 500,000 homes was to be achieved by 1968, slum clearance accelerated and 'sensible local authority rent policies' established (Dale, 2000, p 166). NHS improvements were to be secured 'by giving family doctors closer contact with hospitals and with local health and welfare services' (Dale, 2000, p 169). The Conservatives were also committed to establishing a major new government department formed by the merger of the 'Ministry of Health, the Ministry of Pensions and National and the National Assistance Board' (Dale, 2000, p 169).

Despite Heath's modernising zeal and positive campaigning, the Conservatives proved unable, as had been widely anticipated within party circles, to loosen Labour's grip on power in 1966. On a 41.9% share of the vote, the party secured just 253 seats, giving Labour an overall majority of 97. The party found it difficult to convince a sceptical electorate that the Conservatives, who had been in office for 13 years between 1951 and 1964, could be trusted to oversee the economic and social regeneration of the nation. 'There was', as Gilmour and Garnett (1998) observe, 'never any possibility of the [Labour] Government losing; by polling day the odds against a Conservative victory had stretched to twenty to one. Labour gained 6 per cent more of the vote than the Conservatives, whose vote fell by nearly 600,000 even though the Liberal share of the vote also dropped' (p 225).

The emphasis that Heath and his Heathmen placed on technocratic modernisation owed much to the influence of the Bow Group[7], the independent research society that had been founded by Conservative Cambridge graduates in 1951 to provide a counter-balance to left-leaning thinks tanks such as the Fabian Society. In the economic sphere, emphasis was to be given to carefully calibrated, 'non-ideological' government action that would provide entrepreneurial managers working within a revitalised, competitive capitalist system in Europe and beyond with the necessary incentives and support to generate increased growth and prosperity.[8] The adoption of a modern technocratic narrative within elite Conservative circles proved to be a source of irritation for those party members who longed for a 'clear blue' message that reflected the party's core values and beliefs. The adoption of a 'non-ideological' narrative was seen as nothing less than an unprincipled accommodation with Labour's statist inclinations, not least in social policy. Although Heath's approach, which included a renewed emphasis on selective rather than universal forms of state welfare, appeared to signal a determination to avoid the charge of 'muddling through', the fact that the changes he was promoting were often described in progressive or modern terms, was of little comfort to those seeking a more distinctive neo-liberal direction in Conservative social policy.

The neo-liberal challenge

The Institute of Economic Affairs (IEA) was arguably the most influential body promoting neo-liberal ideas in Britain in the post-war era. Founded in 1955 by Anthony Fisher[9] and Oliver Smedley, the IEA, under the direction of Ralph Harris and Arthur Seldon, published a series of pamphlets and short works that attempted to persuade opinion formers in politics, the media and universities of the merits of free market ideas. Seldon had a keen interest in the welfare state and, along with other economic liberals, contributed to publications promoting the case for market, as opposed to state, provided pensions, healthcare, housing and education.[10] Although the IEA had some limited success in persuading both Labour (Walden, Houghton)[11] and Liberal (Parloe) politicians of the need to curb government economic intervention and reform the welfare state, it was Conservative MPs such as Enoch Powell and Geoffrey Howe who proved to be more in tune with their ideas. Powell, who became the leading advocate of free-market Conservatism in the 1960s, enjoyed a cordial relationship with the IEA.[12] Although highly critical of economic planning and the reliance on prices and incomes policies, Powell was, in common with influential neo-liberal scholars such as Hayek[13] and Friedman,[14] more circumspect with regard to social policy, believing that the state had a legitimate, if limited role to play in the areas of social security, health and education.[15]

In contrast Geoffrey Howe, who had 'worked closely with Seldon and the IEA on issues such as private medical insurance and industrial relations' (Jackson, 2012, p 58), and who was an influential member and chair (1961-62) of the Bow Group, sought a much more radical reduction in state welfare activity. While Howe was perfectly content for citizens to choose to spend more of their private incomes on enhanced welfare provision, he was highly critical of the Conservative Party's failure to oppose the growth of state spending in this area. In a contribution to *Principles in practice*,[16] a book commemorating the tenth anniversary of the founding of the Bow Group, Howe set out a 'neo-liberal' Conservative approach to the welfare state that involved the rejection of egalitarian forms of redistribution and the principle of universalism.

According to Howe (1961), Conservatives must aim 'for a large reduction, in the long run, of the public social services', while accepting 'the permanent responsibility of caring for those who cannot provide for themselves' (p 61). In practice, this involved eliminating:

> those cases where the state is merely disbursing with one hand money which is then taken with the other. We must ensure that the existing services have built into them the mechanism that is necessary to enable them to contract. People who are able and willing to provide for the health and education of their families should be in every way encouraged to do so. People who are at present obliged by the compulsory insurance scheme to 'take in each other's washing' must be allowed, and indeed encouraged, to do their own. (Howe, 1961, p 68)

For Howe, 'Tory social policy' should have three main aims: 'the relief of primary poverty' through humanely administered forms of means-tested cash assistance, the alleviation of secondary poverty arising from the imprudent choices of 'ignorant' or 'neglectful' citizens and the enhancement of the national interest through such means as enhanced educational opportunities for all. In addition, the state was deemed to have a legitimate role to play in funding (through the savings generated from increased forms of selectivity) larger capital projects. 'Most parents can afford to feed their children. The State alone can build new hospitals' (Howe, 1961, p 72). Encouraged by what he saw as signs of Labour's potential conversion to neo-liberal thinking on the welfare state[17] Howe, in a subsequent Bow Group publication, called for increased forms of 'private' finance and provision and an end to the monopolistic, statist 'waiting-list society'. 'We must ensure', he argued, 'that every citizen has the means, in cash and not in kind if possible, to secure basic services. But we must do this in such a way that he is free to supplement public provision from his own increasing private resources, free as a customer to shop around between different institutions' (Howe, 1965b, p 26).

Heath's modern technocratic approach also held little appeal to traditionally minded Conservatives who believed that the ever-expanding welfare state was a symptom of a wider malaise in British society. The 'permissive' shift in British society, which had been 'aided and abetted' by the adoption of more progressive agendas in spheres such as broadcasting and the arts and by legislative changes in areas such as criminal justice, abortion, divorce, homosexuality, gambling and censorship,[18] was seen then as promoting an individualistic, hedonistic, rights-based culture that was leading to the emergence of an 'irresponsible' society. Permissiveness was seen as corroding the 'will to work', which, in conjunction with full employment and the welfare state, was releasing 'workers from the discipline imposed by unemployment, poverty, and the schooling of many generations in the ways of industrial society' (Gamble, 1974, p 113). The radicalisation of university students, the adoption of 'progressive' teaching methods in primary and secondary schools and attacks on the grammar schools were a source of particular concern to these traditional Conservatives. The authors of the so-called 'Black Papers',[19] for example, feared that young people would leave full-time education devoid of the self-discipline and skills needed for adult life.[20]

Heath's 'technocratic' revivalist economic and social strategy, based as it was on a direct appeal to aspirational middle-class 'pacemakers',[21] proved unattractive to neo-liberal-minded Conservative shadow ministers such as Angus Maude, who was dismissed from the shadow Cabinet by Heath in 1966 after criticising the party's lack of ideological direction in an article in *The Spectator*.[22] The unrepentant Maude continued his attack in a Conservative Party Centre lecture in 1967 on 'The consuming society', highlighting what he saw as the party's undue emphasis on materialism and empiricism. He also defended Enoch Powell's decision to deliver his controversial 'rivers of blood speech' in Birmingham in 1968[23] on the grounds that it would help to open up debate in Conservative circles not only about immigration but also about the permissive society and the detrimental levels of cross-party uniformity.[24]

Selsdon Park and the 1970 General Election

Members of the shadow Cabinet met at the Selsdon Park Hotel in south-east London in 1970 in order to decide on, and familiarise themselves with, the policies that would be included in the forthcoming General Election manifesto.[25] This meeting has come to be seen in some quarters as the pivotal moment when neo-liberal Conservative ideas gained ascendency over those of a progressive One Nation Conservative kind.[26] The idea that party policy would henceforth be underpinned by a neo-liberal Conservative ideology owed less, however, to the actual tenor of the discussions that took place over the weekend. Instead it reflected the media's 'spin' on the discussions based on Macleod's suggestion that the party should highlight its stance on law and order when it held its hastily convened press conference on the Saturday afternoon of the conference.[27]

The Sunday and Monday newspapers interpreted the emphasis on law and order as a signal that the party was shifting to the right, which some titles greeted with enthusiasm while others were more circumspect. *The Economist*, for example, described the Conservatives as 'uncompassionate stainless steel Tories' (cited in Campbell, 1993, p 265). The Labour leader Harold Wilson, in a speech in Nottingham a week later, was quick to identify what he regarded as a 'reactionary' shift in Conservative ideology. As Campbell notes, 'the impression that the Tories had adopted a hardline policy on immigration and policing was quickly seized on by Wilson and skilfully combined with the allegation that the Tories were planning to dismantle the Welfare State and return to the capitalist jungle' (1993, p 265). He invented a composite model of the new breed of hard-faced Tory – economically liberal but socially authoritarian – which he christened 'Selsdon Man'. As with the cartoonist Vicky's earlier depiction of Harold Macmillan as 'Supermac' and the subsequent portrayal of Mrs Thatcher as an 'Iron Lady' by the Russian media, this epithet proved advantageous for the intended victim. As Campbell (1993) continues, '"Selsdon Man" was a brilliant phrase, but it rebounded on Wilson, first because it lent the Opposition's earnest catalogue of humdrum policies precisely the cloak of philosophic unity and political impact that they had hitherto lacked, and second because it turned out that the electorate was at least as much attracted as repelled by them' (p 265).

The extent of Heath's conversion to the neo-liberal Conservative cause at this time remains a matter of contention. The fact that Heath did not appear to dissent from this depiction of the party's ideological shift in the run-up to the 1970 General Election provides support for the view that, at the very least, he saw some political advantage in being associated with some of these ideas.[28] Certainly, it could be argued that some neo-liberal insights, which were formulated on the basis of up-to-the-minute expert analysis of contemporary trends and developments, were compatible with Heath's modern, technocratic approach to economic and social policy. However, it was the theme of modernisation that animated Heath and most of his shadow cabinet colleagues. It was a case of pursuing the right policies for the modern age rather than any strict adherence to neo-liberal or One Nation Conservative doctrine.[29]

The party's 1970 General Election manifesto, *A better tomorrow* (Dale, 2000), did, however, reflect the growing influence of neo-liberal ideas on Conservative thinking and policymaking. On the economic front the fight against inflation was to be prioritised, taxes lowered, the size of government reduced and trade unions reformed. The manifesto also promised that the Conservatives would tackle the 'serious rise in crime and violence' (Dale, 2000, p 194), end 'large-scale permanent immigration' and encourage voluntary repatriation (Dale, 2000, p 193). Social service spending was to be better targeted, the sale of council housing encouraged and social security administration strengthened to ensure that the 'shirkers and scroungers' did not bring the service into 'disrepute' (Dale, 2000, p 191).

Neo-liberal sabre rattling of this kind should not be interpreted as signalling the abandonment of the party's conditional support for the welfare state that the One Nation wing of the party had promoted during the post-war era. One of the major themes of the manifesto was that the Conservatives were better able to exercise stewardship over the economy and, as such, would generate the growth needed to 'improve Britain's social services to the full' (Dale, 2000, p 189). The manifesto promised to 'bring about a great increase in home ownership' (Dale, 2000, p 188), tackle homelessness and the problem of slum housing, improve primary school provision, raise the school-leaving age to 16 and expand higher education. A Conservative administration would also provide a pension income to the over-eighties as of right, introduce attendance allowances for the 'seriously disabled' (Dale, 2000, p 191), counter the 'problem of family poverty' (p 191) and improve social work services in the light of the Seebohm recommendations (see Seebohm, 1968). The number of health centres was to be increased and 'more emphasis' placed 'on community services' so that more people could be 'looked after at home where they are happier' (Dale, 2000, p 192). The manifesto also underlined the subtle shift in party thinking about academic selection in state schools. Abolition of the 11-plus was now deemed to be a positive step forward given that 'in most cases the age of eleven is too early to make final decisions which affect a child's whole future' (Dale, 2000, p 190). Local education authorities were now to be given the right to introduce comprehensive schooling if they adjudged this to be 'best for their area' (Dale, 2000, p 190).

Confounding the views of electoral 'experts' and opinion poll evidence, Heath led the Conservatives to a 'surprise' victory in the 1970 General Election, aided, it has been suggested, by the untimely announcement of unexpectedly poor trade figures and England's inglorious exit from the World Cup finals in Mexico at the hands of West Germany.[30] On a national swing of 4.8%, the Conservatives returned to government after a six-year absence with an overall majority of 30 seats.[31]

Into government

Although social policy developments during the Heath era (June 1970 to February 1974) had a decidedly modern technocratic flavour, this involved the incorporation of 'relevant' neo-liberal and One Nation Conservative ideas rather than any outright rejection.

It can be argued that Keith Joseph's reform of the National Health Service,[32] which was designed to resolve some of the underlying difficulties with 'separate' administrative arrangements for GP, hospital and local authority services, is the best example of an ideological light form of 'technocratic modernisation'. As Timmins (2001) points out, Joseph replaced '700 hospital boards, boards of governors, management committees and executive councils, with 14 regional health authorities, 90 area health authorities each with a linked family practitioner committee, and 200 district management teams each with a community health council to watch over it' (p 293). Peter Walker's reform of local government, which was implemented at around the same time, can also be regarded as another example of a decidedly technocratic modernisation approach. Under the Local Government Act of 1972, some 14,000 local authorities were pared back to 420 administrative jurisdictions, though the retention of a significant number of two-tier county and district administrative units[33] only served to perpetuate 'the old administrative antagonisms and the damaging divisions between interrelated services' (Lowe, 2005, p 102).

The Heath government's attempt to merge the tax and benefits system through the introduction of a sophisticated computerised system also seemed to fit within the technocratic modernisation ambit. However, as Sutcliffe-Braithwaite[34] reminds us, neo-liberals such as Friedman[35] and Lees[36] had been promoting such ideas on the grounds that they represented the ideal form of 'social security' for ensuring 'the free functioning of the market' and for preserving work incentives. The Heath government eventually abandoned its ambitious plan in this sphere. The administrative complexities of the proposed scheme proved insurmountable and there were fears of voter backlash from those groups who believed they might lose out as a result of the changes.[37]

There were also a number of social policy measures that had a more distinctive neo-liberal Conservative lineage. The introduction of Family Income Supplement (FIS) in 1972 comes into this category. 'Reneging' on a pre-election promise made by Iain Macleod[38] to the Child Action Poverty Group in March 1972 that a future Conservative government would increase Family Allowances,[39] Keith Joseph opted, instead, to introduce a less costly, selective, anti-poverty measure in the shape of

FIS. Under FIS, low-earning families with dependent children would have their incomes enhanced by up to 50% of the difference between their gross income and the designated income they 'required' to avoid financial hardship.[40]

The introduction of the *Housing Finance Act* in 1972 and the promotion of council house sales also had a decidedly neo-liberal Conservative provenance. The 1972 legislation, which 'went through what was then the longest Standing Committee stage in parliamentary history' (Raison, 1990, p 75), sought to move away from general property-based allowances to the subsidising of individual tenants deemed to be in the greatest need of support. Local authorities lost the right to set their own rents and were obliged, instead, to levy 'fair' rents on all their tenants and to operate a national rent rebate scheme for low-income tenants in both the public and private sector. Labour controlled councils opposed this legislation not least because central government was able to claw back 50% of any rental surplus that councils had previously used for general rent subsidies for spending on other local services. Labour councillors in Clay Cross, Derbyshire, refused to comply with the new regulations, which resulted in the appointment of a special housing commissioner and the eventual surcharging of 11 council members.[41]

The sale of council housing, which been advocated by many economic liberals within the party since the end of the Second World War,[42] was embraced by the Heath government, which believed this could help in the party's long-term aim to create a property-owing democracy. Councils were instructed not to stand in the way of tenants who wanted to purchase their home. Although the number of sales were modest (around 60,000 sales in 1972)[43], the policy proved popular with grassroots Conservative supporters.

Social security fraud, immigration and pension reform were three other policy areas in which neo-liberal Conservative influences could be detected. In response to neo-liberal Conservative fears about the level of fraud in the social security system, which had been heightened by the publication of *The benefits racket* by Robin Page (1971), a former Executive Officer at the Supplementary Benefits Commission,[44] the new government set up the Fisher Committee in 1971. The committee's report[45] (Fisher, Sir, H., 1973) reaffirmed the importance of preventing and detecting abuse not least because of the need to uphold 'general standards of morality in society' (Fisher, Sir, H., 1973, para 37, p 11). Claimants were to be refused benefit if they 'neglected to avail' themselves of appropriate employment opportunities (Fisher, Sir, H., 1973, para 267, p 110) or if they had hindered their prospects of finding work by virtue of their 'conduct and habits' (Fisher, Sir, H., 1973, para 267, p 111). Consideration was also to be given to the use of the *Theft Act* or the *Forgery Act* in the prosecution of some benefit fraudsters, given the low 'maximum penalties' permissible under 'the social security Acts' (Fisher, Sir, H., 1973, Recommendation 76, p 242). However, Timmins (2001) suggests that Joseph and his officials were reluctant to implement 'draconian' reforms of this kind not least because of the detrimental effects this would have on the 'deserving' dependents of supposedly 'undeserving' fraudsters (p 286).

The 1971 *Immigration Act*, which came into force in 1973, tightened previous legislation by introducing a system of work permits for all immigrants. Under this Act, all immigrants and their dependents were to be denied any automatic right of permanent residence. In addition, the Act permitted public funds to be used for voluntary forms of repatriation.

The Conservatives' proposed pension reforms were also influenced by neo-liberal Conservative ideas, not least because of the perceived need to distinguish their approach from Labour's statist 'egalitarian' redistributive scheme. Under Conservative plans, the private sector was to be accorded the major role in the provision of second, earnings-related pensions, with the state's responsibility limited to the operation of a residual scheme on behalf of those employers unable to provide a viable form of occupational cover.[46]

The fact that social expenditure rose to its highest post-war level under the Heath government, with public sector employment increasing by some 10%, lends support to the contention that Heath's adoption of a modern technocratic approach to the welfare state did not signal the demise of One Nation influences.[47] Certainly, there were a number of policy initiatives that can be linked to this strand of Conservative thought. These include the introduction of Attendance Allowance, a new non-contributory 'disability' benefit in 1971 and the decision to grant pensions to all those aged over 80 who had had been unable to build up adequate contribution records in the post-1948 era. Plans were also made for additional investment in education over the next decade. The White Paper, *Education: A framework for expansion*, published in December 1972 (Department of Education and Science, 1972), contained a commitment to provide free nursery places for 50% of all three-year-olds and 90% of all four-year-olds, increased teacher numbers (up by 150,000) and an expansion in higher education provision so that the participation rate for the designated age group would increase from 15% to 22%.[48] Although Margaret Thatcher took some unpopular decisions during her initial period as Education

Secretary (a post she held for the duration of the Heath government), such as the withdrawal of free school milk from older primary school pupils, which earned her the sobriquet 'Thatcher Milk Snatcher',[49] she pressed ahead with some more 'progressive' measures. She raised the school-leaving age to 16 in 1972, oversaw the introduction of the Open University – Chancellor Macleod wanted to 'kill it off as part of his tax-cutting plans' (Timmins, 2001, p 299) – and, despite some personal reservations, was complicit in the forward march of comprehensive schooling. Mrs Thatcher's 'progressivism' even led some delegates at the party's annual conference in October 1972 to complain 'vociferously that not enough was being done to protect grammar schools and permit parental choice' (Moore, 2014, p 227).

In his assessment of social policy under the Heath government, Lowe (1996) argues that there was 'insufficient ruthlessness in the determination of priorities' (p 214). This reflected the underlying tension that still existed between One Nation and neo-liberal Conservatives with regard to the welfare state. The former accepted the need for 'modernisation' but were wary of adopting measures that would alienate Conservative-inclined voters who valued the security that the welfare state had delivered. In contrast, the latter contended that urgent action was needed to counter what had become an ever more costly, egalitarian, aspirational-sapping, dependency-inducing institution. This tension was to be resolved more decisively in a neo-liberal direction during the Thatcher era (1975-90).

The Heath government (1970-74): the wider political context

It is important to remember, as was noted previously, that focusing on social policy developments during any political era, not least Heath's tenure, runs the risk of overstating the importance of this particular area of government activity. It is noticeable, for example, that social policy developments have not featured prominently in many 'holistic' assessments of the Heath government. Economic issues, trade union reform and unrest, entry into the European Economic Community (EEC) and developments in Northern Ireland have attracted far greater attention. In the light of subsequent developments in the Thatcher and Major eras, it is useful in particular to refer to some of the key economic and industrial developments that occurred during the era of Heath government, not least because of the spill-over effects in relation to social policy.

In the initial phase of the Heath administration, the 'quiet' modern technocratic revolution that was put in place in relation to industrial policy and trade union reform was warmly received by neo-liberal-inclined Conservatives. Heath's decision to 'put together an assertively free-market team' (Campbell, 1993, p 302) at the Department of Technology (Geoffrey Rippon, Sir John Eden and Nicholas Ridley) was seen by anti-collectivists as a sign that the new government was 'set to embark' on a 'privatisation programme and the dismantling of the socialist state' (Ridley, 1991, p 4). Their optimism proved to be short-lived. The reshuffle that followed the untimely death of Macleod in July 1970 saw Rippon become Chancellor of The Duchy of Lancaster in order that he could oversee Britain's membership of the Common Market. He was replaced at the Department of Energy by an 'instinctive interventionist' (Campbell, 1993, p 302) John Davies, (a newly elected MP and former Director-General of the CBI who was soon to preside over a new 'super-ministry' – the Department of Trade and Industry).[50] Ridley remained at the new department until April 1972, when he decided to leave the government. He had opposed the 'interventionist' Industry Bill, which would have authorised tax-payer support for ailing industries, and was less than enamoured by Heath's offer of a 'sideways' move to become Minister for the Arts (Ridley, 1991, p 4).

The *Industrial Relations Act* of 1971, which was presented by the Heath government as a much-needed modernisation of the law, and would allow responsible trade unionists to fulfil their legitimate role in society within a clear rights and responsibilities framework, also gave some encouragement to neo-liberal-minded Conservatives who believed this was a useful initial step in reducing the power and influence of the unions. In contrast, those of a modern technocratic persuasion believed that the comprehensive nature of their legislative bill, which included the establishment of an Industrial Relations Court with 'wide-ranging powers to enforce ballots and cooling-off periods on registered unions' (Clarke, 1996, p 331), should be regarded as an end state not a staging post. In practice, however, the Act, failed to achieve its objective of providing a 'cure for Britain's industrial relations troubles' (Taylor, 1996, p.176). The number of working days lost due to strike action nearly doubled following the implementation of the Act.[51] Key trade unions exercised their right not to register with the newly established Industrial Relations Court and employers were reluctant to make use of the court's extensive powers for fear that it would have an adverse effect on already fraught labour relations. Indeed, when the court did become involved in industrial disputes it merely 'turned cooling off periods into hotting-up periods' (Clarke, 1996, p 332). When the court sanctioned the arrest of five shop stewards during the London dock strike of 1972, the situation was only resolved by the 'opportune' intervention of the Official Solicitor who secured the timely release of the so-called 'Pentonville Five' (Clarke, 1996, p 332). As Clarke concludes, the Conservatives had managed to put a 'massive act upon the statute book, at immense political, economic and industrial cost, but with no pay-off' (Clarke, 1996, p 332).

One of the most significant criticisms levelled at the Heath administration was its failure to live up to its manifesto commitments, particularly its pledge not to backtrack in the face of adversity. Neo-liberals were, for example, buoyed up by the government's decision to sanction the liquidation of the Mersey Docks and Harbour Board.[52] They were less enamoured, though, by subsequent economic 'U-turns'. Decisions to rescue financially stricken companies such as Rolls Royce and the Upper Clyde shipbuilders were deemed to be indicative of a loss of political nerve. This interventionist 'turn' also involved the provision of generous financial support for firms to enable them to cope with the rigours of EEC entry under the *Industry Act* of 1972,[53] the introduction of a statutory prices and incomes policy, and increased support for corporatist forms of governance.

The inflationary pressures that built up in 1971/72 following Chancellor Anthony Barber's earlier 'dash for growth', which Ziegler (2011) has described as an 'ill-disciplined stampede' (p 407), presented real difficulties for a government committed to voluntary rather than statutory price and income restraint. Following the miners' unanticipated rejection of a pay offer in 1972, which led to highly effective strike action that threatened to bring national economic activity to a juddering halt, a generous pay settlement was agreed following a swift 'inquiry' by Lord Wilberforce. The failure of subsequent attempts to secure 'corporate' agreement about prices and incomes policy resulted in the decision to introduce statutory measures in November 1972 (stage one involved a 90-day prices and incomes 'freeze'). A more elaborate scheme (stage two) saw the introduction of both a Pay Board and a Prices Board in February 1973, which were scheduled to operate until the following autumn. By the end of stage two, ministers were beginning to feel more hopeful that their economic strategy was bearing fruit. By this time, Britain had joined the EEC, unemployment was declining, the number of days lost to strike action had fallen rapidly and pay restraint was accepted by both employers and unions[54]. However, this optimism was soon to dissipate. Stage three of the government's pay policy started to unravel almost as soon as it had been introduced on 8 October 1973. Although this 'stage' had been designed to ensure that the miners could be offered a more generous pay settlement on grounds of their 'exceptional' circumstances, the government underestimated both their bargaining strength and the depth of rank-and-file opposition to statutory pay policy.[55] Following the National Union of Mineworkers' (NUM) rejection of a 16.5% pay offer in November 1973 and a subsequent overtime ban, a strike was called in February 1974. The government responded by calling its 'fifth state of emergency in three years' (Sandbrook, 2010, p 579). This led to the introduction of various measures designed to conserve fuel stocks, including a three-day working week, petrol rationing, lower speed limits, and a ban on TV broadcasting after 10.30pm on weekdays as well as on 'floodlit' football matches.[56]

Heath was unwilling to agree to the miners' demands for a sizeable pay increase on the grounds that it would involve the abandonment of his incomes policy. He believed that it would be possible to secure a compromise agreement over pay, but such an accord could not be brokered. Following his rejection of an offer by the TUC for the miners to be treated as a special case, Heath decided after lengthy deliberation[57] to call a General Election, which was held on 28 February 1974.

The party's General Election manifesto, *Firm action for a fair Britain* (Dale, 2000, pp 199-226), referred to the various achievements of the outgoing Conservative government and contained a familiar range of social policy commitments such as the provision of 'more houses for rent in areas of housing need' (Dale, 2000, p 215), the possible introduction of a disablement income, the extension of 'free nursery education throughout the country' (p 217), and improvements in services for 'the old, the disabled, the mentally ill and the mentally handicapped at home, in the community and in hospital' (Dale, 2000, p 213). However, the key question that was posed to the electorate was whether a trade union should be able to hold the nation to ransom.

> The choice before the government, and now the choice before the country, is clear. On the one hand it would be possible to accept the NUM's terms for a settlement. The country must realise what the consequences of this would be. It would mean accepting the abuse of industrial power to gain a privileged position.... The alternative is to reach a settlement with the NUM on terms which safeguard the nation's interests as well as the miners. (Dale, 2000, pp 202-3)

As with a subsequent contest in 2010, the result of the election proved inconclusive. The Conservatives achieved the largest share of the vote (37.9% compared with 37.1% for Labour, with the Liberals securing an impressive 19.3% share [up from 7.5% in 1970]). Labour, however, edged ahead in terms of seats.[58] Heath did not concede defeat immediately and sought ways of constructing a 'majority' coalition government. He held talks with the Liberal leader Jeremy Thorpe to see whether they would enter into a coalition government and also offered the Conservative whip to Ulster Unionists MPs.[59] The Liberal demand for proportional representation as a 'yellow line' for their participation in a coalition government proved a step too far for the Cabinet, while the Unionist request for the 'whip' to be extended to the Democratic Unionist Party and the Vanguard Unionist Progressive Party was deemed impractical, as it would 'mean explicitly repudiating the power-sharing executive in Northern Ireland which had come in to existence in January' (Bogdanor, 1996, p 372). As a consequence, it was Harold Wilson who returned to Downing Street as head of a minority Labour administration.

When Wilson called a second General Election of 1974 in October, Labour had solidified its position. There was a general expectation that having 'done well in impossible circumstances', it deserved a further term in office (Ziegler, 2010, p 462). Despite having lost two of the three General Elections he had contested as Conservative leader, there was no concerted attempt from within the party to replace Heath prior to polling day. As the title of the Conservative's manifesto clearly indicated – *Putting Britain first: A national policy from the Conservatives* (Dale, 2000, pp 227-61) – the party's main focus in this campaign was to be on the need to elect a unifying Conservative government, which would, in pursuit of the national interest, 'invite people from outside the ranks of our party to join with us in overcoming Britain's difficulties' (Dale, 2000, p 232). Despite this unifying theme, Heath was unable to prevent Labour from securing another electoral victory. Labour's 39.2% share of the vote (compared with 35.8% for the Conservatives) gave it an overall majority of three seats.[60]

Heath's defeat at this election sounded the death knell for his technocratic modernising approach. The 'subterranean' force of neo-liberal Conservatism was now ready to take centre stage (Bogdanor, 1996, p 377).

FIVE

The Conservative (counter-) revolution: neo-liberal Conservatism and the welfare state, 1974-97

The Conservatives' defeat in the October 1974 General Election served to strengthen the resolve of those who believed that a new 'ideological' and policy direction was needed in order to restore the fortunes of both the party and the nation. This chapter will explore the emergence of the neo-liberal Conservative alternative as the influence of One Nation Conservatism and the technocratic modernisation approach that had been adopted under Edward Heath waned. The apparent failure of Keynesian-style interventionism to provide economic and social stability gave neo-liberal Conservatives the opportunity to press their claims for a more 'radical' alternative to the previous strands of post-war Conservatism. This took the form of both a 'counter'-revolution in the sense of returning to a position prior to the 'suffocating' embrace of post-war social democracy and a revolution in the sense of moving swiftly to the creation of a more individualistic, entrepreneurial, property-owning society in which any remaining embers of socialism would be extinguished.

The seeds of discontent

The perceived failure of the Heath government to move in the neo-liberal Conservative direction outlined in the 1970 General Election manifesto led many of those on the right to campaign more vigorously for the party to abandon the post-war drift towards collectivism. Indeed, even before the infamous 'U-turns' in policy undertaken by the Heath government, there were signs of growing discontent on the right of the party. For example, Rhodes Boyson, Ralph Harris and Ross McWhirter[1] had set up the Constitutional Book Club in 1970 in an effort to bolster the neo-liberal cause. They published a series of pamphlets and books including *Right turn* (Boyson, 1970), *Goodbye to nationalisation* (O'Sullivan and Hodgson, 1971), *Must history repeat itself?* (Fisher, 1974) and *Rape of reason* (Jacka et al, 1975).

The lack of neo-liberal direction in the government's economic policy led Nicholas Ridley, Jock Bruce-Gardyne and John Biffen to establish the Economic Dining Club[2] in 1972, which became a forum for monetarist and supply-side ideas. Subsequently, a more wide-ranging organisation – the Selsdon Group – was formed in the summer of 1973. This group, which included Lord Coleraine, Nicholas Ridley and Ronald Bell,[3] published the 'Selsdon' manifesto at its first official meeting at the Selsdon Park Hotel in September 1973 (The Selsdon Group, 1973). It emphasised the growing sense of crisis in British society and the failure of the government to 'reduce the size of the public sector or do anything really radical about extending the private sector in welfare and education'. It was feared that 'if present trends continue, the electorate will only have a choice between two brands of collectivism at the next General Election: Socialism V. The Tory Corporate State' (The Selsdon Group, 1973, np). To counter this 'intolerable' development, the group called on the party to 'devote itself to the cause of personal freedom and to embrace economic and social policies which extend the boundaries of personal choice' (The Selsdon Group, 1973, np).

The longer-established right-wing think tank, the Institute of Economic Affairs (IEA), also continued to advance the neo-liberal cause with publications such as *Whatever happened to the quiet revolution?* (Bruce-Gardyne, 1974) and *Government and the market economy* (Brittan, 1971). Their hopes that the Heath government, which included neo-liberal sympathisers such as Keith Joseph, might pursue a more anti-collectivist agenda were soon dashed (much to the dismay of one leading light of the IEA, Arthur Seldon, who had even decided to vote Conservative for the first time in 1970 in anticipation of a decisive change in policy).[4]

Under the chairmanship of Peter Lilley (1973-75), the Bow Group[5] also began to devote more attention to neo-liberal Conservative thought, publishing a number of pamphlets extolling the virtues of monetarism including the *Alternative manifesto* (Lilley et al, 1973), *No more tick: A Conservative solution to inflation* (Durant et al, 1974) and *Lessons for power* (Hodgson, 1974). The neo-liberal cause was also championed by a group of influential economic 'monetarists' including Alan Waters (who had been removed from a part-time government position with the Central Policy Review Staff) and Brian Griffiths. They drafted a 'Memorial to the Prime Minister' in 1973, suggesting that the Heath government's misguided expansionary policies would lead to higher inflation and an unsustainable current account deficit.[6]

By the early 1970s, many neo-liberal Conservatives had come to the conclusion that one of the major factors holding back their 'ideological' advance within the party was the lack of a senior party figure to promote their cause. Following Enoch Powell's departure to the political wilderness after his controversial 'rivers of blood' speech in Birmingham in 1968 (which led Heath to remove him from the shadow Cabinet) there was no obvious neo-liberal figurehead. Help was now at hand, though, albeit in the somewhat unlikely shape of Sir Keith Joseph. Despite being one of 'the most discerning and inquisitive consumers of the IEA's literature' (Cockett, 1995, p 168), Joseph's failure to implement some of its neo-liberal policy prescriptions during his tenure as secretary of State for Health and Social Security (1970-74) had, as was noted above, proved a major disappointment to neo-liberal sympathisers. Alfred Sherman 'despaired' of Joseph's timidity in government, describing him as a 'lion in opposition but a lamb in government' (Garnett, 2005, p 11) and as a 'good man fallen amongst civil servants' (Cockett, 1995, p 206).

After the Conservative Party's defeat in the February 1974 General Election, Joseph sought a far from painless rapprochement with leading neo-liberal advocates such as Alan Walters and Ralph Harris.[7] Overlooked for the post as chancellor in Heath's new shadow Cabinet team, Joseph had, at his own request, been granted a roving commission to consider future party policy. Recognising the difficulties he faced in persuading fellow shadow Cabinet colleagues to follow a new economic and social direction, Joseph, decided, after consulting Alfred Sherman,[8] to establish (with the financial support of Nigel Vinson and with the acquiescence of the party leader)[9] a new think tank, the Centre for Policy Studies (CPS), in June 1974. With Joseph as its Chairman, Margaret Thatcher as Vice-Chair and Sherman as Director of Studies, this new organisation sought to promote the case for a 'social market' economy within the Conservative Party.[10] The new think tank 'quickly became the crucible of Joseph's intellectual revolution – a meeting place where those interested in changing the party's thinking could meet to discuss their ideas before separating to write papers and pamphlets' (Campbell, 2000, p 266). To coincide with the establishment of the CPS (and to attract the interest of prospective donors), Joseph delivered the first of a series of influential speeches (drafted in collaboration with Sherman), on economic and social policy at Upminster on 22 June 1974. In this speech, which was reprinted in full in *The Times*, Joseph argued that

> Since the end of the Second World War we have had altogether too much Socialism. There is no point in my trying to evade what everybody knows. For half of that 30 years Conservative Governments, for understandable

reasons, did not consider it practicable to reverse the vast bulk of the accumulating detritus of Socialism on which on each occasion they found when they returned to office. So we tried to build on its uncertain foundations instead. Socialist measures and Socialist attitudes have been very pervasive.

I must take my share of the blame for following too many of the fashions.

We are now more Socialist in many ways than any other developed country outside the Communist bloc – in the size of the public sector, the range of controls and the telescoping of net income. (Cited in Sherman, 2005, p 163)

With regard to the social services, he argued that 'we seem to have generated more problems than we have solved' (cited in Sherman, 2005, p 166).

By arguing that both he and his party were partly responsible for betraying the nation, Joseph was clearly signalling his abandonment of the One Nation Conservative cause.[11] Joseph's suggestion that the leftward 'ratchet' effect of Labour' egalitarian economic and social policies had been accepted rather than challenged by the Conservatives in the post-1945 era helped to legitimise his promotion of neo-liberal, rather than One Nation, Conservatism. As he reflected in a foreword to a collection of his speeches in 1975, 'It was only in April 1974 that I was converted to Conservatism. I had thought I was a Conservative but I now see that I was not really one at all' (Joseph, 1975, cited in Denham and Garnett, 2001, p 250).

Given that Joseph had always been sympathetic to free market ideas, his vociferous support for neo-liberal economic policies is arguably less significant than his growing disillusionment with the impact of the post-war welfare state. During his tenure at the Department of Health and Social Security (DHSS), for example, Joseph began to focus on what he termed as the 'cycle of deprivation'. In a speech to the Pre-School Playgroups Association in London in 1972, he argued that vulnerable children, brought up in families where parental skills were deficient, education opportunities limited and resources scarce, were also likely to become the parents of the next generation of deprived children. Joseph commissioned research to explore whether there was firm evidence of such cyclical disadvantage, hoping that this would pave the way for more targeted forms of assistance. Significantly, this emphasis on individual and familial causes of deprivation served to shift the poverty discourse from the impersonal structural factors promoted by democratic socialists to individualistic (blameworthy) reasons favoured by the neo-liberals.[12] The One Nation principle of *noblesse oblige*, based on a dutiful, compassionate approach to the poor, was now being superseded by a harsher doctrine of individual responsibility that was more in keeping with the views of newer Conservative MPs who believed that if they had managed to succeed in life through 'hard work, individual effort, self-restraint and sobriety', the same outcomes could be achieved by those who were equally determined to improve their own lives (Dorey, 2011, pp 130).

Joseph's speech at Upminster served to alienate many of his Cabinet colleagues, as did a subsequent speech at Preston on 5 September 1974, which was seen as opening up internal divisions over economic policy at a time when party 'unity' was deemed paramount given the proximity of the General Election. Although Joseph toned down a section of the speech (which had been drafted by Sherman with contributions from Walters and Samuel Brittan of *The Financial Times*) relating to incomes policy, his core argument about the need to prioritise the fight against inflation by monetarist means, even at the expense of high levels of unemployment, remained undiluted.[13]

Although Heath made some concessions to neo-liberal Conservative ideas in the October 1974 General Election manifesto, most notably in his declaration that inflation should be viewed as 'a moral and political evil as well as a social and economic evil. Everything else is secondary to the battle against inflation and to helping those who have been wounded in it' (Dale, 2000, p 230), the party's second consecutive defeat only served to galvanise those who believed that a seismic change of direction was required. Certainly Joseph showed no signs of moderating his criticisms of the direction of post-war economic and social policy, which he believed was leading 'towards moral decline'. In a speech to the Edgbaston Conservative Association at the Grand Hotel in Birmingham[14] on 19 October 1974 shortly after the October General Election, he drew attention to the dangers of the permissive society that had engendered a growth in 'delinquency, truancy, vandalism, hooliganism, illiteracy' and a 'decline in educational standards' (Joseph, 1974). While accepting that government still had a duty to help the poor, he expressed concern about the emergence of what has come to be known as a dependency culture: 'I am not saying that we should not help the poor, far from it. But the only really lasting help we can give to the poor is helping them to help themselves; to do the opposite, to create more dependency is to destroy them morally while throwing an unfair burden on society.' Towards the end of his speech, Joseph turned his attention to an issue which was posing a threat to 'our human stock,' namely, the 'high and rising proportion of children being born to mothers least fitted to bring children into the world and bring them up'. These lower-working-class mothers were seen as producing problem children who would become the unmarried mothers of tomorrow or the inmates of 'borstals, sub-normal educational establishments' and prisons. While Joseph accepted that extending 'birth-control facilities to these classes of people' would evoke concerns about the encouragement of immorality, he suggested that it might be the lesser of two evils until 'we are able to remoralise whole groups and classes of people' (Joseph, 1974).

The potentially explosive nature of the phrase 'our human stock', with its eugenic undertones, prompted the *Evening Standard* to break a press embargo and publish the story in its Saturday edition. Although the speech was well received by some fellow MPs, members of the general public and by Sir Laurence Olivier, who 'sent a supportive telegram' (Denham and Garnett, 2001, p 268), questions were raised about the accuracy of Joseph's remarks by the Child Poverty Action Group, some sections of the media and opposition MPs (Denham and Garnett, 2001, pp 268-9). Although Joseph attempted to clarify his proposals for the remoralisation of society in subsequent interviews and speeches, doubts had been raised, even amongst trusted colleagues such as Geoffrey Howe, about his political judgement. The furore surrounding the Birmingham speech seems likely to have contributed to Joseph's subsequent decision not to contest the leadership of the party. When the other leading neo-liberal Conservative candidate, Edward Du Cann, also declined to stand, fearing that his candidature might have given rise to further unwanted media and opposition intrusion into his business affairs,[15] it was left to Margaret Thatcher to put herself forward as the standard bearer of the 'Right'.

Although Heath was confident that he could rebuff the challenge of Margaret Thatcher in the leadership election in January 1975,[16] it was the member for Grantham who emerged triumphant in what had been described as the 'peasants' revolt'. Following an astute campaign masterminded by Airey Neave, Thatcher secured the support of 130 MPs on the first ballot compared with 119 for Heath.[17] Although the margin of victory was insufficient to secure an outright victory under the party's prevailing electoral rules, it provided the platform for Thatcher's second-round triumph where she saw off four new challengers: Willie Whitelaw, Geoffrey Howe, Jim Prior and John Peyton.[18]

Thatcher's accession to the party leadership did not result in an immediate shift to the right in party policy. Although unwavering in her determination to move both party and the nation in a neo-liberal Conservative direction, Thatcher recognised that this could not be achieved overnight. Faced with a disgruntled former leader[19] who was to prove anything but 'a loyal and distinguished member of his successor's team' (Thatcher, 2011a, p 282), as well as a number of 'sceptical' shadow Cabinet members (such as Ian Gilmour, Michael Heseltine, Jim Prior and Francis Pym) who did not share her political philosophy, not to mention the need to persuade a wary electorate that she could be entrusted to restore the nation's fortunes, Thatcher opted for a gradualist strategy. She did make a number of changes to strengthen neo-liberal Conservative representation in key areas. Within the shadow Cabinet, for example, Howe was made shadow chancellor and Joseph retained his broad policy and research brief, while Airey Neave was asked to oversee her personal office. Peter Thornycroft took over as Party Chairman and Angus Maude replaced Gilmour as Chair of the Conservative Research Department (Conservative Central Office, 1976).

The publication of a lengthy statement on party policy, drafted by Chris Patten in October 1976, *The right approach* (Conservative Party Central Office, 1976) represented a concerted attempt to outline the neo-liberal Conservative economic and social agenda that the party would now pursue. It was argued that the time had come to reverse the socialist advance in British society in which high public spending and redistributive taxation had delivered 'neither equality nor prosperity – only inflation, unemployment and growing bureaucratic threats to individual liberties'. A neo-liberal Conservative administration would pursue policies designed to promote 'individual freedom and responsibility':

> We mean to protect the individual from excessive interference by the State or by organisations licensed by the state, to stop the drift of power away from the people and their democratic institutions, and to give them more power as citizens, as owners and as consumers. We shall do this by better financial management, by reducing the proportion of the nation's wealth consumed by the State, by steadily easing the burden of Britain's debts, by lowering taxes when we can, by encouraging home ownership, by taking the first steps towards making the country a nation of worker owners, by giving parents a greater say in the better education of their children. (Conservative Central Office, 1976)

The desire to 'free' citizens from the suffocating embrace of the state through tax cuts, higher profits and rewards and reductions in public expenditure was portrayed as a necessary form of rebalancing rather than as covert support for the doctrine of laissez-faire.

In an effort to reassure traditionalists, and to counter anticipated criticisms that the party was abandoning 'true' conservatism,[20] the report made clear that the current emphasis on individualism should not be interpreted as an attempt to weaken support for the 'complex network of small communities which go up to make society' such as the family, the neighbourhood, the church and voluntary organisations.

In terms of social policy, *The right approach* highlighted the need for 'very large reductions' in spending that would be achieved through the imposition of cash limits and a refusal on the part of central government to 'bail out' those local authorities 'which have been extravagant or have mismanaged their affairs'. The report also highlighted the changes a neo-liberal Conservative government would introduce in relation to specific welfare services. In the case of housing, priority would be given to encouraging home ownership by such means as a 'statutory right to buy' for existing council tenants, a reduction in rent subsidies and reinvigoration of the privately rented sector. In social security, support for 'the retired, the disabled, the sick and the very poor' was seen as a priority for government action. The social security system was deemed to be at its most ineffective in dealing with working-age adults 'with the result that many people are now better off on social security than working'. Raising tax thresholds and cutting the basic rate of tax were seen as short-term solutions to this problem, while tax credits were regarded as a longer-term remedy on the grounds that they would 'simplify' the system and help cut 'through the thickets of means-tested benefits' and reduce administrative costs (Conservative Central Office, 1976).

The growing cost of the NHS was deemed to require increases in prescription and other charges, and an expansion of private and voluntary sector provision. In education, the focus would be on raising standards and extending parental choice within the state sector. A Parents' Charter would be established 'setting out existing and additional rights for parents regarding the education of their children' and schools would be expected to provide a simple prospectus and an annual report that would enable parents to familiarise themselves with the institution's 'educational aims and achievements'. The report also promised to restore direct grants to the schools affected by Labour's decision to abandon this scheme, and to encourage experimental education voucher schemes to see whether this might enhance 'parental influence and choice' (Conservative Central Office, 1976).

It was in the economic rather than social realm, however, that the neo-liberal Conservatives focused most of their attention in the run-up to the General Election of 1979. In a companion document entitled *The right approach to the economy*, (Maude, 1977) the key elements of the party's 'new approach' based on the creation of 'a more stable economic climate' were laid out. This involved strict control of the money supply, curbs on government spending, 'lower taxes on earnings, capital and savings', the 'removal of unnecessary restrictions on business expansion', 'varied rates of pay' to 'reflect supply and demand, skill, effort, experience and risk' and 'better methods of collective bargaining' (Maude, 1977). The report emphasised that the Conservatives were seeking to work with, rather than against, the trade unions: 'We see the trade unions as a very important economic interest group whose co-operation and understanding we must work constantly to win and to keep, as we have done in the past. We see no need for confrontation and have no wish for it' (Maude, 1977). Although this sentiment may have accurately reflected the views of key contributors to the document (Geoffrey Howe, Keith Joseph, Jim Prior and David Howell), some cheerleaders of the neo-liberal Conservative cause such as Norman Tebbit believed that a showdown with the unions was both necessary and inevitable.[21] The industrial disputes that plagued the Callaghan-led Labour government during the 'Winter of Discontent'[22] only served to strength the hand of those inclined to the latter position. A more 'resolute' approach to the 'problem' of the trade unions was included in the Conservative manifesto of 1979 (Dale, 2000, pp 265-82). In an effort to curb 'trade union power and privileges' reforms on picketing, the closed shop and strike ballots were proposed as well as the withdrawal of state support for 'strikers and their families' (Dale, 2000, pp 268-9).

The passages on social policy within this manifesto echoed the themes and direction of *The right approach*. It reiterated the Conservatives' commitment to greater home ownership and confirmed that tenants would be given the 'right to buy' their council home, with discounts ranging from 33% to 50% depending on their length of tenure.[23] The private rented sector was to be stimulated by the introduction of regulations designed to make it much easier for landlords to offer short-term lets. In education, the emphasis was to be on improving the quality of schooling, particularly in relation to basic skills. Those parts of Labour's 1976 *Education Act* that compelled 'local authorities to reorganise along comprehensive lines' and that restricted their freedom to 'take up places at independent schools' were to be abolished, while an Assisted Places scheme would be introduced to enable poorer parents to claim back some or all of the fees associated with sending their child to a designated independent school. There was no promise of extra funding for the NHS, though it was envisaged that better use could be made of existing resources through decentralisation and cutting back bureaucracy. Private provision was to be encouraged by allowing pay beds in NHS hospitals and by restoring 'tax relief on employer-employee medical insurance schemes' (Dale, 2000, p 279). In social security, tax credits would be introduced 'as and when resources become available'. In the interim, efforts would be made to 'simplify the system, restore the incentive to work, reduce the poverty trap and bring more effective help to those in greatest need' (Dale, 2000, p 280).

Improved opinion poll ratings in the autumn of 1976 suggested that Margaret Thatcher's baptism of fire as opposition leader, in which she had often came off second best when confronting two of Labour's 'wiliest' leaders (Harold Wilson and Jim Callaghan) over the dispatch box, and struggled to convince party sceptics that she was more than a 'narrow minded dogmatist' with 'simple minded remedies' (Campbell, 2000, p 2), was finally over. However, Labour's opinion poll revival occasioned by the formation of the Liberal-Labour (Lib-Lab) pact in March 1977, led to uncertainty as to whether Thatcher could seize the opportunity to become Britain's first woman Prime Minister. The pendulum swung back to Thatcher and the Conservatives following Callaghan's reluctance to call an election in the autumn of 1978 and the negative impact of the 'Winter of Discontent'.

In the General Election of May 1979, the Conservatives secured an overall majority of 43 seats, having achieved 43.9% of the popular vote (339 seats) compared with just 36.9% for Labour (269 seats).

The first Thatcher government (1979-83)

Implementing a neo-liberal Conservative economic agenda

Reform of the welfare state was not the main concern for the first Thatcher government. Instead, the emphasis was very much on the economic themes that had been highlighted in *The right approach to the economy*, such as trade union reform and privatisation. Thatcher's cautious approach to change was reflected in the composition of her Cabinet, which included ministers who were fully signed up to the neo-liberal Conservative cause (such as Geoffrey Howe, Keith Joseph and John Biffen) as well as those of a One Nation (Ian Gilmour, Mark

Carlisle) or 'modern technocratic' (Michael Heseltine, Peter Walker) disposition. Significantly, those who came to be known as 'drys' by virtue of their commitment to the pursuit of neo-liberal Conservative goals such as rolling back the state, cutting taxes, curbing inflation and reducing public expenditure were appointed to key economic portfolios. In contrast, those perceived as 'wets'[24] on account of their 'paternalistic' 'One Nation' sympathies, which led them to oppose 'extreme measures, such as severe anti-union laws, and unfamiliar conditions such as high unemployment' (Young, 1993, p 199), were dispatched to less strategically significant departments such as education and agriculture.

In his first budget in June 1979, the new Chancellor Geoffrey Howe demonstrated his clear determination to pursue a neo-liberal Conservative economic agenda by making it clear that interest rates and monetary policy[25] would be used to control inflation and that the Public Sector Borrowing Requirement (PSBR) would be brought under control. As Green (2006) points out, the 'tight control of the money supply' meant that 'labour costs could not simply rise, whether in the shape of an expanded labour force or increased wages and benefits for those in work. If they did, for example as a consequence of trade union wage claims, then employers and firms would run into the barrier of the non-availability of funds or the prohibitive cost of borrowing' (p 63). The basic rate of income tax was cut from 33% to 30% (with the aim of introducing a 25% rate in the medium term) and the top rate was reduced from 83% to 60%. A unified, higher VAT rate of 15% was introduced to reflect the government's preference for indirect, as opposed to direct, taxes. Interest rates were to rise from 12% to 14%, while prescription charges were increased from 20p to 45p. The budget also sought to cut public expenditure, which had risen as a result of the government's decision to honour the recommendations of the Clegg Commission on public sector pay (which led to a 25% rise over 12 months – see Campbell, 2000, pp 438-9) and a manifesto commitment to increase police and service pay. Later in the year, Howe also took the bold step of abolishing exchange controls. As Campbell (2003) notes:

> This was arguably the single most important step that the Thatcher Government took to give practical effect to its belief in free markets: by doing away with the restrictions on the movement of capital which had been in place since 1939, the Government dared to expose the British economy to the judgement of the global market. (p 50)

In Howe's second budget in March 1980, the medium-term financial strategy (which had been formulated by Nigel Lawson, the then Financial Secretary to the Treasury) was laid out, committing the government to 'a monetary growth target of around 6%' by 1983-84. As part of this strategy, the Chancellor continued to bear down heavily on public spending. Prescription charges were increased to £1, sickness and unemployment benefits were made taxable and supplementary benefit payments to strikers' families were cut by £12 a week on the questionable assumption that such claimants would receive an equivalent amount in strike pay from their trade union. Howe's third, and most controversial, budget in March 1981 came at a time when output was falling and manufacturing was in steep decline. Interest rates and exchange rates remained high at this time (not least as a result of sterling becoming a petro currency in the wake of North sea oil) and unemployment was rising. While previous 'interventionist' governments would have opted to stimulate the economy at such a time, Howe, prompted by a resolute Prime Minister and her chief economic adviser Alan Walters, pressed ahead with his anti-inflationary strategy (much to the dismay of 364 economists who had written to *The Times* calling for the government to abandon its 'monetarist' experiment).[26] The PSBR was reduced by £4,000 million through such means as the non-uprating of personal tax allowances, which, given that inflation was hovering at around the 15% mark, represented a hefty tax 'increase'.

The harsh economic medicine being administered to the nation led to the first significant Cabinet 'rebellion' at a meeting to review the government's public spending strategy shortly before the summer recess on 23 July 1981. A paper was presented to the meeting by Howe and Leon Brittan 'outlining a further package of spending cuts for 1982-3' (Campbell, 2003, p 119). Virtually the whole Cabinet[27] united in rejecting the proposals. In the light of the sharp rise in unemployment, which was set to top three million, and the eruption of rioting in Brixton in April 1981 (and subsequently in Toxteth and Moss Side), the 'rebels' urged Thatcher and her Chancellor to take their foot off the neo-liberal accelerator if the party was to retain a serious chance of winning the next General Election. It was left to Thatcher's loyal deputy, Willie Whitelaw, who in his role as Home Secretary had been dealing with the aftermath of the riots, to defuse this potentially damaging challenge to Margaret Thatcher's leadership by reiterating the importance of Cabinet loyalty to the leader, an intervention that enabled 'Thatcher to close the meeting without conceding any ground' (Campbell, 2003, p 120). A subsequent critique in the shape of a strongly worded memorandum from trusted aides John Hoskyns[28] and David Wolfson and speechwriter Ronnie Millar in August, drawing attention to deficiencies in the Prime Minister's leadership and management qualities, only served to galvanise Thatcher's resolve, albeit in a predictable way.[29] By the time the Cabinet sat again in the autumn, 'wets' such as Gilmour, Soames and Carlisle had been axed. Prior had been shipped off to Northern Ireland, while 'dry' newcomers such as Lawson (energy), Tebbit (employment), Cecil Parkinson (Paymaster General and Party Chairman) joined the government.

The first Thatcher government adopted a two-pronged approach to trade union reform based on non-intervention in pay negotiations, which it hoped would encourage workers (and employers) to arrive at 'realistic' pay settlements, and in legislative changes that would curtail the powers of organised labour. Disputes at British Steel and in the civil service confirmed that the 'non-interventionist' strategy would take time to bear fruit. The strike at British Steel in January 1980 over a 2% pay offer and looming job cuts that led to secondary picketing at private steel works resulted in improved offers of 6% and, subsequently, 10%. Eventually a 16% award was agreed following an inquiry conducted by former Labour Cabinet minister Harold Lever. Although this result seemed like a defeat for the government, it did set in train a longer-term 'rationalisation' of the industry under Ian MacGregor, who cut the workforce by half and returned the company to the private sector.[30] The government also had to deal with a civil service strike in the early part of 1981, which was triggered by a 7% pay offer that the unions deemed unacceptable.[31] The Cabinet minister with responsible for the civil service, Christopher Soames, attempted to settle this damaging dispute by increasing the offer to 7.5%, thereby breaching government pay guidelines. Thatcher opposed this settlement and threatened to resign rather than accept a deal that undermined the government's cash limits policy. However, she backed down a few weeks later and agreed to the deal.[32] Significantly, Thatcher and her ministers were wary of tackling the miners head on at this time. They agreed a 13% pay settlement in November 1980 and quickly withdrew pit closure plans when strike action was threatened in February 1981. However, plans were being put in train at the Civil Contingencies Unit chaired by Willie Whitelaw to prepare for a future conflict, which Thatcher was determined to win.[33]

Recognising the shortcomings of the 1971 Industrial Act, the neo-liberal Conservatives opted for Fabian-style changes to trade union law that involved 'tying down the trade unions with a thousand silken cords' (Clarke, 1996, p 3) rather than administering a swift single blow to the neck. Thatcher's desire to avoid premature confrontation with the trade unions helps to explain why Jim Prior, who was far from being a cheerleader for the neo-liberal Conservative cause, was initially entrusted with the task of bringing forward the new government's legislative agenda. Under the 1980 *Employment Act*, secondary picketing was outlawed and so-called 'closed shop' arrangements (where employees were obliged to join the designated trade union in their workplace) could only be enforced if the workers concerned had agreed to the arrangement through a ballot.

Acknowledging that Prior was unlikely to be a reliable ally for her longer-term trade union reforms, Thatcher appointed Norman Tebbit (affectionately known as the Chingford 'skinhead' or 'Rottweiller'[34] because of his 'confrontational' approach to political debate) as her new Employment Secretary in September 1981 (following Prior's redeployment to the Northern Ireland office). Tebbit's 1982 *Employment Act* did not herald any significant change to the government's gradualist strategy, though it did confirm that continuous reform would remain the order of the day until the threat of 'political' trade unionism had been quelled. Under the 1982 Act, the definition of a lawful strike was restricted in the main to disputes arising between employers and their own contracted employees, thereby restricting 'sympathy' action by other workers. The Act also made it more difficult to operate a closed shop. Individuals who were dismissed from their jobs for refusing to join a union also became entitled to generous rates of compensation.

The first Thatcher government also took some initial steps in what came to be known as privatisation. Although many rank-and-file and backbench Conservatives had remained hostile to nationalisation throughout the post-war era, the party had tended to take a pragmatic stance on public ownership.[35] The initial forms of privatisation undertaken by the Thatcher government were not focused on the loss-making major nationalised industries such as British Rail, British Steel and the National Coal Board, but rather on smaller enterprises that were thought suitable for denationalisation. These included a number of companies that had been brought under public control through Labour's National Enterprise Board, such as ICL computers, Ferranti engineering, Amersham International and Cable and Wireless.[36]

First-term neo-liberal Conservatism and the welfare state (1979-83)

Although Thatcher was unwilling to contemplate any major reconstruction of the welfare state during her first term in office for fear that it might detract from more urgent economic considerations,[37] this did not mean that this sphere of activity remained immune to change. The publication of *The government's expenditure plans 1980-81* (HM Treasury, 1979) signalled its commitment to cutting public expenditure, which was deemed to be at the 'heart of Britain's economic difficulties'. To the alarm of his departmental officials, Patrick Jenkin, the Secretary of State at the DHSS, proved to be a willing advocate of reductions in social security spending. Jenkin agreed to the severing of the link between pensions and average earnings (announced in Howe's first budget), the freezing of Child Benefit, the withdrawal of earnings-related additions for unemployment and sickness benefits and a 5% cut in invalidity and other benefits, as a prelude to making them taxable. Employers were also required to bear some of the cost of statutory sick pay. Other changes were introduced to secure cost savings rather than to fulfil any 'ideological' blueprint. The semi-independent Supplementary Benefits Commission was abolished and replaced with a more transparent, rule-based administrative system. Increased payments for families with dependent children were introduced, though these were to be 'funded' by reductions in pensioner benefits.[38]

In contrast to his 'hawkish' approach to social security, Jenkin was keen to protect the NHS budget and succeeded in persuading the Chancellor of the political necessity of matching Labour's proposed spending plans. As a result, he was able to secure a three-year respite from Treasury demands for economies, which were restricted solely to increased prescription and dental charges.

Jenkin proved, willing, however, to consider alternative forms of funding for the NHS and in 1981 set up a working party to examine such possibilities. Jenkin's successor, Norman Fowler, was not, however, persuaded of the advantages of moving to an alternative funding system, given that 'taxation would still have to finance a giant share of the service' (Timmins, 2001, p 388). He was also sensitive to the potential political fallout from any such move. He underlined this stance in a subsequent Cabinet discussion of a Central Policy Review Staff paper relating to the control of public expenditure in September 1982, which advocated moving away from a tax financed health service to some form of private health insurance. The leak of this report at the time of an ongoing pay dispute with the nurses led to accusations that the government was intent on privatising the NHS, a suggestion that had to be vigorously refuted by Fowler and eventually by the Prime Minister herself at the party's annual conference in October 1992 when she famously declared that the NHS was 'safe' in Conservative hands.[39] Henceforth, despite Thatcher's personal inclination to 'revolutionise' the NHS, it was 'reform', albeit infused with neo-liberal rather than social democratic ingredients, that was to become the established modus operandi for future health policy.

Given projected falls in both primary and secondary school numbers, education was targeted as an area for budget savings. The introduction of the *Education Act* in 1980, under which local authorities were no longer obliged to provide schoolchildren with milk, meals and transport, helped to meet the initial £280 million spending reductions in this area of government activity. Cuts to the tune of 13% over three years were also imposed on the university sector, though the 'selective' nature of these measures meant that the pain was particularly acute for universities such as Aston and Salford, which experienced severe funding reductions.[40]

There were some modest attempts to nudge education in a neo-liberal Conservative direction by halting the advance of compehensivisation and by enhancing parental choice through the use of vouchers. Labour's previous stipulation (under the 1976 *Education Act*) requiring councils to submit plans for comprehensive education was abolished, while Mark Carlisle introduced, in the face of significant Cabinet opposition, an Assisted Places scheme to help poorer children attend independent schools. Moreover, in an attempt to improve parental choice in state education, Carlisle's successor, Keith Joseph (with the assistance of his two special advisors, Stuart Sexton [who had been closely involved with the Black papers referred to earlier] and Oliver Letwin), sought to introduce a system of school vouchers. Joseph was, however, forced to abandon this policy after acknowledging that his department was unable to overcome the numerous practical problems involved in implementing such a scheme.

In housing, hefty cuts were made in capital expenditure and in the subsidies provided to local councils. Public sector housing was seen as an area ripe for neo-liberal Conservative reform. The growth of subsidised local authority housing was seen as distorting the housing market by deterring investors from supplying privately rented accommodation. Subsidised provision of this kind was also seen as engendering a 'low rent' culture among tenants, who believed they had a 'right' to live in expensive areas at tax payers 'expense'. According to Ridley (1991):

> Absurdly low rents, and a monopoly position in providing rented housing, allowed some councils to make their tenants entirely dependent upon them. They received a rotten service – repairs and maintenance and improvements were minimal – yet the tenants were trapped in their houses by

the lack of availability of alternative accommodation to rent, and by such cheap rents that no other landlord could match them, even if he had a house to offer them. The tenants felt beholden to the council, and most paid the price expected of them giving their political support to them. (p 87)

The 1980 *Housing Act* attempted to deal with this issue by 'encouraging' local authorities to charge higher rents by withdrawing central government subsidies from local authorities, though the longer-term consequence of this was to push up the cost of Housing Benefit.[41]

The government's flagship 'right to buy' policy was also introduced under the 1980 *Housing Act*. Council tenants of three years' standing or more were given the right to buy their council homes at substantial discounts. Opposed by Labour, this policy proved popular with many tenants. By 1983, some 500,000 tenants had exercised their 'right to buy'. As Timmins (2001) notes, this policy proved to be 'though no one knew it then, the biggest single privatisation of the Thatcher era, raising £28 billion over thirteen years – more than the sale of gas, electricity and British Telecom put together' (p 378).

It seems unlikely that the Thatcher government's welfare reforms played a significant role in her second electoral victory in 1983 in which the Conservatives achieved 'a majority just two short of Labour's 1945 post-war record of 146, at a time when three million people were out of work' (Timmins, 2001, pp 391-2). Thatcher's electoral triumph can be better explained by her success in 'turning around' the economy[42], a divided opposition[43] and by her effective handling of the Falklands conflict, which, Moore (2014) contends, persuaded the electorate of 'her special gifts of leadership' (p 752).

Although the Conservative share of the vote in the 1983 General Election (42.4%, 397 seats) was slightly less than in 1979, it proved sufficient to extend the party's overall majority. Labour's performance proved to be its worst since 1918 (27.6% of the votes, 209 seats). It only narrowly succeeded in holding on to second place in the poll, with the alliance a whisker away in third place (25.9% of the vote, 23 seats).[44]

The second Thatcher government (1983-87)

The Conservative manifesto 1983 (Dale, 2000) confirmed the party's determination to move the country in a neo-liberal Conservative direction. On the economic front, voters were advised to stick with the government that had presided over a national recovery in the face of a world recession and rapid technological change. The Conservatives would, it was argued, continue to restore 'sound money', secure a 'better balance between trade unions and the rest of society', bring 'efficiency to the nationalised industries' and develop 'effective policies to mitigate the curse of unemployment' as well as 'resist unreasonable pay claims in the public sector' (Dale, 2000, pp 287-8). While rising unemployment was seen as regrettable, this was deemed to be an inevitable consequence of being 'one of the least efficient and over-manned of industrialised nations' (Dale, 2000, p 290) and of continued trade union resistance to economic change. Further reform was deemed necessary to ensure that trade union power was used 'democratically and responsibly' (Dale, 2000, p 289).

In terms of social policy, the manifesto rejected the claim that the Conservatives were seeking to 'dismantle the welfare state' (Dale, 2000, p 296). Their declared aim was to 'return more choice to individuals and their families' (Dale, 2000, p 296) while ensuring that efficient state-funded provision was focused more sharply on 'those who are least able to help themselves'.

The manifesto pledged 'to protect retirement pensions and other linked long-term benefits against rising prices' (Dale, 2000, p 297), though voters were reminded that the government's ability to help those in need 'depends on the wealth that the country produces' and that '40p in every pound of public spending is already devoted to health and social security' (Dale, 2000, p 298). The party's commitment to creating a 'property-owning democracy' (Dale, 2000, p 296) was underlined by a pledge to 'give many thousand more families the chance to buy their homes' by extending and expanding the 'right to buy' scheme (Dale, 2000, p 297). In education, the Conservatives promised to 'seek ways of widening parental choice and influence over their child's schooling' (Dale, 2000, p 299). In the NHS, efficiency savings were seen as the key to ensuring 'that all patients receive the best possible value for the money that is spent'. To this end, health authorities would be encouraged to put services such as 'laundry, catering and hospital cleaning out to competitive tender', and more stringent control exercised over management costs and staff numbers.

Into government

Second-term economic and industrial issues

Economic and industrial issues continued to be at the forefront of the Conservative government's agenda during the period 1983-87. In terms of the latter, the government's finely orchestrated showdown with the

National Union of Mineworkers (NUM) proved to have the most long-term significance. In preparing for this dispute, the government adhered closely to what came to be known as the 'Ridley formula' for defeating the miners. As Milne (2004) explains, this involved the 'build up of coal stocks and imports, the encouragement of non-union road hauliers to move coal, the rapid introduction of dual coal-oil firing at all power stations, the withdrawal of social security benefits from strikers' families and the creation of a large, mobile squad of police' (Milne, 2004, p 9). The announcement of a number of pit closures by Ian Macgregor (the former chair of British Steel, who had been appointed chair of British Coal in 1983) triggered local walk-outs in Yorkshire and led the miners' leader Arthur Scargill to call a national strike in March 1984 without a ballot (in defiance of the requirements of the new *Trade Union Act* of 1984). This led to the eventual sequestration of union funds that hampered the NUM's ability to provide long-term financial support to those taking part in strike action. Although the strike lasted for nearly a year, this was a dispute that the NUM was unable to win despite a vigorous campaign that was supported by a wide cross-section of the British public. Lack of support from the Labour Party and the Trades Union Congress, as well as the decision of some miners to form a breakaway Union of Democratic Mineworkers in December 1984, fatally wounded the NUM cause. The Conservative-led victory over the miners signified a watershed in British industrial relations. Over time, the days lost to industrial action fell sharply, union membership plummeted and the 'political' influence of the trade unions declined markedly.

There was a change of emphasis in the neo-liberal Conservative approach to privatisation during the second term of the Thatcher government. The 'denationalisation' narrative of the first term, which had focused on the need to counter the problems associated with efficiency and monopoly in public provision, was supplanted by an emphasis on the 'cultural' and political benefits that privatisation could bring. Giving ordinary citizens the opportunity to buy shares and build up their own personal wealth was seen as a way of creating a 'One Nation' capital-owning democracy.[45] The sale of shares in British Telecom and British Gas were exemplars in this regard. Despite protests from the Labour Party and the trade unions, a slick advertising campaign by Dorland (a subsidiary of Saatchi and Saatchi, which had played an influential part in the upturn in the party's fortunes in 1979)[46] and an attractive share price ensured that the first tranche of BT shares were heavily oversubscribed when offered for sale in November 1984. As Campbell (2003) points out, 'more than a million small investors applied for shares, including 95 per cent of BT employees, defying the advice of their union; most of these had never owned shares before, but the sale was weighted to favour those who applied for the smallest number' (p 237). In the same way that bookies express delight when a new punter returns home with sizeable winnings after their first day at the races (which it is hoped will lead to a lifetime of gambling), the government derived much satisfaction from the success of the first part of its popular capitalist strategy (the BT share price rose by 90% on the opening day of trading, yielding £4 billion in revenue). A subsequent sale of British Gas shares, which proved equally popular with the public following a 'Tell Sid' advertising campaign, raised £5.4 billion in 1986.[47]

By extoling the virtues of popular capitalism, the neo-liberal Conservatives also sought to persuade the public of the benefits that could accrue if a market-orientated approach were adopted towards the welfare state. However, there were few signs that the Thatcher government was ready to accelerate its neo-liberal Conservative overhaul of the welfare state. Indeed, some of those most committed to more fundamental reform began to express their frustration at the lack of progress. According to Ridley (1991), the Prime Minister 'ought to have put in place alternative methods of provision based on the private sector which gave the people both choice and the quality of service they wanted. Her steps in this direction were too late, too hesitant, and not radical enough' (p 257).[48]

Second-term social policy

The lack of major second-term structural reform of the welfare state should, not, however, lead one to conclude that the attitude of the Thatcher government towards collective provision of this kind was softening. Efforts to constrain spending were maintained under Thatcher's new Chancellor Nigel Lawson, while opportunities to shift policy in a neo-liberal Conservative direction were pursued in the areas of social security, the NHS, education and housing when it was deemed practicable to do so.

Social security was a key Treasury target for savings, given that it represented a sizeable proportion of government expenditure. While the Minister for Health and Social Security, Norman Fowler, was prepared to curb unnecessary departmental spending, he remained committed to preventing 'unnecessary' cuts.[49] He launched a major, cost-neutral, review of social security in 1985, which focused on four areas of spending – pensions, housing benefit, supplementary benefit and allowances for children and young people. The subsequent Green Paper (Department of Health and Social Security, 1985) recommended some significant changes including the withdrawal of the State Earnings Related Pension Scheme (SERPS), the 'abolition' of Supplementary Benefit ([SB], to be replaced by Income Support), the introduction of a Social Fund (which would replace various discretionary SB grants with loans), a new Family Credit benefit (to replace Family Income Supplement) and a modified Housing Benefit scheme. Older people and families with children stood to gain from these changes 'at the expense of the unemployed, those without children and particularly those under twenty-five, whose benefit was cut markedly in an attempt to cajole them to either stay in the parental home or get into work' (Timmins, 2001, p 399). Various objections were raised about these proposals, particularly the abolition of SERPS. Treasury concerns that the abolition of SERPS would prove costly in the short run coupled with questions about the viability of alternative, private forms of support led to the retention of a modified version of this scheme in the subsequent *Social Security Act* of 1986. While Fowler's review of some key features of the social security system confirmed it was perfectly possible to steer the service in a neo-liberal direction, it also suggested that this was likely to be a lengthy process.

The Prime Minister's earlier pledge to 'protect' the NHS meant that the 'reform' agenda in this sphere of social policy had to be carefully formulated. The strategy that was followed was to reassure the public that the service would remain 'free' at the point of delivery but made more cost-effective. A number of efficiency measures were introduced into the NHS during the second Thatcher government. In line with manifesto commitments, health authorities were required to generate annual efficiency savings and to compare their performance in terms of length of hospital stay, treatment costs and waiting lists with other authorities. In September 1983, they were also required to put non-medical services such as cleaning, catering and laundry out to competitive tendering – a process that generated £86 million worth of 'savings' by 1986.[50] As part of the cost containment process the government had put in place, Derek Rayner was seconded from Marks and Spencer in 1979 to advise on how NHS expenditure could be reduced in areas such as transport, advertising and staff accommodation. Another private sector retailer, Roy Griffiths (the then Managing Director of the food chain Sainsbury's), headed up a major inquiry into NHS administration in 1983 and recommended the introduction of a more commercial style of management based on command and control as opposed to the 'inefficient', 'consensual' arrangements that were currently operating.

Plans were also unveiled for the reform of General Practice in a Green Paper entitled *Primary health care: An agenda for discussion* (Department of Health and Social Security, 1986), which aimed to give patients more choice and a better standard of service by reforming GP financial arrangements. The subsequent White Paper, *Promoting better health* (Department of Health and Social Security, 1987), confirmed the government's 'managerial' direction of travel, with Family Practitioner Committees being required 'to set disease prevention targets, to carry out surveys of consumer satisfaction and to monitor, with the help of professional advice, patterns of prescribing and hospital referrals' (Klein, 1995, p 167). The title of the White Paper also reflected the government's recognition that the costs of the NHS could be reduced by a greater emphasis on the prevention of ill health.

Given Keith Joseph's lengthy tenure as Secretary of State in the Department of Education one might have anticipated a robust neo-liberal agenda to emerge from this sphere of social policy. However, despite his personal enthusiasm for spending cuts and reform, Joseph found it difficult to press ahead with the changes he wanted. After formally conceding defeat on his plans to introduce education vouchers at the party's annual conference in 1983, Joseph was subsequently forced to withdraw his proposals to require high-income parents to contribute towards the university tuition fees of their children (1984) following vociferous parental and backbench opposition.[51] He also had to contend with a protracted industrial dispute with the teaching unions following his decision to stand firm over a `final' pay offer (which was only resolved by the offer of a more generous settlement by his successor Kenneth Baker).

Joseph enjoyed greater success in providing parents with more information about the performance of individual schools. The reports compiled on all schools by Her Majesty's Inspectorate (HMI) were placed in the public domain and schools were required to provide parents with an annual report on their activities. Joseph also published a Green Paper on higher education (Department of Education and Science, 1985), which highlighted the need for universities to respond more directly to the nation's economic priorities rather than to 'blue skies' research. Joseph's desire to counter what he regarded as the 'socialist' research agendas of the Social Science Research Council (SSRC) led him to appoint Lord Rothschild to consider whether such research might in future be undertaken by the private sector. Joseph's hope that Rothschild might recommend the closure of the SSRC did not, however, materialise and he had to settle for the symbolic renaming of the organisation as the Economic and Social Research Council, which he hoped might prove more amenable to the commissioning of investigations (and results) more in keeping with the neo-liberal Conservative view of the world.[52]

In the sphere of housing, the success of the 'right to buy' policy during the first term led the second Thatcher administration to maintain the momentum that had been built up by offering even more generous discounts. The majority of new house building was to be concentrated in the private sector, while housing associations were to take a major role in the limited amount of new public sector construction that was envisaged on the grounds than they were more effective landlords than their local authority counterparts. Public sector rents continued on an upward trajectory as result of reduced central government subsidies. By 1986-87, only a quarter of all local authorities were still receiving such subsidies.[53]

The third Thatcher government (1987-90)

The manifesto

The title of the Conservative Party's 1987 General Election manifesto, *The next moves forward* (Dale, 2000, pp 311-51), served to reaffirm its determination to press ahead with the neo-liberal economic and social 'revolution' that had proved 'outstandingly successful' during the first two terms (p 351). It was predicted that continuing along this path would eventually give rise to a 'capital-owning democracy of people and families who exercise power over their own lives in the most direct ways' (p 316). On the economic and industrial front, the Conservatives reaffirmed their commitment to bear down on inflation, cut taxes and borrowing, 'reduce the share of the nation's income taken by the state' (p 326), press ahead with their 'successful programme of privatisation' (p 3), extend share ownership and continue their 'popular' programme of trade union reform by enhancing the individual rights of union members.

In social policy further pressure was applied to the neo-liberal accelerator pedal. Major reform was promised, for example, in education. A National Curriculum was to be introduced for all five- to 16-year-olds, with regular testing of pupils at the ages of seven, 11 and 14 prior to GCSE examinations at 16. Over a five-year period, the governors and head teachers of all secondary schools (and many in the primary sector) would be given budgetary control. Schools would be required to admit as many pupils as could be accommodated to stimulate parental choice, with 'good' schools being encouraged to 'expand beyond present pupil numbers'. State schools would also be given the right to opt out of local authority control and receive funding directly from the Department of Education and Science. In higher education, a new University Funding Council would be set up to allocate funding and the possible introduction of top-up loans for students was mooted.

The Conservatives also promised to increase home ownership, stimulate the private rented sector, give council tenants the right to 'choose' their landlord and create Housing Action Trusts, which would be empowered to take over, and then renovate, run-down housing estates. It was envisaged that the latter initiative would lead to the control of such dwellings passing to 'housing associations, tenant co-operatives, owner-occupiers or approved private landlords' (Dale, 2000, p 319). In the NHS, there was to be greater emphasis on prevention, better financial and training support for staff, more capital building, reductions in long-term hospital stays, more 'business-like' management to help improve efficiency and minimise waste and a reduction in waiting times. In social security, the aim was to provide a secure standard of living for retirement pensioners through a combination of state and occupational pensions and personal savings. More help was to be provided for low-income families, unemployment and benefit traps were to be tackled and the 'tangled web of income-related benefits which has grown up piecemeal over forty years' reformed (Dale, 2000, p 339). Finally, and significantly in the light of subsequent events, an attempt was to be made to 'strengthen local democracy and accountability' (Dale, 2000, p 344) by replacing domestic rates with a Community Charge for local services that was to be levied on all adults aged 18 or over with reductions for students and benefit recipients.

The 1987 General Election and Thatcher's last stand

Margaret Thatcher achieved a third successive electoral victory in the June 1987 General Election, although her majority was cut to 101 seats and the share of the vote declined to 43.4%.[54]

A number of commentators have argued that it was only in Thatcher's third term that a determined effort was made to undertake a neo-liberal inspired reform of the welfare state.[55] Unquestionably, there was a flurry of activity in areas such as education, health and community care, which owed much to the fact that the 'completion' of the economic and industrial transformation of Britain had been achieved during the first two terms. However, the third-term 'social' initiatives owed much to the preparations that had been made during the first two terms.

The *Education Reform Act* of 1988[56] activated the educational changes that had been outlined in the party's manifesto with one significant addition – the abolition of the Inner London Education Authority. State schools would in future follow a 10-subject National Curriculum (favoured by Baker but not by Thatcher[57], who wanted the focus to be on English, Maths and Science), with designated attainment standards (knowledge, skills and understanding) that would be measured through national testing for pupils aged seven, 10, 14 and 16. The test results would be published to provide parents with more information on the relative performance of a particular school. Schools would also be able to apply for grant maintained status, subject to parental approval being expressed through a ballot. Non-grant maintained schools were to be given increased financial autonomy. Parental choice was to be enhanced by allowing popular schools with 'spare' capacity to admit more pupils. Privately sponsored (but still mainly state-funded) City Technology Colleges were to be established to improve the educational attainment of pupils living in disadvantaged areas, where the comprehensive system was deemed to be failing. This initiative failed to take off and only 15 such institutions were established.[58] Thatcher was disappointed by Baker's over-elaborate educational reforms and chivvied his successor, John Macgregor, to overhaul some of Baker's changes. Although Macgregor was able to cut the number of subjects covered by the National Curriculum and to reduce testing in line with Thatcher's preferences, the Prime Minister was frustrated that her third-term school reforms, which were designed 'to ease the state still further out of education', proved so difficult to achieve (Thatcher, 2011b, p 597). She was also dismayed to find that so many well-respected academics had come to regard her government's approach to the universities as little more than the 'philistine subordination of scholarship' (Thatcher, 2011b, p 599). It is hard, however, to refute this claim in the light of the decisions to abolish academic tenure, the promotion of a more entrepreneurial ethos and the introduction of business-like modes of governance.

The new Health and Social Security Secretary, John Moore (who was only left with responsibility for the latter service after his department was split in two in July 1988), was a committed neo-liberal Conservative who favoured a smaller state and greater selectivity. He criticised the so-called poverty lobby (and the Institute for Fiscal Studies)[59] for their failure to distinguish between poverty, which he contended had virtually been abolished, and inequality, which was deemed to be an essential feature of liberal societies. Moore,[60] along with the influential American commentator Charles Murray (1980), can be credited with ensuring that the US definition of the term 'welfare' (which is used 'exclusively' to describe 'less eligible' means-tested benefits claimed by 'undeserving' groups such as lone mothers who are ineligible for contributory social security payments) came to greater prominence in UK social policy discourse.[61]

Although there were no major structural reforms of social security during Moore's term of office (efforts were directed to embedding Fowler's earlier reforms), his commitment to the neo-liberal Conservative cause was evident in a number of his policy pronouncements. As part of the 1987 spending round, for example, he agreed to the freezing of Child Benefit (an allowance he would have liked to have seen abolished)[62] and, following the introduction of guaranteed youth training places, he moved speedily to withdraw Income Support from all 16- and 17-year-olds in September 1988.

Given its popularity with the British public, the NHS proved to be the biggest challenge to neo-liberal Conservatives who wanted to 'reform' this 'sacred' part of the welfare state. During the first two terms, radical changes such as outright privatisation or the introduction of an insurance-based funding scheme had been ruled out. As a consequence, the government was always vulnerable to the charge that it was neglecting the NHS unless it made the generous financial provision needed to cope with the ageing of the British population, technological advances and the growing costs of a labour-intensive service. After its third-term victory, the government was subjected to renewed criticism about under-funding, including a well-publicised missive from the Presidents of the Royal Colleges in December 1987. In response to growing concern about under-funding, Tony Newton, who was deputising for John Moore, announced additional emergency NHS funding.

Thatcher's frustration at the failure to make progress on workable reforms to create a more 'efficient' health service led her to take personal charge of the process. During an interview on the BBC's *Panorama* programme in January 1988, she announced that she would chair a review of the NHS. The other members of the review team were John Moore (subsequently Kenneth Clarke), Tony Newton (subsequently David Mellor) Chancellor Nigel Lawson (who believed that the NHS remained a highly effective service in terms of cost containment),[63] John Major (the other Treasury representative), three civil servants, Roy Griffiths (Thatcher's health service adviser) and members of the Policy Unit. Its preferred option was to reform the NHS along the lines suggested by the influential health economist Alain Enthoven (1985). This involved the creation of an internal market with a clear division between purchasers (tax-funded health authorities and providers (GPs and hospitals). It was envisaged that a division of this kind would increase efficiency and help to contain costs. It was only after Clarke joined the team in July 1989, following Moore's departure from the government because of ill health, that a workable scheme was devised in which District Health Authorities were to become purchasers of care from self-governing hospital trusts. GPs would also become fundholders and would be able to 'buy' services for their patients from a range of 'competitor' providers. These ideas were incorporated into the White Paper *Working for patients* (Department for Health, 1989) and the subsequent *National Health and Community Care Act* of 1990, which Clarke was able to implement with few concessions despite concerted opposition from the medical profession,[64] the trade unions and the Labour Party.

The changes to community care that occurred under the 1990 Act also reflected the neo-liberal Conservative reform agenda. Although the principle of public funding was retained, the pattern of delivery was altered to ensure greater reliance on non-state providers. In response to a rapid growth in social security support for residential care (up from £10 million in 1981 to £2 billion by 1991), the government adviser, Roy Griffiths, was charged with coming up with cost-effective changes. His initial recommendations, which included the appointment of a Minister for Social Care, local authority oversight and a ring-fenced budget, were not greeted with any enthusiasm by the government. As a compromise, local authorities were given budgetary and regulatory responsibilities (for example, need assessments and inspections) for social care but they were expected to make extensive use of private and third-sector providers in the hope that this would stimulate competition and innovation and drive down costs.

The Conservatives also continued to seek ways to reduce the state's role in the construction, ownership, administration and regulation of housing. The 1988 *Housing Act* allowed private landlords and housing associations to take over the running of council-owned properties provided the tenants had given their consent through a ballot. In practice, such transfers were rarely initiated by local tenants but rather by Conservative-controlled local authorities keen to dispose of their properties. The Act also permitted the establishment of Housing Action Trusts, but these did not prove particularly successful (only five had been established by 1994). Rent controls were abolished and the interests of landlords were strengthened by the introduction of 'assured' and shorthold tenancies. The rents of tenants not eligible for Housing Benefit also rose sharply as central government subsidies were pared back and local authorities were prevented from subsiding rents through general revenues.

Thatcher's position as Prime Minister and party leader seemed impregnable after her third consecutive General Election victory in 1987. She seemed set fair to fulfil her long-term objectives of stemming the post-war socialist advance, shrinking the welfare state and reigniting the entrepreneurial spirit of the nation. However, a combination of events led to her dramatic downfall in 1990. The post-election economic boom proved short-lived and the unpopularity of the 'Poll Tax' (Community Charge),[65] which was seen as imposing unfair burdens on those with modest means, resulted in her political judgement being questioned. More significantly, she was weakened by a series of ministerial resignations, some of which were tendered by individuals who had once been among her staunchest supporters. Having already 'lost' Michael Heseltine and Leon Britton following the Westland Helicopter saga in 1986,[66] as well as Norman Tebbit (who had left the government at the end of her second term to care for his wife who had been seriously injured in the Brighton bombing in 1984), Thatcher now had to contend with additional departures. Chancellor Nigel Lawson, who resented her reliance on the advice of Alan Walters rather than his own over issues such as membership of the Exchange Rate Mechanism, left the government, as did Norman Fowler, Peter Walker and Nicholas Ridley (who was forced to resign after making some disparaging comments about 'the Germans' in *The Spectator*). Thatcher's denouement occurred when her longest standing, and arguably most 'put upon' minister, Geoffrey Howe (who had been 'demoted' to Leader of the House and Lord President of the Council in 1989 after a spell at the Foreign Office), resigned from the government after yet another prime ministerial tirade against the European Union.[67]

Unease among a number of backbench MPs about Thatcher's direction of travel led to two leadership challenges. The first, from the 'stalking horse' Sir Anthony Meyer in November 1989, was easily rebuffed. The second, and more significant one, from Michael Heseltine, led to her downfall. Although Thatcher managed to defeat her ex-Cabinet colleague by 204 votes to 152, her failure (by just four votes) to meet the victory 'threshold' triggered a second ballot. After initially indicating that she was prepared to 'fight on', she subsequently changed her mind and decided to tender her resignation following a series of individual meetings with Cabinet colleagues (and even with one Labour MP, Frank Field) that convinced her that she could not even command unqualified support even from 'loyalists' such as Peter Lilley. Although Thatcher's 'anointed' successor, John Major, fell two votes short (185 votes) of the absolute majority he needed to defeat Michael Heseltine (131 votes) and Douglas Hurd (56 votes) in the second leadership ballot, he was elected as the new leader following the withdrawal of his two rivals.

The neo-liberal 'revolution' and the welfare state under Thatcher

The idea that the Thatcher government, committed as it was to the free market and individualism, had succeeded in transforming the welfare state between 1979 and 1990 was treated with scepticism by neo-liberal enthusiasts such as Alfred Sherman and Nicholas Ridley. Both contended that ministers did not make sufficient effort to dismantle this institution. In contrast, a number of academic commentators have suggested that although there was a concerted attack on the welfare state at this time, it proved to be a storm-resilient institution.[68] While it is unquestionably the case that total social spending remained broadly constant during the Thatcher era and that institutions like the NHS managed to survive the neo-liberal assault, the impact of the changes that occurred during this period should not be underestimated. The 'decision' to adopt a gradualist, 'Fabian' approach to welfare state reform in the belief that this would lead eventually to a residual range of publicly funded social services delivered by providers primarily from the private and voluntary sectors proved to be an astute one. 'Grandmother' footstep reforms avoided the political pitfalls of seismic 'revolutionary' change without compromising the broader long-term objective of reversing the post-war social democratic grip on British society. While it is difficult to assess the precise impact of a gradualist strategy of this kind, neo-liberal Conservatives can point to New Labour's embrace of much of their economic agenda policy and their subsequent adoption of a 'consumerist' (rather than egalitarian or ethical) defence of the welfare state as evidence of a slow leap 'forward' for the political Right. Moreover, neo-liberal Conservatives will take heart from more recent surveys of public attitudes[69] that suggest that a neo-liberal mind-set is beginning to taking hold in the British population, particularly in relation to the issue of welfare state 'dependency'. Neo-liberal Conservatives are likely to be particularly encouraged by the fact that younger age groups seem to accept that they now need to be personally responsibility for meeting their own welfare 'needs' and that they regard individual, rather than structural, explanations of poverty and disadvantage as more plausible.

Consolidating the neo-liberal Conservative revolution: the Major era, 1990-97

Like a football manager appointed midway through the season to revive a club's fortunes following the '(in)voluntary' retirement of a once successful coach, John Major, a self-professed One Nation Conservative,[70] was faced with the unenviable choice of deciding whether to retain the playing squad he had inherited from his predecessor but alter the tactics or make wholesale changes in both areas. He opted to retain most of the Thatcher Cabinet while simultaneously pushing the party back to its 'compassionate roots' (Major, 2000, p 214). In pursuit of this strategy, Major recognised that he would run the risk of alienating some die-hard Thatcherites who would regard any deviation from 'deep' neo-liberal Conservatism as a retreat to the comfort zone of One Nation Conservatism. However, Major was convinced that a change of tone was essential if the party was to shed its image as a 'vehicle for intolerance', prejudice and unfairness (Major, 2000, p 213) and thereby enhance its prospects of securing a fourth consecutive electoral victory.

In pursuit of his 'nudge' strategy, Major decided to 'unfreeze' Child Benefit, 'compensate haemophiliacs who had been infected with the HIV virus as a result of contaminated blood transfusions' (Major, 2000, p 212) and, more significantly, jettison the Poll Tax. While the Poll Tax had the superficial attraction of ensuring that 'everyone should pay something towards the cost of services that everyone used' (Major, 2000, p 216), it was recognised that a 'universal flat-rate tax could only be sustainable at a level the poorest could bear' (Major, 2000, p 216). Given that low payments of this kind would not generate sufficient revenue or be 'economic to collect', it was concluded that a new scheme needed to be devised. A fairer eight-banded property tax scheme with discounts for single-person households was eventually formulated by Michael Heseltine (the new Secretary of State for the Environment) for implementation after the General Election. To quell public hostility towards this tax, Major instructed his new Chancellor, Norman Lamont, to use central government funding (some £4.5 billion in total) to ensure that community charges reached reach 'sane levels' in the interim (Major, 2000, p 218).

While there were no dramatic changes in social policy up until the 1992 General Election,[71] Major did attempt to formulate a more 'progressive' version of the neo-liberal Conservative approach to the welfare state. While supportive of the principle of privatisation and the contracting out of some state welfare services, Major believed that the public needed to be reassured that any significant reform of a public services such as education or health should not be viewed as a prelude to privatisation.[72] Accordingly, reforms were presented as a long overdue attempt to ensure that citizens received high-quality services from their providers at a cost the taxpayer could afford. Although Major accepted that the majority of public sector workers were dedicated and hard-working, he believed that that too many services continued to be delivered in 'patronising and arrogant' ways (Major, 2000, p 245). As he contended,

> Some officials seemed to have the attitude that as the service was 'free', everyone should be grateful for whatever they received, even if it was sloppy. There was a mentality in parts of the public service that that no one had responsibility to give better services to the public, unless, of course, they were bribed with more pay or shorter hours. Complaints were treated with an anonymity and disdain that would have fast brought a private company to its knees for lack of customers. Working methods were often slapdash and inefficient, because there was neither the stimulus of competition nor true accountability for performance. New ideas were seen as threats. Services were run carelessly, wastefully, arrogantly and, so it seemed to me, more for the convenience of the providers than the users, whether they were parents, pupils or patients. (Major, 2000, p 245)

In order to transform the 'quality and standing of public services' (Major, 2000, p 258), Major introduced a Citizen's Charter in 1991, under which public service providers were required to comply with agreed performance targets (monitored by independent inspectors), deal with complaints in a timely and responsive way and provide redress where appropriate.[73] Charter marks (which could be held for three years) were to be awarded to public service organisations that were deemed to have delivered high-quality services.

The Conservatives' 1992 General Election manifesto, *The best future for Britain* (Dale, 2000), served to confirm that Major would continue to pursue a modern neo-liberal Conservative direction in both economic and social policy. In terms of the former, it was announced that the party would maintain price stability, 'keep firm control over public spending', reduce taxes in a speedy and prudent way, and ensure that 'market mechanisms and incentives' were allowed to operate as effectively as possible (Major, 2000, p 362). Efforts would be made to 'encourage the wider distribution of wealth throughout society' by sustaining home ownership and promoting a 'capital owning democracy' (Major, 2000, p 365). The privatisation programme would continue, with British Coal, local authority-owned bus companies and airports and British Rail being targeted for full or partial ownership transfers. Deregulation would continue and trade union reforms were promised in order to strengthen the rights of individual members and reduce 'wildcat' strikes. In social policy, an expanded role for citizens' charters was envisaged to promote a consumerist ethos among service users. In education, the need for a strong school–parent relationships was emphasised as well as a 'good grounding' in basic skills. The need for a 'widening' of opportunities 'without compromising academic standards' was also highlighted. A further expansion of higher education and training (Major, 2000, p 376), including the ending of the artificial 'binary' divide between universities and polytechnics, was also promised.

The manifesto also pledged to increase spending on the NHS in real terms, 'develop the NHS Trust movement' and ensure that the 'benefits of fund-holding arrangements were available' to all GPs (Major, 2000, pp 390-1). Under the Patient's Charter, the wait for hip or knee replacements or cataract treatment was to be reduced from two years to 18 months from March 1993 and better information would be provided relating to service availability and standards of care. In housing, the importance of home ownership was emphasised and a range of innovative schemes such as a 'nation-wide "rents to mortgages" scheme' and a do-it-yourself shared-ownership initiative (Major, 2000, p 397) were to be developed to extend this form of tenure. Similar initiatives were also to be developed to improve opportunities for those renting in the private sector, such as a 'rent a room' scheme under which a home owner could let a room 'tax-free' to a lodger. Initiatives to tackle the problem of rough sleepers were to be introduced, while existing schemes to improve the quality of affordable housing such as the voluntary transfer of 'batches' of council properties to housing associations and the establishment of Housing Action Trusts would be continued.

An improved and modernised social security system was also promised, with extra help being directed towards 'less well-off' pensioners, disabled people and low-income families. The government's commitment to Child Benefit was underlined by a pledge to raise this benefit each year in line with prices while the introduction of new or revamped disability benefits was seen as a way of directing extra help to this growing group of claimants. A Child Support Agency was also to be established to ensure that absent parents contributed to the upkeep of all their dependent children, not just those with whom they currently resided.

While the Major government was convinced of the need to maintain the momentum of public sector reform, the anti-state and anti-poor rhetoric of the Thatcher era was discarded and replaced by a narrative that focused on effectiveness and efficiency.

The 1992 General Election

Although the majority of political pundits predicted that Major would lose the 1992 General Election, voters seemed to heed Conservative warnings that the return of a Kinnock-led Labour government would undermine the achievements and reforms of the Thatcher era and signal a return to outmoded policies that would impoverish and divide the nation (Major, 2000, p 417). The departure of Mrs Thatcher, the withdrawal of the Poll Tax and the understated assurance exuded by Major himself helped to focus media attention on the shortcomings of the Labour leader Neil Kinnock[74] and on his party's tax and spend 'bombshells'. Voters opted to hold tightly onto the hand of 'nurse', in the shape of Major and the Conservatives, for fear of something worse (Kinnock and the Labour Party).[75] On a 77.7% turnout, the Conservatives secured more votes (14,092,891) than any other party in British political history. However, their 42.3% share of the vote (compared with 35.2% for Labour) only yielded 'a miserly majority' of 21 seats (Major, 2000, p 307).

The Major government, 1992-97

At the party's first post-election conference in Brighton in October 1992, there was little evidence in many of the conference speeches of the more emollient version of neo-liberal conservatism that Major had seemed keen to pursue. In his own speech, Major condemned 'sponging' New Age Travellers – a group that was also targeted by the new Social Security Secretary Peter Lilley in his now infamous rendition of a song ('I've got a little list') adapted from the Gilbert and Sullivan opera *The Mikado*. According to Lilley, New Age Travellers were apt to 'descend like locusts demanding money with menaces' from law abiding citizens. He also took aim at 'bogus asylum seekers', 'councillors who claim the dole to run left wing campaigns', 'young ladies who get pregnant to jump the housing queue' and 'dads who won't support the ladies they have "kissed"'.[76] Single mothers were also subjected to criticism in other well-publicised speeches by John Redwood (Minister for Wales), Michael Howard and George Young.[77]

These attacks on what were regarded as 'undeserving' claimants were prompted in part by the need to curb social security spending in the light of a projected £50 billion budget deficit in 1993 that had been triggered by Britain's decision to withdraw from the Exchange Rate Mechanism on 'Black Monday' (16 September 1992), during which £15 billion worth of reserves were used up in what proved to be a fruitless attempt to protect the value of the pound. Neo-liberal Conservative groups such as No Turning Back (a staunchly neo-liberal Conservative organisation that had been established in 1985 to carry forward the torch of 'Thatcherism') were quick to offer deficit-reducing solutions such as the abolition of SERPS and greater reliance on non-state provision for those whose financial needs arose from unemployment or disability.[78]

The deteriorating state of the public finances led Michael Portillo, the Chief Secretary to the Treasury, to announce a fundamental review of welfare spending in February 1993 with a view to identifying those areas of provision where resources could be better targeted or where the state might withdraw altogether. Lilley, a close ally of Portillo, accepted the case for expenditure restraint and reform. He was particularly attracted to the principle of 'conditionality',[79] in which the 'right' to benefits was dependent on claimants making determined efforts to find, and retain, paid work. Jobseekers Allowance, which was eventually introduced in 1996, required claimants to demonstrate that they had been actively seeking work by providing documentary evidence that they had been in contact with prospective employers. Those deemed to have made insufficient efforts to find paid work faced the prospect of having their benefits cut or withdrawn. Lilley also drew up plans for a pared back SERPS scheme and announced plans to replace invalidity and sickness benefits with a less generous Incapacity Benefit scheme. Entitlements to Unemployment Benefit were reduced from 12 months to six months and Housing Benefit allowances were cut. In an effort to encourage more claimants to return to work, Family Credit payments were enhanced and 'back to work bonuses' were introduced.

The consolidation of earlier neo-liberal Conservative education reforms proved far from straightforward. The decision of the new Education Secretary John Patten to press ahead with national testing of English for all 14-year-olds despite professional concerns about its effectiveness led to a national teachers' boycott of *all* testing. The dispute was only resolved following the intervention of one of the government's 'fire-fighters', Sir Ron Dearing, the newly appointed head of the School Curriculum and Assessment Authority.[80] The introduction of a new external inspection regime for schools also proved controversial. The first Head of the Office for Standards in Education, Chris Woodhead, adopted a confrontational approach to inspections that differed markedly from the 'collaborative' methods favoured by HMI. Following the first round of inspections, Woodhead announced that improvements were needed in 50% of primary schools and 40% of secondary schools. Schools deemed to be 'failing' were liable to be put into 'special measures' or even closed.

The government faced an uphill battle in its efforts to persuade state schools, particularly in the primary sector and in Scotland, to apply for grant maintained status, which had been proposed in the 1987 manifesto. Despite financial incentives, just 4% of all schools had become grant maintained by 1997. In addition, a national nursery voucher scheme intended to increase parental choice failed to stimulate much interest when it was introduced in 1997.

Neo-liberal Conservative ideas were, however, more warmly embraced by the entrepreneurial management teams that had come to prominence in the university sector. They proved more than willing to trade off academic autonomy and scholarly endeavour for the promise of secure or enhanced forms of funding. The binary divide between universities and polytechnics ended in 1993 when the latter were permitted to opt for 'university' status.

Consolidation of the Thatcher legacy also proved far from straightforward in the NHS, where the new minister Virginia Bottomley had to deal with growing public and professional concern that the introduction of the purchaser–provider split and GP fundholding were undermining the ethos of the service. Although some additional funding was made available to meet the initial costs of these reforms, especially the greatly increased managerial wage bill, this was not sustained. As Timmins (2001) notes,

> NHS growth dropped from a real terms increase of almost 6% in 1992-3 to a tenth of that a year later. Bottomley got it up to 3.78 percent the following year, but it then slid away to barely 1.5% in 1995-6 and 0.6% in the run up to the 1997 election. (p 516)

To counter the growing uneasiness about the adverse impact of the reforms, Bottomley's successor, Stephen Dorrell, published a White

Paper, *The National Health Service: A service with ambitions*, (Department of Health, 1996), which attempted to reassure both the general public and clinicians that the government was more interested in providing a first-rate health service than in introducing 'market' reforms.

Fewer consolidation problems emerged in the area of housing. An additional 300,000 council houses were sold off in this period and 170,000 tenants acquired a new landlord under the government's voluntary transfer scheme.[81] Housing associations cemented their place as the largest provider of new 'social' housing, supplying nearly 168,000 homes between 1992 and 1996 compared with just 10,500 in the local authority sector.[82] The rents for such properties steadily increased, however, given that housing associations were forced to rely on more expensive forms of private finance, rather than public subsidies, to finance their building programmes. The deregulation of the private rented sector also appeared to 'revive' this part of the housing sector.[83]

John Major also championed a return to more traditional forms of practice in areas such as education and social work. In his 1992 party conference speech, he declared that if his critics sought to portray him as 'old fashioned, well so be it'. As he pointed out:

> 'I have this message for the progressives who are trying to change the exams. English exams should be about literature, not soap opera. And I promise you this. There'll be no GCSEs in Eldorado[84] – even assuming anyone is still watching it!… Let us return to basic subject teaching, not courses in the theory of education. Primary teachers should learn how to teach children to read, not waste their time on the politics of gender, race and class.'

In his conference speech a year later, Major launched his infamous 'Back to Basics' campaign in which he sought to 'activate' the traditionalist agenda he had promoted in 1992. Much to Major's consternation, though, his attack on 'progressivism' was seen by many sections of the media as a deep-rooted desire to return to the 'stability' and 'moral' climate of the 1950s following the permissive excesses of the 1960s and '70s. Although Major had no desire to berate single mothers or 'preach sexual fidelity' to private citizens (Major, 2000, p 555), this proved to be the narrative that found favour in the media. Following a concerted media campaign, the junior minister Tim Yeo (who had previously drawn attention to the 'damage' caused by broken families) was forced to resign from his post in January 1994 after it was revealed that he had fathered an 'illegitimate' child. Intense media coverage was also devoted to the death of another junior minister, Stephen Milligan, following a sexual misadventure. Further exposés relating to ministerial wrongdoing – including allowing innocent businessmen to be imprisoned in order to cover up 'illegal' government actions surrounding 'arms for Iraq' (the Matrix Churchill case), the receiving of cash for the asking of parliamentary questions (Graham Riddick, David Tredinnick, Tim Smith and Neil Hamilton), and accepting 'undeclared' hospitality from a Saudi Arabian arms dealer (Jonathan Aitken) – led to the Major government becoming engulfed in questions of 'sleaze' in the run-up to the 1997 General Election.

Since becoming leader in 1992, Major had endured a continuous struggle with the 'Eurosceptic' wing of the party. The party's agreed (manifesto) position on ratifying the Maastricht Treaty (which Major had signed in 1991 after securing an opt-out from the social chapter and joining the currency union) unravelled following a backbench revolt (aided and abetted by Margaret Thatcher) that had gathered momentum following the decision of the Danish electorate to reject, in a referendum, their own government's backing of the new accord. Following the loss of a key Commons vote, Major only succeeded in gaining parliamentary 'approval' for ratification by calling for, and winning, a vote of confidence.[85]

Following persistent sniping, Major opted for a 'pre-emptive strike' against his critics by calling a snap leadership contest in June 1995. Although he secured a comfortable victory over his sole, Eurosceptic, rival John Redwood, there was a general perception that the party lacked the cohesion to function as an effective government. Faced with a vibrant, media-savvy 'New Labour' leader, Tony Blair, who promised to combine a neo-liberal economic policy with a sprinkling of social democratic social justice, it was no longer a question of whether the Conservatives would lose the 1997 General Election but merely the likely margin of their defeat.

Assessing the Major era, 1992-97

Between 1992 and 1997, the Major governments attempted to consolidate the neo-liberal Conservative reforms of the welfare state that had been introduced by the previous Thatcher administrations. Although Major was more sympathetic to the welfare state given his own first-hand experience of the protection it could afford to ordinary citizens in times of need, and was keen to dismantle opportunity barriers in order to secure a 'classless' society, he remained committed to the neo-liberal reform agenda that the previous governments had set in motion. Major believed that market disciplines such as performance-related pay, competition, audit and external inspection would improve the quality of public services and keep a downward pressure on costs. Major's best-known 'cultural' initiative – the Citizen's Charter – was intended to embed an active consumerist, as opposed to passive citizenship, mind-set among the British public. Although it can be argued that the charters failed to excite the public, they may well have contributed to the 'cultural' revolution that was, arguably, the main achievement of both the Thatcher and Major governments. By the end of the 1990s, it seemed that public support for the welfare state had become decidedly instrumental rather than ideological.

The neo-liberal direction in Conservative economic and social policy was reaffirmed in the party's General Election manifesto of 1997 – *You can only be sure with the Conservatives* (Dale, 2000). Once again, the virtues of the free market, low taxes, privatisation, deregulation, minimal inflation, trade union reform, and law and order were proclaimed. In social policy, the drive for a smaller state 'doing fewer things and doing them better' (Dale, 2000, p 441) was to continue. A more affordable and efficient social security system was promised, as was a further round of council house sales. Higher standards and greater choice were promised in both education and healthcare. It was clear, however, that this message no longer resonated with the public, who voted decisively for New Labour. In a dramatic change in the party's fortunes, the Conservatives secured just 30.2% of the popular vote in 1997, losing 182 seats. It was the biggest swing to an opposition party since Labour's post-war landslide in 1945.

Conclusion: breaking the One Nation stranglehold – neo-Liberal Conservatism and the welfare state

Neo-Liberal Conservatives contend that the 'social democratic' economic and social policies pursued by both Labour and acquiescent, paternalist, One Nation Conservative governments in the 30-year period following the Second World War quashed enterprise and aspiration (which proved particularly detrimental to a beleaguered middle class) and stifled economic advance and created a state dependency culture. A swing of the pendulum in a laissez-faire direction was deemed necessary if this creeping socialist advance was to be halted. Rejecting the One Nation Conservative contention that pragmatic forms of state intervention could bolster rather than undermine free market activity, the neo-liberal Conservatives set in train their economic and social counter-revolution when the political tide turned in their favour at the end of the 1970s.

The neo-liberal Conservative approach to the welfare state that became so influential in the 1980s and 90s did, however, share some common ground with the One Nation Conservative tradition that had preceded it. Both schools of thought agreed that an egalitarian universal welfare state was undesirable and that public funds should be concentrated on assisting those most in acute need by providing a safety net for those who had fallen on hard times through no fault of their own. However, while One Nation Conservatives were also prepared to extend the scope and generosity of state provision in areas such as education and healthcare on the basis that this had become the settled will of the British people, neo-liberal Conservatives believed that the British public could, and indeed should, be persuaded to take greater responsibility for their own welfare needs. The rapid post-war expansion of the welfare state was seen as having fostered a damaging culture of state dependency in which the drum beat of 'citizenship' had led large numbers of non-needy citizens to rely on tax-financed state support. One of the reasons why Margaret Thatcher so despised the word society was not because of an underlying hostility towards voluntary civic engagement but rather because this term was too often used as a code word for the idea that individuals and families should, in the face of unmet need, seek assistance from the state in the first instance rather than rely on their own resources, ingenuity and endeavour.[86] However, for One Nation progressives such as Gilmour and Macmillan,[87] (who had witnessed at first hand the toxic effects of laissez-faire economic policies in the 1930s) the neo-liberal turn in government policy at this time was seen as 'alien' to the true spirit of Conservatism.

Despite their ideological predispositions, the neo-liberal Conservatives recognised the political backlash they would face if they attempted to move too swiftly towards the residualisation of the welfare state. As a consequence, an incremental strategy was adopted in the hope that some of the other 'individualistic' changes that they had put in train (right to buy, wider share ownership and lower taxation) would eventually create a citizenry more willing to accept fundamental reform of the welfare state.

SIX

Progressive neo-liberal Conservatism and the welfare state, 2005-15

The election of David Cameron as the new Conservative leader in 2005 signalled the emergence of what can be termed the 'progressive' neo-liberal Conservative approach to the welfare state. John Major's defeat in the 1997 General Election at the hands of New Labour under the charismatic leadership of Tony Blair led to 13 years of opposition for the Conservative Party. During this period, the Conservatives began to take a greater interest in social issues. The first part of this chapter traces the compassionate turn in Conservative thinking under the leadership of William Hague, Iain Duncan Smith and, to a lesser extent, Michael Howard in the period from 1997 to 2005.

The compassionate turn?[1] Neo-liberal Conservatism and the welfare state, 1997-2005

John Major's decision to resign as leader on 2 May 1997, the day after his party's crushing defeat in the 1997 General Election (in which seven Cabinet ministers lost their seats), meant that those Conservatives returning to the opposition benches were faced with the immediate prospect of a leadership contest. Ken Clarke, Peter Lilley, William Hague, Michael Howard and John Redwood all threw their hats into the ring. After the elimination of Lilley, Howard and Redwood in early rounds of voting, Hague, Thatcher's preferred candidate, defeated Clarke by 92 votes to 70 in the final run-off, thereby confirming 'that being anything other than a Eurosceptic was an insurmountable bar to leading the party' at the time (Snowden, 2010, p 45).

The Hague era (19 June 1997 to 13 September 2001)

William Hague faced the unenviable task of trying to re-energise public support for the Conservatives in the face of a 'New Labour' government that was proving hard to oppose, given its success in laying claim to the 'common' ground of British politics. By renouncing socialism, embracing the neo-liberal economic agenda and substituting a commitment to social justice for the pursuit of equality, New Labour had left the Conservatives floundering. Although the Conservative shadow Cabinet team had a strong neo-liberal presence including as it did Lilley (Chancellor), Howard (Foreign Office), Brian Mawhinney (Home Secretary), Redwood (trade and industry), Iain Duncan Smith (social security), Cecil Parkinson (Party Chairman) and Francis Maude (culture, media and sport), Hague was keen, at first, to demonstrate his willingness to move on from the Thatcher/Major era by authorising internal reforms aimed at enhancing the participation of grassroots members[2] and by encouraging the development of a more tolerant and compassionate political narrative that was formerly promoted by One Nation Conservatives.

Hague's attraction to the theme of compassionate Conservatism was heavily influenced by the more nuanced approach to social issues that the Republicans had been pursuing in the United States.[3] As Montgomerie (2004) notes, 'compassionate conservatism has two complimentary sides: one seeking to modify conservatism, the other seeking to modify society's idea of compassion' (p 7). In terms of the former, conservatism was deemed to be compatible with an ethic of care and a concern for the disadvantaged. In the case of compassion, it was seen as important not just to support those in poverty but to help them to become more self-sufficient, not least through the greater involvement of publicly funded voluntary organisations and faith groups. Compassionate conservatives were also strongly committed to the principle of subsidiarity. As Olasky (2000) explains in relation to US social policy:

> Compassionate conservatives choose the most basic means of bringing help to those who need it. The goal is to look within the family first; if the family cannot help, maybe an individual or group within the neighbourhood can; if not, then organizations outside the neighbourhood but within the community should be called upon. If it is necessary to turn to government, compassionate conservatives typically look first to municipal, then to county, then to state, and only then to federal offices. (p 17)

Peter Lilley and compassionate Conservatism

Peter Lilley's[4] R.A. Butler memorial lecture at the Carlton Club on 20 April 1999 (which was delivered on the same evening that many party members were celebrating the 20th anniversary of Margaret Thatcher's first election victory at the Hilton hotel)[5] proved to be one of the most notable attempts by a senior Conservative to persuade party colleagues to adopt a more 'compassionate' approach to the welfare state in the post-Thatcher era. Described by fellow shadow Cabinet colleague Michael Howard as 'the most dangerous and damaging speech I have ever read in my entire career' (Snowden, 2010, pp 60-1), Lilley reminded his audience that in the immediate post-war period the Conservative Party had been associated with 'selfishness, greed and high unemployment'. Despite R.A. Butler's attempt to 'reconcile the welfare state and Conservatism in the public mind', it remained the case that 'half a century later the public's greatest area of unease about Conservatives is our supposedly hostile attitude to the welfare state and particularly to health and education'. In an effort to remedy this perception, Lilley suggested that the party needed to 'openly and emphatically accept that the free market has only a limited role in improving public services like health, education and welfare'. To reassure the public that the party had a benevolent approach to the welfare state, Lilley argued that Conservatives should draw attention to some of their non-market values, not least their acceptance of the principle that the rich should support the poor, that the 'strong' should 'aid the weak' and that the funding of public services was a reflection of such an ethos. He argued that the provision of healthcare free at the point of delivery was superior to private forms of insurance that tended to leave poorer citizens with the 'worse health records' facing the 'highest premia'. He also highlighted the need for diverse, free, taxpayer-funded, compulsory schooling (albeit with greater diversity of provision than would be necessary in healthcare) on the grounds that society had 'a common interest in ensuring that the rising generation' could 'develop their talents to the full so they can contribute fully to society and support themselves'. For Lilley, the Conservative Party needed to make clear to the public that they now trusted 'teachers, doctors and nurses' to improve service quality and would no longer rely on inappropriate market means to drive up performance.

Instead of opening up a post-Thatcherite agenda on the welfare state, Lilley's speech only served to harden the resolve of those neo-liberal Conservatives who believed that any concerted attempt to distance the party from the Thatcher legacy would be counter-productive as well as treacherous. The furore surrounding Lilley's speech[6] persuaded Hague to abandon any attempt to pursue an overly 'progressive' position on social issues. According to Snowden, by siding with those who were unwilling to 'question the party's Thatcherite inheritance', Hague surrendered the opportunity to 'address the causes of the party's unpopularity' (p 61).

It should also be noted that Hague's initial desire to pursue a more socially inclusive and less judgemental approach to lifestyle choices, did not, as Dorey (2003) reminds us, translate into notable policy shifts. Few Conservative MPs supported New Labour's attempt to 'equalise' the age of consent at 16 for both homosexuals and heterosexuals under a clause in the Crime and Disorder Bill. Indeed, one prominent member of the House of Lords, Baroness Young, denounced it 'as a "paedophile's charter"' (Dorey, 2003, p 134). Similarly, the decision to impose a three-line whip on Conservative peers to counter the New Labour government's attempt to repeal Section 28 of the 1988 *Local Government Act*, which prohibited the 'promotion of homosexuality' in schools, was hardly indicative of any relaxation of the party's long-standing 'traditionalism' with regard to family and sexual issues.[7]

Hague's support for marriage and the nuclear family was underlined by his opposition to New Labour's abolition of the married couples' tax allowance and by his public utterances concerning the superiority of the 'traditional' two-parent family over lone-parent or 'broken' families, in terms of providing children with emotional and financial security. While respecting the right of couples to cohabit, Hague believed that it would be inappropriate to grant them 'the same pension rights, or rights pertaining to the division of property, as married couples' (Dorey, 2003, p 136). Hague's response to New Labour's revisionist welfare narrative, which called for a greater focus on responsibilities rather than rights, also led him to pledge his support for tougher forms of conditionality, including the withdrawal of benefits from unemployed claimants who refused an offer of employment, when his party returned to government. The shadow Secretary of State for Social Security, David Willetts, also supported more 'vigorous' welfare measures when he suggested that lone mothers should have their personal allowances reduced if they failed to make reasonable effort to seek paid employment when their youngest child started secondary school.[8]

By the time of the 2001 General Election, it had become clear that Hague had reverted to a conventional neo-liberal Conservative position on economic and social policy. The party's General Election manifesto, *Time for common sense* (Conservative Party, 2001), promised lower taxes, especially for 'hardworking families', deregulation and proper control of public spending. In the case of social policy, there was a focus on individual responsibility and restricting state dependency. A major attempt to encourage more voluntary sector welfare provision was also announced on the grounds that these non-state organisations were better 'able to help people in real need' (Conservative Party, 2001, p 33). The Conservatives also promised to set up an Office for Civil Society 'to give families, faith communities and voluntary groups a voice at the heart of government' (Conservative Party, 2001, p 33).

Enhanced choice for social service users was also highlighted. 'Free' schools, run by faith groups, charities and private companies, were to be encouraged as a way of enhancing parental choice. Patients were to be given guaranteed maximum waiting times for cardiac or cancer treatment and a greater choice in selecting a hospital for their treatment. Non-state providers were also to be funded by the NHS to provide 'routine', standardised treatments such as cataract surgery or hip replacements. Labour's 'tax penalties' on employers or individuals who 'free up resources in the NHS and help to 'reduce waiting times' (Conservative Party, 2001, p 20) by taking out private health insurance would also be reversed.

Tougher rules were also to be introduced in the field of social security for working-age adults. Benefits were to be withdrawn from unemployed claimants who refused to work under a proposed 'can work, must work guarantee' (Conservative Party, 2001, p 34). Stricter anti-fraud measures were also proposed.

Europe and asylum seeking also featured prominently in both the manifesto and the campaign. The decision to focus on European issues (in Europe not run by Europe/saving the pound) was linked to the party's success in the 1999 European elections.[9] The issue of 'bogus' asylum seekers (a safe haven, not a soft touch) was also seen as a way of shoring up the party's core vote.[10] Although Hague had hoped to restore his party's fortunes in the 2001 General Election, the result left him deflated. On a historically low turnout (59.4%), the Conservatives 'gained' just one seat and only secured a marginal increase in their share of the popular vote (31.7%).[11]

Like Major before him, Hague quickly tendered his resignation as party leader after losing the election. Five candidates participated in the party's fifth leadership contest in 12 years – Michael Ancram, Iain Duncan Smith, David Davies, Kenneth Clarke and Michael Portillo.[12] Portillo, who stood as the change candidate on an unequivocal 'modernising' platform (he was supported by two up and coming 'progressives', David Cameron and George Osborne),[13] emerged victorious after the first round of voting.[14] Portillo was unable, however, to build on his first-round support, narrowly failing to qualify for the final 'shoot-out' after securing 53 votes in the second round of voting (compared with 59 for Clarke and 54 for Duncan Smith). The final contest, which was to be decided by the votes of ordinary party members, saw the decidedly neo-liberal Conservative and Eurosceptic candidate Duncan Smith (who had been endorsed by Margaret Thatcher and *The Daily Telegraph*) ease to victory over his better-known, pro-European rival by 155,933 votes to 100,864.[15]

The rise and fall of the quiet man: the Iain Duncan Smith era (September 2001 to November 2003)

Duncan Smith was fully committed to the compassionate Conservative agenda. With the support of Rick Nye (formerly of the Social Market Foundation) and Greg Clark (who was to head up a new policy unit), Duncan Smith was keen to ensure that the party adopted a more sympathetic and supportive approach to disadvantaged groups in society. In a speech at the party's spring conference following a well-publicised visit to Easterhouse, one of the most deprived areas of Glasgow, in February 2002, Duncan Smith informed his audience that:

> A nation that leaves its vulnerable behind, diminishes its own future. Britain will never be all that it should be until opportunity and security mean something to people in Easterhouse. To make this country theirs as much as it is ours. That is a mission fit for a new century. (Duncan Smith, 2002, p 31)

Duncan Smith's brand of compassionate Conservatism was not deemed, however, to require a retreat from the Fabian-style counter-revolution that had started during the Thatcher era. A policy unit pamphlet, *Leadership with a purpose: A better tomorrow* (Conservative Policy Unit, 2002) was published to coincide with the party's annual conference in 2002 in order to provide a guide to Duncan Smith's prospective social agenda.[16] After acknowledging the success that the Thatcher governments had achieved in delivering economic prosperity by adhering to the neo-liberal policy advice contained in *The right approach* in the mid-1970s (Conservative Party, 1976), it was now deemed apposite for the next Conservative government to create 'a better society' (Conservative Policy Unit, 2002, p 2). New Labour's promise to transform society was deemed to have 'failed' and as a consequence it now fell to the Conservatives to tackle the five contemporary 'giants' that posed a threat to British society - rising crime, inadequate healthcare, failing schools, child poverty and growing dependency on the state.

The slaying of these modern day giants[17] did not require the creation of a welfare state, but, rather, its reform. While public funding of services would still be required, more diverse forms of delivery involving greater reliance on the voluntary and private sectors were deemed necessary to ensure that citizens would have better access to a diverse range of 'excellent' services. To this end, a decentralised NHS was proposed 'in which the component institutions – GPs, hospitals and clinics' would no longer be managed from Whitehall, 'according to a national blueprint', but would, instead, manage 'themselves in response to the demands of individual patients' (Conservative Policy Unit, 2002, pp 20-1). In addition, citizens were to be released from the so-called 'responsibility trap'. 'Virtuous' citizens who were willing to provide for their own healthcare and pensions from their own savings or earnings were to be 'rewarded' for their actions, not subjected to additional taxes. An enhanced role for both the voluntary and informal sectors was also envisaged, given that current levels of state support were deemed unsustainable. The growth of state support was seen as having not only undermined 'the personal networks of family and community that are best placed to support people through their lives', but also as fuelling a culture of dependency.

> We will place our trust in communities, strengthening the voluntary institutions that can give personal help to people at times of their lives when they are vulnerable; and recognising the contribution that members of families make to the care of each other. (Conservative Policy Unit, 2002, p 3)

A combined approach of this kind was intended

> ... to do what Conservatives have always sought to do: to reinforce individual liberty and civil society, rather than allow the precious underpinnings of civilised life to be eroded by intrusive, ineffective and alienating government intervention. We are in favour of people and society, rather than of ever-growing government. (Conservative Policy Unit, 2002, p 4)

Given his own deeply held religious convictions, it is not surprising that Duncan Smith's brand of 'compassionate' Conservatism was underpinned by an unshakeable belief in the positive role that both the 'traditional' family and faith groups could play in society. This was reflected in the party's decision to oppose New Labour's Adoption and Children's Bill in 2002, which would have permitted unmarried couples, whether gay or straight, to adopt children. Although a three-line whip was imposed on MPs, this did not prevent Portillo, Maude and Clarke defying their party and voting with the government, while John Bercow, the shadow Work and Pensions Minister, resigned from the government.[18] Duncan Smith's subsequent appeal for party unity only served to heighten internal concerns about his leadership capabilities. Duncan Smith was seen as lacking 'the charismatic public persona necessary for success in the media age' and proved unable to improve his party's standing in the opinion polls (Hayton, 2012, p 51). Although Duncan Smith made some progress in demonstrating that the Conservatives had an interest in a wider range of issues than Europe, immigration and low taxation, his compassionate Conservative message all too often appeared to be based on doing things *to*, rather than *for*, those experiencing poverty. As a result, it proved an uphill struggle to counter Theresa May's telling observation at the 2002 party conference that the Conservatives were still perceived by large swathes of the electorate as the 'nasty party'.

Beset by criticisms of his ineffective handling of internal party affairs, the fallout from the 'Bettysgate' affair[19] and a failure to restore his party's standings in the polls, which some MPs thought might presage the terminal demise of the Conservatives as a political force, Duncan Smith was eventually forced to secure a vote of confidence from his parliamentary colleagues after 25 Conservative MPs exercised their new right[20] to call for a leadership contest in the autumn of 2003. Although Duncan Smith amassed 75 votes, he was opposed by 90 of his fellow Conservative MPs. The leadership of the 'quiet man'[21] had come to an end after just two years. As Bale (2010) remarks, Duncan Smith had

> ... presided over a party that at times had descended into institutional chaos, a party that was unable to call on the services of many of its most talented individuals, a party that eventually lost the confidence of the economic interests that funded it, and a party whose ideas were still some way away from the preferences of the electorate whose votes it needed to return to power. (p 193)

Lukewarm compassionate Conservatism? The Michael Howard era (6 November 2003 to 6 December 2005)

In 'selecting' Michael Howard, another deep blue neo-liberal Conservative[22] to succeed Duncan Smith following a 'bloodless coup',[23] it seemed improbable that the party would pursue the 'modernising' agenda that some MPs and the increasingly influential think tank Policy Exchange[24] believed was necessary to restore the party's electoral prospects. However, 'modernising' socially inclusive themes were much to the fore in the speech[25] that Howard delivered to launch his leadership bid at County Hall in October 2002. After being confirmed as the new party leader, Howard sought to develop a more 'moderate' line on social and moral questions by allowing, for instance, free votes on New Labour's civil partnership legislation and on the Gender Recognition Bill, which granted transsexuals enhanced legal protection including the 'right to marry in their adopted sex' (Hayton, 2012, p 113).[26] While this strategy did little to resolve internal party divisions over such questions, it did help to create the impression that the Conservatives were prepared, at least in principle, to move with the times rather than simply be a party of 'reaction'.

In terms of economic issues and the welfare state, though, there was little to suggest that Howard would stray too far away from more orthodox neo-liberal Conservative standpoints, although he was keen to stress the party's desire to provide help for those in genuine need and to extend opportunities for all. In a two-page advertisement published in *The Times* on 2 January 2004, Howard reaffirmed his belief in a free but responsible society, where people are 'not nannied or over-governed', and where government acts to remove opportunity barriers. He firmly rejected the idea that the disadvantages experienced by some poorer groups in society could be attributed to the actions of more wealthy citizens who were in good health or who had been better educated. He did, however, acknowledge though that one of the duties of a Conservative government was 'to look after those who cannot help themselves' (Howard, 2004). In a subsequent speech at Policy Exchange in February 2004, Howard set out his vision of the 'British dream', in which all citizens should be able to succeed through hard work and the exercise of their talents and be given the opportunity to have greater choice and influence over the 'healthcare they receive' and the 'schools their children are educated in'. The NHS was deemed to be 'too impersonal, too inflexible, too centralised and too bureaucratic'. He confirmed his commitment to a smaller state and lower taxation and the need to ensure that discrimination based on ethnicity, beliefs or sexuality was eradicated. Although he remained convinced that 'conventional' marriage and the traditional family provided the 'best environment' for bringing up children, he acknowledged that there was now a move towards alternative arrangements. He expressed his support for civil partnerships, but not for same-sex marriage.

For Howard, the Conservatives needed to be seen as a party that was committed to reforming, not dismantling, the welfare state. To this end, he promised to 'match' New Labour's spending plans while simultaneously increasing user choice and cutting waste. In terms of the former, a 'right to choose' campaign was launched in 2004 offering citizens the opportunity to use public funds, augmented where necessary by personal savings, to access private welfare provision. In the case of the latter, David James, a businessman, was asked to examine waste in the public sector. James identified £35 billion of efficiency savings (including the loss of 230,000 public sector jobs), a sum that Howard and his shadow Chancellor Oliver Letwin suggested could be used to reinvest in frontline services such as the police and prisons, to reduce borrowing and to cut taxes, particularly for older people.

Howard remained acutely sensitive to the suggestion that the Conservatives were still intent on rolling back the welfare state. The party's prospective parliamentary candidate for Sedgefield, Danny Kruger, was forced to stand down after indicating that the Conservatives were presiding over the 'creative destruction' of the welfare state, while the Deputy Chair and MP for Arundel and South Downs, Howard Flight, resigned as Deputy Chair of the party[27] after hinting at a private meeting of the Conservative Way Forward Group that the next Tory government were intending to impose draconic welfare cuts after the General Election.[28]

The 2005 General Election

The Conservatives' 2005 General Election manifesto – *Are you thinking what we're thinking? It's time for action* – reaffirmed Howard's promise to match Labour's spending on services such as the NHS and schools (Conservative Party, 2005). This was accompanied by a pledge to cut waste. Annual savings of £12 billion in 2007-08 were to be achieved by freezing civil service recruitment, cutting '235,000 bureaucratic posts' and abolishing '168 public bodies' (Conservative Party, 2005, p 3). Reforms in various areas of welfare were also outlined. In education, school heads and governors were to be granted 'full control over admissions and expulsions', the national curriculum was to be slimmed down and university tuition fees (that had been introduced by New Labour) were to be abolished. In the NHS, patient choice was to be improved and local professionals would be empowered to run local services. Primary Care Trusts were to be reduced, Strategic Health Authorities abolished and the numbers of 'quangos, inspectorates and commissions' cut (Conservative Party, 2005, p 11).[29] Those choosing to pay for private treatment would be compensated for half the cost of the standard NHS procedure in recognition of the tax contributions that such patients had already made to the NHS. In housing, the right to buy scheme was to be extended to housing association tenants.

In accordance with the advice of the party's Campaign Director, Lynton Crosby, the manifesto also emphasised the uncompromising stance that a future Conservative government would take in the areas of crime (the recruitment of 5,000 additional police officers), immigration (24-hour surveillance at ports of entry) and Europe (setting a date for a referendum on the European Constitution).

Despite growing voter antipathy towards the New Labour government over issues such as the Iraq war and tuition fees, Tony Blair was still able to guide his party to an unprecedented third consecutive victory in 2005[30] with an overall majority of 66 seats. As Bale concludes, although Howard prevented the Conservatives from falling into third place behind the Liberal Democrats, 'he failed to move the Party out of the ideological and institutional rut which it had been stuck with since the early 1990s' (Bale, 2010, p 253).[31]

David Cameron and the 'progressive' neo-liberal Conservative approach to the welfare state

Howard did not resign immediately after the party's third consecutive General Election defeat, but was persuaded to stay on as leader until a decision had been reached about proposed changes to the leadership election rules.[32] A leadership contest was eventually activated under the old rules in October 2005. During Howard's 'interregnum', David Cameron, who played a leading role in drafting the party's so-called 'Victor Meldrew'[33] manifesto of 2005, emerged as the favoured moderate and modernising leadership candidate. After early rounds of MP voting that saw the elimination of Kenneth Clarke in the first ballot and Liam Fox in the second, Cameron went on to beat the early frontrunner David Davis in the final run-off.[34] Cameron's success has been attributed to a rousing speech at the party's annual conference in Blackpool in October[35] and a recognition by electors of the need to back a modern rather than traditional candidate.[36]

Given Labour's success in rebranding itself as New Labour,[37] Cameron believed that his own party could benefit from a similar makeover. Accepting that the party was seen as being out of touch with the views of ordinary voters and of being indifferent to the needs and aspirations of those experiencing multiple disadvantages, Cameron sought to focus on the party's positive stance on the NHS and the family and move away from its 'negative' approach to issues such as Europe and immigration.[38]

Cameron's repositioning was not deemed to require any modifications to the party's neo-liberal Conservative approach to economic policy either on grounds of principle or electoral advantage (New Labour's conversion to the merits of neo-liberalism meant that there were no longer any significant ideological differences between the parties over the economy). In contrast, the construction of a new, softer, social narrative was deemed necessary to 'detoxify' the Conservative 'brand' and to highlight how the party's agenda in this sphere differed from the overly statist strategy of New Labour.

In seeking to detoxify the Conservative brand, Cameron could have decided to adopt the 'progressive' One Nation moniker that held sway in the 1950s and '60s. Although sympathetic to the progressive One Nation desire to be seen as a modern, rather than reactionary, force in British politics,[39] Cameron wanted to develop a bolder, more enterprising, doctrine that involved the recalibration, rather than the rejection, of neo-liberal conservatism. He did not want to be perceived as making his party 'less conservative or tacking to the left', but rather one that understood 'the concerns and challenges, the hopes and aspirations of contemporary Britons' (Maude, 2013, p 2).

Progressive neo-liberal Conservatism is arguably the best descriptor of the enterprising doctrine that Cameron and his acolytes attempted to develop. Although Conservatives have traditionally been sceptical about the notion of progress because of its association with the abstract, improving doctrines of socialism and liberalism as opposed to the pragmatic forms of organic change (see Chapter One), Cameron was keen to embrace this concept, apply a distinctive Conservative hue to it and challenge Labour's claim to be the exclusive promoters of this forward-looking concept.[40] As was noted earlier, this 'progressive' strand of thinking did not involve the rejection of the neo-liberal economic strategy that had been introduced by the Thatcher governments and consolidated under Major's administrations. The Cameron team remain wholly persuaded of the advantages that could accrue to the nation from a flourishing, properly regulated, 'free' market.[41] Accordingly, the economic crisis of 2007/08 did not lead to any fundamental questioning of the neo-liberal approach. Instead, responsibility for the crisis was attributed to the New Labour government's failure to provide effective regulation of the banking industry and its profligate approach to public spending, which had, it was claimed, left the nation vulnerable to economic shocks.

It was in the broad area of social policy that Cameron sought to mark out the progressive elements of his doctrine. There were three key aspects of Cameron's progressive social narrative: social 'inclusion'; state welfare, social justice and poverty; and the 'Big Society'.

Social 'inclusion'

A more sympathetic, less judgemental, approach was to be adopted towards those who chose alternative lifestyles of a 'non-harmful' kind. While the party was to remain resolute in its support for marriage and the 'two-parent' family, this was to be combined with a more inclusive approach to alternative family arrangements such as lone parenthood, provided that such parents 'played by the rules' and strove for economic independence.[42] In addition, the condemnatory attitudes towards gay people that had come to the surface in Conservative circles as a result of the introduction of Section 28 of the *Local Government Act* of 1988 were now to be rejected. Henceforth, the party would adopt more positive forms of support for civil partnerships and gay marriage.[43] A more enlightened approach towards those experiencing poverty was also deemed necessary in order to counter public perceptions that the party believed that all working-age adults claiming means-tested benefits were 'scroungers' and 'skivers'.

State welfare, social justice and poverty

State welfare

The party's approach to state welfare, social justice and poverty was also to be refashioned. In the case of state intervention, Cameron wanted to be seen as the leader of a party that was not ideologically anti-collectivist but, rather, like Disraeli and Baldwin before him,[44] supportive of those forms of interventionism that were deemed conducive to the common good. In this way, Cameron hoped to distance his party from hard-line neo-liberal opposition to the state that had left potential voters fearful that highly valued forms of collective provision such as the NHS were to be pared back or privatised. For Cameron (2009), much state welfare intervention up until the 1960s was 'not only well-intentioned and compassionate but generally successful'. As such, the task for the progressive was not to oppose all forms of state intervention per se, but rather identify and support those measures that would enhance well-being and jettison those government interventions that were detrimental. Significantly, however, Cameron was keen to distinguish his approach to state intervention from what he regarded as the ineffective, outmoded, ideologically motivated, egalitarian statist strategy that New Labour had been pursuing in government. For Cameron, the restoration of Britain's 'broken society' (a phrase that he had purloined from his fellow leadership contender Liam Fox)[45] required a bolder and more imaginative approach than the blinkered one followed by New Labour. Government would take the lead in terms of funding and 'enabling', but service delivery would increasingly fall to the voluntary and private sectors.

Social justice

Cameron also sought to distinguish his progressive form of neo-liberal Conservatism from the 'reactionary' variant that had come to prominence in the Thatcher era by embracing a non-egalitarian, form of social justice.[46] Rejecting the trenchant critiques of social justice advanced by earlier thinkers such as Hayek and Powell, which had strong appeal for the economic liberal wing of the party,[47] Cameron believed that it was now necessary for the party to recognise that it had paid insufficient attention to the painful social consequences that had resulted from the 'regenerative' neo-liberal economic reforms of the Thatcher era. A future Conservative government would now seek to break down opportunity barriers and promote social mobility. Significantly, though, this new-found commitment to social justice did not extend to narrowing the gap between rich and poor or the adoption of the 'bounded' conception of inequality associated with One Nation Conservatism.[48] As Bercow (2002) explains,

> ... for too long Conservatives have ducked expressing their belief in social justice for fear of being disbelieved or derided. This taboo must be broken. There are those of us who believe passionately in social justice. However, while many on the left seek equality of outcome, we do not. While they think inequality is synonymous with injustice, we do not. Social justice is not about stopping the people from becoming too rich; it is about stopping them from becoming too poor. (p 21)[49]

Poverty

This embrace of a progressive social justice narrative also informed Cameron's approach to the problem of poverty. The Social Justice

Policy Group (SJPG, which was one of six review groups that David Cameron established in 2005 to 'think the unthinkable')[50] provided much of the impetus for the shift in party thinking on poverty. Chaired by former party leader Iain Duncan Smith, and granted significant autonomy, the SJPG worked under the umbrella of the Centre for Social Justice, a think tank that the former party leader had helped to establish in 2004. The SJPG 'produced' a range of influential reports.[51] *Breakthrough Britain: Overview* (Centre for Social Justice, 2007a) considered the question of why during a 'period of unprecedented prosperity' (p 13) had a social recession, marked by increased poverty and welfare state dependency, taken hold?[52] After conducting a nationwide study, the SJPG identified five 'pathways into poverty – worklessness and economic dependency, family breakdown, addictions of various kinds, education failure and indebtedness'. Although the SJPG was keen to avoid 'pejorative and judgemental' moralising about the choices that those experiencing poverty had made, it was adamant that any remedial policy had to have a moral underpinning. Accordingly, the report highlighted the importance of marriage, the family and paid work in combating poverty.[53]

The second series of reports focused on policy solutions to the problem of poverty. Rejecting both non-intervention and outmoded 'state' remedies, the SJPC favoured an integrative approach in which citizens would be expected to 'take responsibility for their own choices', while government would provide support that would enable people to 'make the right choices' (Centre for Social Justice, 2007a, p 7). Some 190 policy recommendations were put forward, including fiscal support for those living as couples, and informal, private and voluntary sector childcare initiatives to 'break the cycle of disadvantage in the early years of a child's life' (Centre for Social Justice, 2007a, p 7). Family Services Hubs were proposed for every community and more flexible Child Benefit payments would enable parents to stay at home to care for a child deemed to at 'risk'. More personalised, localised and intensive support schemes based on paid work[54] were also envisaged as a way of enabling 'vulnerable' adults to break free from benefit dependency.

The third report (Centre for Social Justice, 2009) focused on Britain's 'broken' benefits system, which was characterised as disincentivising work, personal saving and home ownership while penalising pro-social behaviour such as marriage and cohabitation. A new Universal Credit scheme was proposed that aimed to 'maximise the number of working age households with at least one member in work' and to ensure that 'all households receive a fair minimum income' (Centre for Social Justice, 2009, p 11). It was envisaged that some 4.9 million households would benefit to the tune of £1,000 per year after the introduction of Universal Credit.

The deliberations of the SJPG proved highly influential in shaping the progressive neo-liberal Conservative narrative about poverty that took hold under Cameron. It was now accepted, for example, that poverty should be viewed as a relative concept. As Cameron made clear in a speech delivered in 2006:

> In the past we used to think of poverty in absolute terms – meaning straightforward deprivation…. That's not enough. We need to think of poverty in relative terms – the fact that some people lack those things that others in society take for granted. So I want the message to go out loud and clear – the Conservative Party recognises, will measure and will act on relative poverty. (Cited in Hickson, 2008, p 358)

Cameron also wanted to distance himself from what he saw as New Labour's narrow, mechanistic approach to poverty, which had focused on halving the number of children living in households below 60% of median incomes. It was argued that this strategy had led to too great an emphasis on those living on the margins of poverty as opposed to those with more intractable problems. A broader, more holistic, anti-poverty strategy, based on non-financial as well as financial factors, was now seen as the way forward.[55] Cameron's determination to ensure that his party would come to be regarded by the time of the next General Election as the one most committed to tackling poverty and disadvantage was underlined in his speech to the party's annual conference at Manchester in October 2009:

> 'Labour still have the arrogance to think that they are the ones who will fight poverty and deprivation…. Who made the poorest poorer? Who left youth unemployment higher? Who made inequality greater? No, not the wicked Tories. You, Labour: you're the ones that did this to our society. So don't you dare lecture us about poverty. You have failed and it falls to us, the modern Conservative party to fight for the poorest you have let down.'

The 'Big Society'

The promotion of a 'Big Society' was the third key component of Cameron's progressive neo-liberal Conservative manifesto. This emphasis on society was intended to distinguish Cameron's vision of Conservatism from the highly individualistic form of neo-liberalism that had characterised the Thatcher years and had resulted in a suspicion that many active forms of civil engagement were indicative of a desire to move society in a social democratic direction. Equally, the emphasis on society rather than the state was intended to signify that it was possible to move society in a progressive direction without resorting to the unwieldy and inflexible state initiatives favoured by the New Labour government. The positive case for civil society was advanced by a number of progressive Conservative thinkers such as Phillip Blond (2010) and Jessie Norman (2010), who sought to re-establish the importance of what Burke had termed the 'little platoons' within society.[56] In his book, *Red Tory*, for example, Blond (2010) highlighted how civil society and the communitarian ethos were being smothered by market individualism and an overbearing state. He recommended a number of economic reforms to combat this trend, including a greater reliance on regional banking, the break-up of large business monopolies and the encouragement of mutual enterprises as well as more local control and ownership of welfare services.

Given the breadth and depth of civic activity in contemporary British society, the progressive neo-liberal Conservatives have tended to focus their attention on those individual or philanthropic collective endeavours that are undertaken in order to promote the broader community or public good rather than more explicitly sectional interests. As Ishkanian and Szreter (2012) point out:

> There are several kinds of intermediary associations which also occupy that space between state, family and market, which Big Society is *not* seeking to invoke or support, notably the political organisations representing the sectional interests of industry, employers and parts of the business community, the trade unions and the professional associations.... (pp 4-5, emphasis in original)

By invoking the notion of a Big Society, the Progressive neo-liberal Conservatives (PNLCs) hoped that citizens would become inspired to take greater responsibility for tackling issues in their local community rather than relying on the state to sort 'out their locality's needs' (Ishkanian and Szreter, 2012, p 4). Government would lend its support to such activity by liberalising planning laws and providing practical support so that members of local communities would be in a position to take over the running of community facilities such as parks, libraries and other services.

The 2010 General Election

The Big Society theme underpinned the party's 2010 General Election manifesto. Its very title, *Invitation to join the government of Britain*, (Conservative Party, 2010) was intended to convey the idea that citizens were not just being asked to vote for the Conservative Party but to join with it so that the most effective ways of resolving the issues and problems facing the nation could be put into practice.

> We offer a new approach: a change not just from one set of politicians to another; from one set of policies to another. It is a change from one political philosophy to another. From the idea that the role of the state is to direct society and micro-manage public services, to the idea that the role of the state is to strengthen society and make public services serve the people who use them. In a simple phrase, the change on offer is from big government to Big Society. (Conservative Party, 2010, p vii)

Major reform of the welfare state was seen as crucial if the ethos of the Big Society was to take root. Public sector productivity was to be increased by encouraging a more diverse range of service providers and by 'extending payment by results and giving more power to consumers' (Conservative Party, 2010, p 27). In a measure deemed to be 'the most significant shift in power from the state to working people since the sale of council houses in the 1980s', public service providers were to be given the right to 'own the services they deliver' (Conservative Party, 2010, p 27).

The manifesto also promised to introduce more family friendly policies such as flexible working and parental leave. Enhanced support for older people was to be achieved by linking the basic state pension to earnings and by continuing to provide the winter fuel payment as well as free bus passes and TV licences.

A new Work programme was to be introduced for 'everyone who is unemployed including the 2.6 million people claiming Incapacity Benefit' (Conservative Party, 2010, p 15). In an effort to 'create a welfare system that is fair but firm', long-term claimants were to be 'required to "work for the dole" on community work programmes' (Conservative Party, 2010, p 16), while benefits were to be withdrawn from those who refused to participate in a new Work Programme. A maximum three-year benefit sanction was proposed for those who persistently turned down 'reasonable job offers' (Conservative Party, 2010, p 16). As part of an emergency austerity drive to cope with the projected budget deficit, the pension age was to be raised to 66 in 2016, state subsidies to Child Tax Funds curtailed, and tax credits withdrawn from high-earning families.

The manifesto stressed that the Conservatives were 'the party of the NHS'. The Conservatives have, it was argued, 'consistently fought to protect the values the NHS stands for and have campaigned to defend the NHS from Labour's cuts and reorganisations' (Conservative Party, 2010, p 45). The party pledged to increase health spending in real terms each year, extend patient choice and put professionals 'in charge of commissioning local health services' (Conservative Party, 2010, p 46).

Improved standards in education were also promised. The Academy programme introduced by New Labour had been focused on improving 'failing' schools in disadvantaged areas. The Conservatives wanted to extend this to all primary and secondary schools. In order to improve parental choice, the establishment of 'free' schools was to be encouraged. Parents, teachers, charities and businesses would be permitted to establish innovative publicly funded 'free' schools after gaining approval from the Secretary of State. More rigorous school inspections were to be carried out by OFSTED and any school that remained in 'special measures' for over a year faced the prospect of being 'taken over immediately by a successful Academy provider' (Conservative Party, 2010, p 53). Extra funding (pupil premiums) would be provided to schools educating children from 'disadvantaged backgrounds'.

In housing, the Conservatives promised that they would attempt to fulfil Eden's earlier pledge 'to create a property-owning democracy where everyone has the right to own their own home' (Conservative Party, 2010, p 75). To this end, it was proposed to raise the stamp duty threshold to £250,000 for first-time buyers. The manifesto also contained prospective measures to make it easier for social tenants 'to own or part-own their home' and for the problem of homelessness to be addressed more effectively.

Despite encouraging opinion poll ratings and the unpopularity of Gordon Brown's Labour government, which had been striving to come to terms with the adverse consequences of the global economic crisis, the Conservatives still faced an uphill battle to win the 2010 General Election. As Ashcroft (2010) points out, 'the Conservatives needed to gain seats and swing the popular vote on a scale that had been achieved only once since 1945 – by Tony Blair and New Labour in 1997' (p v). Although Cameron managed to gain an additional 96 seats on a 3.7% swing, securing 36.1% of the popular vote, he fell 20 seats short of an overall majority.

Into coalition

Following lengthy but largely amicable discussions with the Liberal Democrats (who had secured 57 seats on a 23% share of the vote), a Conservative-led coalition government was formed on 11 May 2010.[57] While such an alliance might have seemed unimaginable under previous party leaders such as Michael Howard and Charles Kennedy,[58] the fact that David Cameron and Nick Clegg 'had spent the period before the 2010 election trying to cajole their parties towards ideological positions which, if not identical, were at least closely compatible' helps to explain why this political 'union' proved possible (Dorey et al, 2011, p 185). The limited ideological divide between the progressive neo-liberal Conservatives and their 'Orange Book' Liberal Democrat coalition partners[59] ensured that the coalition agreement that was eventually drawn up did not require the Conservatives to jettison any of their core manifesto proposals.[60] In the case of public service modernisation, for example, Prime Minister David Cameron and his deputy Nick Clegg declared, in their joint introduction to *The coalition: Our programme for government* (Cabinet Office, 2010), that their collective enterprise had the 'potential for era-changing, convention-challenging, radical reform' (Cabinet Office, 2010, p 7). In terms of welfare state reform, it was even argued that 'Liberal Democrat and Conservative ideas' were 'stronger combined' (Cabinet Office, 2010, p 8).

Sharing a 'conviction that the days of big government are over; that centralisation and top-down control have proved a failure' (Cabinet Office, 2010, p 7), the coalition partners promised a 'sweeping reform of welfare, taxes and, most of all, our schools – with a breaking open of the state monopoly' (Cabinet Office, 2010, p 7). In terms of the NHS, 'Conservative thinking on markets, choice and competition' combined with the Liberal Democrat belief in localism was seen as bringing about 'an emphatic end to the bureaucracy, top-down control and centralisation that has so diminished our NHS' (Cabinet Office, 2010, p 8).

Once installed in government, the Conservative-led coalition wasted little time in pressing ahead with major reforms in the key areas of education, social security and, more surprisingly, in healthcare.

Education

The new Secretary of State for Education, Michael Gove, a leading advocate of the progressive neo-liberal Conservative cause, was determined to bring about a rapid reform of state education in England and Wales even though he, and his special adviser Dominic Cummings, recognised that the means needed to achieve this objective were likely to be opposed by members of the educational 'establishment', which came to be disparagingly known as 'the blob'.[61] As with many politicians, Gove's own biography – an adopted child who progressed from a lower middle class background in Aberdeen via a private school scholarship, presidency of the Oxford Union, and a successful media career to become a Cabinet Minster – is important in terms of explaining his reforming zeal. He has, for example, compared his own good fortune with that of a child attending a contemporary Merseyside comprehensive in which 'just 1 per cent of the children had managed to get five C passes at GCSE, including English and maths' which he suggests is the 'minimum a 16-year-old needs to have a decent chance in life' (Gove, 2013, p 28). For Gove, 'there is nothing fixed about any child's future. Deprivation need not be destiny. If the right professionals – under the right leadership, with the right level of ambition – are given the freedom to teach the subjects they love in a disciplined environment, then any child can succeed' (Gove, 2013, p 28).[62] For Gove, the central task for a progressive neo-liberal Conservative education secretary was to oversee significant improvements in educational standards and expectations, transform the curriculum and examination system and ensure that pupils in the state sector are able to leave school with the knowledge and skills that enable them either to secure a place at one of the 'leading' universities, which were still disproportionately the preserve of privately educated pupils, or secure an apprenticeship or high-quality vocational training that led to an alternative worthwhile career.

Lending support to Bale's (2010) contention that ministerial impetus can be an influential 'driver of change', Gove moved at breakneck speed to push through a series of school reforms. Under the *Education Act* of 2010, which came into force just 77 days after the General Election, all primary and secondary schools were permitted to opt for Academy status. Funded by the Education Funding Agency, these schools would enjoy significant autonomy in relation to the pay and conditions of staff, the curriculum, and the length of the school day, although they would be prohibited from selecting pupils on academic grounds unless they had previously been able to (a selective private grammar school that opts to become a publicly funded Academy would be one such example). A green light was also given to the establishment of all-ability, non-profit 'free' schools, modelled on developments in the United States (charter schools) and Sweden,[63] which were seen as a way of enhancing parental choices in locations where there was deemed to be a dearth of 'good' schools. Half of the 24 free schools that were opened in the initial phase of this scheme (September 2011) were located in 'deprived' areas. By the end of September 2014, over 250 free schools were in operation.

Gove also attempted to overhaul state schooling through an enrichment of the National Curriculum by a greater emphasis on 'traditional' subjects and the acquisition of knowledge. Gove oversaw 'rigorous' reforms of GSCE and A level examinations, changes to teacher-training programmes, the recruitment of highly qualified and enthusiastic trainee teachers through Teach First[64] and increased use of performance-related pay. The pupil premium was also introduced to encourage 'better' schools to offer places to students from low-income families as a way of revitalizing' state education.

Gove encountered a number of difficulties in implementing some of his proposed reforms. He was forced, for example, to abandon his attempt to reintroduce 'O' (Ordinary) levels for 16-year-olds and backtracked from his proposal to use a single exam board to set assessments in core subjects. He has also had to intervene to 'rescue' a number of failing free schools. Notwithstanding these setbacks, Gove ploughed on relentlessly, despite seeming increasingly unpopular with many teachers and parents. Given his close relationship with David Cameron, it was surprising that the Prime Minister decided to replace Gove as education secretary in the summer reshuffle of 2014 with the more emollient Nicky Morgan because of fears expressed by the party's election strategist, Lynton Crosby,[65] that Gove's antagonistic relationship with teachers could 'inflict severe damage' on the party's electoral prospects in 2015. Nevertheless, it seems likely that in time Gove might yet join that select band of ministers who are regarded as having 'changed the weather' in social policy.

Social security

Given Iain Duncan Smith's keen interest in poverty and welfare reform as the founder of the Centre for Social Justice and Chair of the Conservative's Social Justice Policy Group, it was not surprising that David Cameron appointed the former party leader as Secretary of State for Work and Pensions. Mirroring Michael Gove's reforming zeal, Duncan Smith saw his key role as rescuing those experiencing the debilitating effects of poverty and 'benefit dependency' which he believed state-centric Labour governments had allowed to take hold in British society. Influenced by the work of the American scholar Lawrence Mead (2001) and by numerous interactions with those living and working in deprived communities, Duncan Smith concluded that the benefits system needed to be reformed if the cycle of poverty and disadvantage experienced by working-age adults was to be halted. He contended that there was a pressing need for a more robust benefit system that would incentivise and help people to secure paid work.

As with Gove's educational reform strategy, Duncan Smith believed that speedy legislative change was needed if his progressive, 'socially just', anti-poverty crusade was to bear fruit. As was noted previously, much of the preparation work for the prospective legislative changes had been undertaken in opposition by the Social Justice Policy Review Group. A Green Paper, *21st century welfare*, was published in July 2010 (Department for Work and Pensions, 2010a), followed by a White Paper just four months later (*Universal Credit: Welfare that works* – Department for Work and Pensions, 2010b). By March 2012, the *Welfare Reform Act* had passed into law.

The introduction of Universal Credit was to be the cornerstone of Duncan-Smith's 'welfare' reform (Department for Work and Pensions, 2012). Originally due to be phased in by 2013, this 'simpler' and 'fairer' benefit was designed to 'improve' the transition from unemployment to paid work. As part of this reform, a number of existing benefits such as Income Support, income-based Jobseeker's Allowance, income-related Employment and Support Allowance, Housing Benefit, Child Tax Credit and Working Tax Credit would be phased out while others such as Attendance Allowance, cold weather payments, pension credits, Child Benefit and carers' allowances were to be retained in a modified form.

As with many major policy initiatives of this kind, the introduction of Universal Credit proved problematic, not least because of an untested IT system (claimants are required to register their applications electronically). The time scales for full implementation have been steadily extended.[66] The scheme exceeded its initial administrative set-up costs (£2.4 billion) and was criticised by the National Audit Office (2013) for displaying weak management, ineffective control and poor governance. Duncan Smith responded to these challenges by appointing a new management team in May 2013, led by Howard Shiplee,[67] to oversee the delivery of Universal Credit.

In 2011, Duncan Smith introduced a new Work Programme[68] under which so-called 'prime' contractors (which might be public, private or third sector organisations) would be required to assist those who had experienced a lengthy period of unemployment (nine to 12 months) to find, and retain, paid work. The contractors were to be remunerated on a payment-by-results basis. Under another scheme to help young people find work, the Work Experience programme, participating companies were required to provide a voluntary unpaid work placement of between two and eight weeks for young people aged between 16 and 24 who would continue to receive Jobseeker's Allowance while participating in the scheme.[69]

Work Capability Tests, which were initially introduced by the New Labour government under the *Welfare Reform Act* of 2007, have also formed a key part of the coalition's social security reform agenda. Working-age adults claiming Employment and Support Allowance, Incapacity Benefit, Severe Disablement Allowance or Income Support on grounds of illness or disability have been subjected to a Work Capability Assessment, undertaken by private contractors such as Atos and Capita,[70] which aims to distinguish between those whose medical condition is so severe as to warrant exclusion from paid work and those who are able, with appropriate support, to return to the labour market.

Unlike the NHS, the social security budget was not exempted from the coalition government's 'deficit reduction' programme, which was based largely on spending cuts rather than tax increases. Working-age adult claimants were expected to bear the brunt of these cuts, which Duncan Smith was keen to portray as fair, proportionate and carefully crafted. These included the introduction of a uniform £500 per week benefit 'cap' to all claimant couples from April 2013, limiting the annual increase for non-pensioner claimants to a below inflation level of 1% per annum for the next three years, introducing a seven-day wait for benefit payments and a fixed level of non-pension Department for Work and Pensions spending.[71]

Controversial changes to the Housing Benefit rules under which claimants deemed to be under-occupying their current accommodation would be required to make a higher contribution towards their housing costs (the so-called 'bedroom' tax) were also defended on progressive grounds. It was argued that this would free up public sector housing for families in greater need by encouraging less needy tenants to move to smaller properties.[72]

Older citizens, by way of contrast, were afforded greater 'austerity' protection. Increased financial security for the next generation of state pensioners was deemed necessary on grounds of social justice. This was to be achieved by the introduction of a simplified single-tier pension that would operate according to a 'triple lock' mechanism that will ensure future payments are increased by no less than 2.5% per annum or higher if either prices or wages exceed this amount.[73]

Some of the social security measures directed at higher-income earners were also intended to demonstrate the progressive ethos of coalition policy. For example, Child Tax Credits were withdrawn from families with incomes above £26,000 per annum (down from £41,300) and Child Benefit was 'taken away' from families with one higher-rate taxpayer with effect from 2013. Sensitive to opposition claims that they might be abandoning their pre-election claim to be the party of social justice, the progressive neo-liberal Conservatives also announced that they would mount a concerted attack on tax avoidance (legal) as well as tax evasion (illegal). Both Cameron and Osborne have criticised high earners who engage in 'aggressive' forms of tax avoidance.[74] Cameron even resorted to the naming and shaming of the comedian, Jimmy Carr, who was alleged to have been involved in an elaborate off-shore tax avoidance scheme.[75] The neo-liberal progressive Conservative commitment to social justice was also questioned following the decision of Chancellor Osborne to reduce the rate of income tax from 50% to 45% for those earning over £150,000 per year in 2013-14, ostensibly on the grounds of the limited revenue generating capacity of the higher rate.[76]

Health

Since becoming party leader, David Cameron has made strenuous efforts to convince the British public that progressive Conservatives are fully supportive of the NHS. In a speech delivered in 2009, David Cameron declared his 'wholehearted commitment to the NHS. Conservatives rely on the NHS, work in the NHS, volunteer to help the NHS. This party wants to improve the NHS for everyone.' This upbeat message was reaffirmed in the party's General Election manifesto of 2010, *An Invitation to join the government of Britain* (Conservative Party, 2010), which stipulated that the Conservatives were 'the party of the NHS, we will never change the idea at its heart that healthcare in this country is free at the point of use and available to everyone based on need, not ability to pay' (Conservative Party, 2010, p 45). To underline the strength of its commitment to the NHS, the party pledged to protect the NHS from the fallout from the financial crash by promising to increase spending on healthcare in real terms.

Once in government, however, the Conservative-led coalition government has found it difficult to establish a 'progressive' NHS narrative. According to Matthew D'Ancona (2013), this failure can be attributed in part to the fact that both David Cameron and George Osborne did not foresee the level of public and professional unease surrounding the major overhaul of the NHS that the new Health Secretary Andrew Lansley was poised to unleash.[77] Although the Conservative Party's 2010 manifesto had highlighted the need for significant change to combat the statist mind-set of the NHS, the coalition agreement appeared to have 'retreated' from this position with its pledge to 'stop the top-down reorganisations of the NHS that have got in the way of patient care' (Cabinet Office, 2010, p 24). Nevertheless, just two months after its formation, the coalition government published a 'transformative' White Paper, *Equity and excellence: Liberating the NHS*, (Department of Health, 2010). The White Paper underlined the new government's desire to move away from what they saw as New Labour's remote, target-driven, centralised control of the service. It proposed to abolish Primary Care Trusts and Strategic Health Authorities[78] and give GP groups budgetary responsibilities to commission health services. Monitor, the independent regulator of Foundation Trusts, was to extend its role to encompass economic oversight of 'access, competition and price-setting in the NHS' (Cabinet Office, 2010, p 25),[79] while Health Watch England would champion patient interests. Crucially, Andrew Lansley's plans were intended to increase competition within the NHS by allowing independent contractors to provide an increasing range of services. In particular, Lansley was keen to see existing NHS staff forming themselves into social enterprises so that they could bid for NHS contracts. Co-ownership ventures of this kind are seen as a spur to innovative and efficient provision.[80]

Lansley's plan fuelled the suspicion that the progressive Conservatives were still intent on privatising rather than modernising the NHS. Fears about back-door 'privatisation' led the Labour Party, the trade unions and a wide range of professional bodies to mount a stringent challenge to Lansley's reforms. Objections were even raised by the influential ConservativeHome website maintained by Duncan Smith's former adviser, Tim Montgomerie. The Health and Social Care Bill had a rough ride through both the Commons and the House of Lords. Around 2,000 amendments were tabled in both houses, which resulted in some minor changes including a relaxation of the implementation timetable, reaffirmation of the Secretary of State's overall responsibility for the service and enhanced safeguards about the professional standards that new independent NHS providers would be expected to meet.[81] The Bill passed into law in March 2012. The only significant casualty from this bruising legislative process was the architect of the reforms,

Andrew Lansley, who was replaced as Health Secretary by Jeremy Hunt in September 2012.

Half-time report (2013)

In an 'official' mid-term review of coalition achievements in government, the NHS reforms were deemed to have given 'patients and communities more choice and a stronger voice'. The 'combination of investment and reform' has, it was argued, started 'to deliver significant improvements in outcomes and productivity' (Cabinet Office, 2013, p 24). Positive assessments were also offered in relation to social security and education policy. In the case of the former, the goal of creating a socially just welfare system in which 'people are better off in work than on benefits' was taking shape. Universal Credit was seen as 'radically' simplifying 'the benefits system', and making work pay 'for hundreds of thousands of people stuck in unemployment and poverty traps' (Cabinet Office, 2013, p 16). The numbers claiming incapacity benefits had fallen by 145,000 as a result of more rigorous work capability tests. In addition, the 'most ambitious employment' scheme 'Britain has ever seen – the Work Programme – provided on a payment-by-results basis' was seen as having 'already helped 200,000 people to find a job' (Cabinet Office, 2013, p 14). In the case of education, the 'progressive' aim of removing obstacles that stand in the way of social mobility so that 'children can go as far as their talents and efforts will take them' (Cabinet Office, 2013, p 22) was being fulfilled by 'a new generation of free schools', the extension of Academy schools, the introduction of a Pupil Premium, more exacting school inspections (even a satisfactory performance was now deemed to be too low an aspiration) and reformed school league tables.

As was noted previously, in the run-up to the 2010 General Election, the Progressive neo-liberal Conservatives placed great importance on the creation of a 'Big Society', believing that it was 'not the grand plans of politicians and bureaucrats that will ultimately deliver social progress and build social capital, but the ingenuity, innovation and entrepreneurial spirit of the British people' (ibid, p.33). The 'half time' report declared that there had been some positive developments in this area. The introduction of Big Society Capital, which provides financial support for neighbourhood groups, charities and social enterprises, the establishment of a Social Action Fund to support volunteering, and the setting up of the National Citizen Service[82] (which it was anticipated would have 90,000 participants by 2014) were all seen as important first steps in reinvigorating civil society.

From their own 'intrinsic' evaluation of their first phase of government the Progressive neo-liberal Conservatives contend that they have not strayed markedly from the social policy agenda that they set out prior to the 2010 General Election. This involved an acceptance of the neo-liberal critique of 'bloated' welfare states, although this was tempered by a desire to avoid victim blaming and the use of reactionary rhetoric. The aim was to develop a softer tone towards the victims of malfunctioning state remedies. Significantly, the Progressive neo-liberal Conservatives have been keen to highlight some concrete examples of their 'progressive' credentials such as the decision to press ahead with gay marriage legislation despite vociferous objections from socially conservative party members and the active steps taken to counter poverty[83] and enhance social mobility.[84] 'Extrinsic' commentators have, however, begun to question the 'progressive' narrative of the coalition government by highlighting the growing number of citizens who are seeking support from food banks[85] and evidence indicating that the costs of austerity are falling disproportionately on the poorer groups in society.[86]

It remains to be seen whether David Cameron's progressive variant of neo-liberal Conservatism will continue after the May 2015 General Election. Even with a new electoral mandate, he may face calls from his fellow Conservatives, who have raised concerns over gay marriage, the EU, immigration and the rise of UKIP to return to a more 'Thatcherite' version of neo-liberal Conservatism.[87]

The Conservative Party and the welfare state: clear blue water?

After examining developments in the Conservatives' approach to the welfare state over the past 70 years, is it possible, finally, to identify what might be regarded as an unambiguous, enduring and authentic party perspective? Is there clear blue water? In theory, this might seem a possibility. Conservatives tend to concur over issues such as human nature, the inevitability and desirability of inequality, the importance of tradition and voluntary action, the necessity of personal freedom, the maintenance of social order, the undesirability of rapid change, the need for free markets and the private ownership of property. Moreover, it is certainly possible to identify some ideas about the welfare state that unite all shades of Conservative thinking, such as the duty to provide a safety net for those at risk of destitution and the inappropriateness of allowing this institution to be used for the purpose of social(ist) engineering or as a vehicle for major forms of redistribution between rich and poor.[1] However, it is maintained here that the party's approach to the welfare state has ebbed and flowed constantly over time. As a result, the best way to understand the Conservatives' approach to the welfare state is not on the basis of a holistic family perspective but, rather through the eyes of one of four competitive 'siblings' who share much in common but differ over a number of key issues. At a particular point in time the voice of one sibling will tend to dominate.

As we have seen, in the period between 1950 and 1964 One Nation Conservatism was the ascendant voice. From this perspective, the welfare state had quickly established itself as part of the national furniture. The main tasks were now to shape it in ways that complemented cherished Conservative values such as personal freedom and opportunity and ensure that the cost of welfare provision was kept in check.

During the Heath era, in which technocratic modernisation held sway, reform of the welfare state was seen as essential if the broader plan for the modernisation of Britain was to be achieved. Although Heath was personally sympathetic to the One Nation Conservative cause, he was prepared to take ideas from any shade of Conservative thinking that might aid his modernisation agenda. Heath's failure to achieve this objective provided an opportunity for the voice of another 'sibling' to come to the fore.

For neo-liberal Conservatives, the economic, social and moral rejuvenation of the nation was deemed to require far greater emphasis on the individual, the free market and the promotion of an entrepreneurial spirit. The welfare state was now seen as being increasingly out of step with core Conservative principles. While accepting that the welfare state still had a role to play in supporting those who had fallen on hard times as a result of sickness, disability or frailty, the neo-liberal Conservatives believed that the 'rights' bestowed on working-age adults, particularly those living in 'non-traditional' households, had engendered a damaging culture of dependency. Work obligations and tighter benefit rules were seen as necessary if familial cycles of dependency were to be avoided. In addition, citizens were to be emancipated from the dead hand of the paternalist welfare state by being provided with opportunities to buy their own council homes and to become shareholders. The motivations and work practices of unionised public sector employees were also questioned. They were now to be viewed increasingly as self-interested knaves rather than selfless saints[2]. Private sector disciplines and, where possible, non-state sector contractors, came to be seen as the best way of improving both efficiency and effectiveness in the public realm.

It is the views on the welfare state of the youngest sibling that are currently attracting the most attention. The progressive neo-liberal wing of the family came to public attention after David Cameron became leader of the Conservative Party in 2005. Cameron was determined to jettison what he saw as the toxic social legacy of the Thatcher era, while retaining the economically liberal elements of the Thatcher era. More compassionate attitudes were to be displayed towards social minorities and the role of civil society was to be enhanced, not least in relation to the provision of welfare services. This was deemed to require some significant changes to the welfare state; a shift that became all the more urgent in a so-called 'age of austerity'. This has involved some painful reductions in welfare spending, although the progressive neo-liberal Conservatives have been keen to stress that the cuts imposed are proportionate and socially just.

Questions remain, though, as to how far the progressive neo-liberal Conservatives differ from their older sibling. Is their compassionate rhetoric merely a disguise for some damaging and far-reaching changes to the welfare state? Such changes are likely, however, to be portrayed as a form of 'creative destruction', which will allow the Big Society to flourish and the state to shrink to a size that better reflects the 'true' spirit of Conservatism. Given the contemporary Labour Party's reluctance to offer a radically different welfare vision for the future, it appears that the progressive neo-liberal Conservatives are now, like their predecessors, setting the contemporary welfare state agenda. How long this particular variant of Conservatism will remain in the ascendency is open to question. However, if history is any guide, it seems likely that another influential form of Conservatism, either old or new, will quickly fill the vacuum.

Postscript

Despite predictions from pollsters and pundits alike that the May 2015 General Election would, like that of 2010, give rise to a hung parliament, the Conservative Party succeeded in securing 331 seats, giving them an overall working majority of 12 seats on the basis of a 36.9% share of the popular vote. Although Labour secured a marginal improvement in its own share of the vote compared with 2010 (30.4% as opposed to 29.0%), the rise of the Scottish National Party (which won 56 of the 59 seats contested in Scotland) and to a lesser extent, UKIP (which drew significant numbers of working-class voters away from Labour in a number of key seats), left them with fewer MPs than they had in 2010 (232 as opposed to 258). The Liberal Democrats, the Conservative's junior coalition partner from 2010-15, experienced a dramatic reversal of fortune gaining just 8 seats compared to the 57 they had won in 2010 (their share of the vote plummeting from 23.0% to 7.9%).

The result has enabled the Conservatives to implement their own policy agenda rather than having to secure a coalition agreement. Their manifesto provided clear indications that the party would continue with its 'progressive' approach to the welfare state. It contained pledges to improve the quality of schooling, introduce free child care of up to 30 hours per week for working parents of three- or four-year-old children, continued support for a properly funded NHS 'free' at the point of delivery, extending the 'right to buy' to housing association tenants and protecting the living standards of pensioners (Conservative Party, 2015). A helping hand would continue to be extended to those working-age adults outside the labour market, provided they were deemed to be making the requisite effort to return to economic independence.

In both their manifesto and during the election campaign the Conservatives made a concerted appeal to aspirational working-class and lower middle-class voters to desert Labour on the grounds that they, the Tories, were now better able to represent their material interests. Their approach mirrored the one employed by Fredrik Reinfeldt who led the Moderate Party to electoral success in Sweden in 2006 and 2010 by proclaiming that they, not the Social Democrats, were the party of the workers. It remains to be seen whether Labour will respond to this challenge by seeking to modify their historic role as a champion for those experiencing poverty and disadvantage in order to avoid being negatively portrayed as a 'welfare party'. In any event, it seems likely that the Conservative Party under David Cameron will continue to present themselves as a 'progressive' force in British politics, confident that any future modifications to the welfare state will not be perceived by key sections of the electorate as a return to the hard-faced Toryism of yesteryear, but rather as an example of their determination to follow a 'socially just' path designed to bring benefit to all parts of the nation.

Selected ministerial posts in Conservative or Conservative-led governments, 1940-2015

Period 1: The coalition (10 May 1940 to 23 May 1945) and national caretaker government (23 May 1945 to 26 July 1945) era

Prime Minister

Winston Churchill: 10 May 1940 to 26 July 1945

Chancellor of the Exchequer

Sir Kingsley Wood: 12 May 1940 to 21 September 1943
Sir John Anderson: 24 September 1943 to 26 July 1945

Education (Board of Education, 1940-44; Department of Education, 1944-45)[1]

Hewald Ramsbottam: 3 April 1940 to 20 July 1941
R.A.Butler: 20 July 1941 to 3 August 1944
Richard Law: 3 August 1944 to 25 May 1945

Health

Malcolm MacDonald: (National Labour) 13 May 1940 to 8 February 1941
Ernest Brown: (National Liberal) 8 February 1941 to 11 November 1943
Henry Willink: 11 November 1943 to 26 July 1945

Social security

Ministry of Pensions

Sir Walter Womersley:[2] 7 June 1939 to 26 July 1945

Ministry of Social/National Insurance

Sir William Jowitt: (Labour) 8 October 1944 to 23 May 1945
Leslie Hore-Belisha: (National Independent) 25 May 1945 to 26 July 1945

Period 2: From Churchill to Douglas Home (26 October 1951 to 16 October 1964)

Prime Minister

Winston Churchill: 26 October 1951 to 6 April 1955
Anthony Eden: 6 April 1955 to 10 January 1957
Harold Macmillan: 10 January 1957 to 19 October 1963
Alec Douglas-Home: 19 October 1963 to 16 October 1964

Chancellor of the Exchequer

R.A.Butler: 26 October 1951 to 20 December 1955
Harold Macmillan: 20 December 1955 to 13 January, 1957
Peter Thornycroft: 13 January 1957 to 6 January 1958
Derick Heathcoat-Amory: 6 January 1958 to 27 July 1960
Selwyn Lloyd: 27 July 1960 to 13 July 1962
Reginald Maudling: 13 July 1962 to16 October 1964

Education (Department of Education, 1951-64)

Florence Horsborugh: 2 November 1951 to 18 October 1954[3]
David Eccles: 18 October 1954 to 13 January 1957
Lord Hailsham: 13 January 1957 to 17 September 1957
Geoffrey Lloyd: 17 September 1957 to 14 October 1959
David Eccles: 14 October, 1959 to 13 July 1962
Sir Edward Boyle: 13 July 1962 to 1 April 1964
Quintin Hogg: 1 April 1964 to 16 October 1964

Health

Harry Crookshank: 30 October 1951 to 7 May 1952
Iain Macleod: 7 May 1952 to 20 December 1955
Robert Turton: 20 December 1955 to 16 January 1957
Dennis Vosper: 16 January 1957 to 17 September 1957
Derek Walker-Smith: 17 September 1957 to 27 July 1960
Enoch Powell: 27 July 1960 to 20 October 1963
Anthony Barber: 20 October 1963 to 16 October 1964

Social security

Ministry of Pensions

Derick Heathcoat-Amory: 5 November 1951 to 3 September 1953

Ministry of National Insurance

Osbert Peake: 31 October 1951 to 3 September 1953

Ministry of Pensions and National Insurance[4]

Osbert Peake: 3 September 1953 to 20 December 1955
John Boyd Carpenter: 20 December 1955 to 16 July 1962
Niall Macpherson: 16 July 1962 to 21 October 1963
Richard Wood: 21 October 1963 to 16 October 1964

Housing and local government

Harold Macmillan: 30 October 1951 to 18 October 1954
Duncan Sandys: 19 October 1954 to 4 January 1957
Henry Brooke: 4 January 1957 to 9 October 1961
Charles Hill: 9 October 1961 to 13 July 1962
Keith Joseph: 13 July 1962 to 16 October 1964

Period 3: The Heath era (19 June 1970 to 4 March 1974)

Prime Minister

Edward Heath: 19 June 1970 to 4 March 1974

Chancellors of the Exchequer

Iain Macleod: 20 June 1970 to 15 July 1970
Anthony Barber: 25 July 1970 to 28 February 1974

Education[5]

Margaret Thatcher: 20 June 1970 to 4 March 1974

Health

Secretary of State for Health and Social Security[6]

Keith Joseph: 20 June 1970 to 4 March, 1974.

Social security

Secretary of State for Health and Social Security

Keith Joseph: 20 June 1970 to 4 March 1974

Housing[7]

Peter Walker: 15 October 1970 to 5 November 1972
Geoffrey Rippon: 5 November 1972 to 4 March 1974

Period 4: From Thatcher to Major (4 May 1979 to 2 May 1997)

Prime Minister

Margaret Thatcher: 4 May 1979 to 28 November 1990
John Major: 28 November 1990 to 2 May 1997

Chancellors of the Exchequer

Sir Geoffrey Howe: 4 May 1979 to 11 June 1983
Nigel Lawson: 11 June 1983 to 26 October 1989
John Major: 26 October 1989 to 28 November 1990
Norman Lamont: 28 November 1990 to 27 May 1993
Kenneth Clarke: 27 May 1993 to 2 May 1997

Education[8]

Mark Carlisle: 5 May 1979 to 14 September 1981
Keith Joseph: 14 September 1981 to 21 May 1986
Kenneth Baker: 21 May 1986 to 24 July 1989
John MacGregor: 24 July 1989 to 2 November 1990
Kenneth Clarke: 2 November 1990 to 10 April 1992
John Patten: 11 April 1992 to 20 July 1994
Gillian Shepherd: 20 July 1994 to 2 May, 1997[9]

Health

Secretary of State for Health and Social Security

Patrick Jenkin: 5 May 1979 to 14 September 1981
Norman Fowler: 14 September 1981 to 13 June 1987
John Moore: 13 June 1987 to 25 July 1988

Secretary of State for Health[10]

Kenneth Clarke: 25 July 1988 to 2 November 1990
William Waldegrave: 2 November 1990 to 10 April 1992
Virginia Bottomley: 10 April 1992 to 5 July 1995
Stephen Dorrell: 5 July 1995 to 2 May 1997

Social security

Secretary of State for Health and Social Security

Patrick Jenkin: 5 May 1979 to 14 September 1981
Norman Fowler: 14 September 1981 to 13 June 1987
John Moore: 13 June 1987 to 25 July 1988

Secretary of State for Social Security[11]

John Moore: 25 July 1988 to 23 July 1989
Tony Newton: 23 July 1989 to 10 April 1992
Peter Lilley: 10 April 1992 to 2 May 1997

Housing (Department of the Environment)

Michael Hestletine: 5 May 1979 to 6 January 1983

Tom King: 6 January 1983 to 11 June 1983
Patrick Jenkin: 11 June 1983 to 2 September 1985
Kenneth Baker: 2 September 1985 to 21 May 1986
Nicholas Ridley: 21 May 1986 to 24 July 1989
Chris Patten: 24 July 1989 to 28 November 1990
Michael Heseltine: 28 November 1990 to 11 April, 1992
Michael Howard: 11 April 1992 to 27 May 1993
John Gummer: 27 May 1993 to 2 May 1997

Period 5: The Cameron era (11 May 2010 to 7 May 2015)

Prime Minister

David Cameron: 11 May 2010 to 7 May 2015

Chancellor of the Exchequer

George Osborne: 12 May 2010 to 7 May 2015

Education (Department for Education, 2010 to present)

Michael Gove: 11 May 2010 to 15 July 2014
Nicky Morgan: 15 July 2014 to 7 May 2015

Health

Andrew Lansley: 11 May 2010 to 4 September 2012
Jeremy Hunt: 4 September 2012 to 7 May 2015

Social security (Department for Work and Pensions)[12]

Iain Duncan Smith: 12 May 2010 to 7 May 2015

Housing[13]

Eric Pickles: 12 May 2010 to 7 May 2015

Notes

Acknowledgements

[1] The University now has additional sites at Medway and Tonbridge.

Preface

[1] See, for example, Bruce (1961), Gilbert (1970), Thane (1982), Digby (1989), Finlayson (1994), Harris (2004), Fraser (2009).

[2] See, for example, Hay (1975), Deakin (1994), Laybourn (1995), Sullivan (1996), Timmins (2001), Lowe (2005), Glennerster (2007), Page (2007).

[3] Two notable exceptions in terms of the Conservative Party are Raison (1990) and Bridgen and Lowe (1998).

[4] Authors differ as to the precise periods the consensus operated. Cases have been made for 1940-79, 1944-76, 1945-57 and even 1972-75; see Dutton (1991), Kavanagh and Morris (1994), Lowe (1990), Marwick (2003).

[5] See, for example, Pimlott (1988), Kavanagh (1992), Kavanagh and Morris (1994), Seldon (1994), Jones and Kandiah (1996).

[6] See Mishra (1977), Page (2010b).

[7] See Jordan (1973).

Chapter One

[1] See Cecil (1912).

[2] See O'Sullivan (1999), Allitt (2009).

[3] See Eccleshall et al (1984), Vincent (1992), Ludham and Smith (1996), Norton (1996b), Letwin (2008).

[4] See Gray (2009).

[5] See also Shore (1952, ch 1).

[6] See Freeden (2003).

[7] See Scruton (2014, ch 3).

[8] See Burke (1969), King (2011).

[9] See Willetts (1992, pp 101-2).

[10] See Scruton (2001, pp 30-6).

[11] See Burke (1969), Bromwich (2014), Norman (2014).

[12] See Clarke (1947).

[13] See Oakeshott (1962).

[14] See Maude (2005).

[15] See Pinker (2003), Dale (2010, pp 259-60).

[16] See Ball (2013, p 50).

[17] See Thorpe (2004), Torrance (2010).

[18] See Blake (1998), Charmley (2008).

[19] See Green (1993), Ellis (2010).

[20] See Green (2002, Introduction).

[21] See Willetts (1992), Norton (1996a), Blake (1998), Green (2002), Charmley (2008), Ball (2013).

[22] See Bulpitt (1986).

[23] See Boothby et al (1927), Macmillan (1933, 1938), Green (2002, pp 72-113).

[24] For example, a series of 'placatory' meetings between the two sides of industry were held between 1928 and 1933 (the Mond-Turner talks) to seek more harmonious relations between the unions and employers following the passage of the controversial *Trades Disputes and Trade Unions Act* in 1927, which the unions had vehemently opposed.

[25] The so-called Geddes axe, which was applied to public expenditure, most notably in the sphere of education in 1921, is an exemplar in this regard; see Harris (2004).

[26] See Abel (2004).

[27] See Campbell (2004).

[28] Baldwin was Prime Minister of the Conservative government from 1923-24 having succeeded Bonar Law (who had been forced to resign because of terminal illness). Baldwin led the Conservative administration from 1924-29 and took over the leadership of the National government in 1935 following Macdonald's resignation due to poor health. Baldwin retired from active politics in 1937; Neville Chamberlain succeeded him as Prime Minister.

[29] See Matthew (2011).

[30] See Ball (2004).

[31] See Blake (1998), Williamson (1999).

[32] See Gilbert (1970), Fraser (2009).

Chapter Two

[1] See Addison (1977, ch III).

[2] See Addison (1992, p 308).

[3] See Ramsden (1980).

[4] See Ramsden (1980).

[5] See Harris (1997).

[6] See Addison (1977, p 217).

[7] See Addison (1977).

[8] See Raison (1990, p 6), Garnett and Hickson (2009, p 42).

[9] See Calder (1971, p 408).

[10] See Hinchingbrooke (1943).

[11] See Tory Reform Committee (1944).

[12] See Raison (1990).

[13] See Addison (1977, p 231).

[14] There was a cross-party agreement that seats becoming vacant during wartime would not be contested by non-incumbent parties. However, the Conservatives were opposed by the newly formed left-leaning Common Wealth party in four of these February by-elections (Midlothian North – Tom Wintringham, Watford – Raymond Blackburn, Ashford – Catherine Williamson, Portsmouth North – Thomas Sargant) and by two left-wing independent Labour candidates in the other two (King's Lynn – Major Fred Wise, Bristol Central – Jennie Lee). Observance of this truce proved difficult in practice. Following a flagrant breach of the electoral 'understanding', the Bristol East branch of the Labour Party was suspended following its active support for Jennie Lee (see Addison, 1977).

[15] See Addison (1977, pp 225-6).

[16] See Brooke (1992).

[17] See Board of Education (1931).

[18] See Board of Education (1938).

[19] Aided schools would receive Local Education Authority (LEA) funding for all day-to-day running costs and half of the capital costs needed to improve sub-standard school buildings. Controlled schools would receive full LEA financial support; see Timmins (2001, p 81).

[20] See Howard (1987, pp 107-39).

[21] See Stewart (1999).

[22] See Brooke (1992).

[23] See Brooke (1992), Stewart (1999).

[24] See Beveridge (1944).

[25] See Ministry of Reconstruction (1944a).

[26] See Harris (1997, p 362).

[27] See Ministry of Reconstruction (1944a). A second White Paper (Ministry of Reconstruction, 1944b) dealt with workmen's compensation.

[28] See Macnicol (1980).

[29] See Thane (1982, pp 241-42).

[30] See Ministry of Reconstruction (1945).

[31] See Jefferys (1991).

[32] See Jefferys (1991).

[33] The Conservatives interpreted the accord as one that applied to virtually all forms of party political activity.

[34] See Page (2007).

[35] See Addison (1977).

[36] See Addison (1992, p 383).

[37] See also Ball (1998, pp 102-3).

[38] See Toye (2013, p 222).

[39] See Addison (1992, p 364).

[40] See Toye (2013, p 222).

[41] See Bonham (1954), Butler and Stokes (1969), Addison (1977).

[42] 'Operation Doorstop' delivered 230,000 new members in a 12-month period following its introduction in October 1946, while 'Operation Knocker' saw membership rise from 1.2 million to 2.25 million in just two months after its launch in April 1948. A fighting fund appeal was also launched in the autumn of 1947 and yielded £1 million in donations in the space of 12 months. See Bale (2012).

[43] See Cooke and Parkinson (2009).

[44] The Young Conservative movement was also established in 1945. By the end of 1949, it had nearly 2,400 branches and a membership in excess of 160,000. A Public Opinion Research Department was set up under Dudley Clarke in 1948 to develop a more sophisticated form of polling analysis and strategy; see Hoffman (1964).

[45] See Dorey (2011, pp 76-7).

[46] The three significant features of the 1927 *Trades Dispute and Trades Unions Act* that the Attlee government had removed were a ban on civil service unions affiliating to the Labour Party, the prohibition of the closed shop in the public sector and a requirement that trade unionists opt in to, rather than out of, paying the political levy; see Addison (1992).

[47] See Pitchford (2011).

[48] See Ramsden (1995, pp 160-1).

[49] See Webster (1988), Klein (1995).

[50] See Addison (1992).

[51] See Conservative and Unionist Central Office (1950).

Chapter Three

[1] The other members were Robert Carr, 'Cub' Alport, Richard Fort, Gilbert Longden and John Rodgers; see Walsha (2000, 2003).

[2] The pamphlet was scheduled to be published in time for the party conference later that year – see Seawright, 2005.

[3] See Walsha (2000) and Seawright (2010).

[4] See Evans (2009).

[5] See Hennessy (2014).

[6] See Seawright (2010).

[7] See Gilmour (1978, 1982), Gilmour and Garnett (1998).

[8] See Green (2002, ch 3).

[9] See Campbell (2013).

[10] See Macmillan (1938).

[11] See Greenleaf (1983).

[12] See Dorey (2011, ch 2).

[13] See Law (1950).

[14] In the subsequent discussion, the term One Nation will be used exclusively in this 'progressive' sense.

[15] See Raison (1990, p 30), Jones (2000).

[16] See Ball (2011).

[17] See Pitchford (2011).

[18] The figure of 321 includes 19 'Conservative'-supporting National Liberal MPs who were elected at this time. Fifty-five National Liberal candidates stood in both the 1950 and 1951 General Elections.

[19] See Boxer (1996).

[20] See Bridgen and Lowe (1998).

[21] See Bridgen and Lowe (1998, p 47).

[22] See Ramsden (1995).

[23] See Torrance (2010).

[24] Both Baldwin and Neville Chamberlain had managed firms that had co-partnership arrangements; see Williamson (1999), Self (2006).

[25] The sobriquet 'pots and pans' was attached to this budget as a result of the decision to extend purchase tax to a range of kitchen utensils and other household items.

[26] See Jefferys (1997, p 51), Thorpe (2010).

[27] See Ball (1998, p 110).

[28] See Ramsden (1995),Pitchford (2011).

[29] See Bridgen and Lowe (1998).

[30] See Lowe (1989).

[31] See Webster (1988, pp 204-11), Sheard (2013, pp 84-6).

[32] See Bridgen and Lowe (1998, pp 132-35).

[33] See Raison (1990, p 40).

[34] See Thorpe (2004, chs 17-18).

[35] See Jefferys (1997, pp 60-4), Thorpe (2010, ch 20).

[36] See Jefferys (1997, p 65), Thorpe (2010, pp 385-7)

[37] See Sandbrook (2005, p 89), Thorpe (2010, pp 423-4).

[38] See Jefferys (1997, p 143).

[39] See Lowe (1988).

[40] See Bridgen and Lowe (1998, pp 104-12).

[41] See Timmins (2001, p 194), Raison (1990, p 46).

[42] See Lowe (1998, Table 7.3, p 193).

[43] See Bridgen and Lowe (1998, pp 50-1).

[44] See Raison (1990, p 55).

[45] See Crowson (2002).

[46] See Kynaston (2013, ch 8).

[47] See Jefferys (1997, p 91).

[48] See Thorpe (2010, p 512).

[49] See Jefferys (1997, p 139), Bridgen and Lowe (1998, p 57).

[50] This was undertaken to comply with the Chancellor's so-called pay pause.

[51] See Shepherd (1997).

[52] See Bridgen and Lowe (1998, p 156).

[53] See Knight (1990).

[54] See Bridgen and Lowe (1998, ch 3).

[55] See Deacon and Bradshaw (1983).

[56] In the Orpington by-election, a resurgent Liberal Party overturned a Conservative majority of 14,760 to take the seat by 7,885 votes; see Ramsden (1996, pp 154-6), Sandbrook (2005, p 347).

[57] See Sandbrook (2005, pp 483-9), Thorpe (2010, pp 546-7).

[58] See Thorpe (2010, pp 540-6), Davenport-Hines (2013).

[59] See Thorpe (2010).

[60] See Sandbrook (2005, ch 18).

[61] See Jefferys (1997, ch 8), Sandbrook (2005, ch 1).

[62] See Ramsden (1996).

[63] See Dale (2000, pp 143–60).

Chapter Four

[1] Immigration once again proved to be a key issue at this by-election. Gordon Walker had previously been ousted from his Smethwick seat in the 1964 General Election by the Conservative candidate, Peter Griffiths, who had stood on an explicitly racist platform; see Crowson (2002).

[2] See Ramsden (1996, pp 253-61).

[3] See Sewill (2009).

[4] A formal voting system had been introduced by the departing leader Douglas-Home following concerns about the unsatisfactory nature of the informal selection procedures (the so-called 'magic circle') that had been employed previously; see Thorpe (2007, ch 15).

[5] The Heathmen are described by Roth (1978) as modern, middle-class, managerial Conservatives such as Robert Carr, Geoffrey Rippon, Tony Barber and John Davies. See also Campbell (1993, p 377).

[6] The Labour Prime Minister Harold Wilson called a General Election in 1966 in the hope of securing a larger majority.

[7] See Barr (2001).

[8] See Gamble (1974, pp 92-102).

[9] Fisher's personal fortune derived from his innovative Buxted broiler chicken business, which had 'transformed the eating patterns of the British public'; Cockett (1995, p 125).

[10] See Seldon (1957, 1967a, 1967b), Prest (1960), Lees (1961), Peacock and Wiseman (1964), Buchanan (1965), West (1965).

[11] See Houghton (1967).

¹² John Wood, who become Deputy Director of the IEA in 1969, edited a number of Powell's books, including *A nation not afraid: The thinking of Enoch Powell* (Wood, 1965).

¹³ See Hayek (1944).

¹⁴ See Friedman (1962), Friedman and Friedman (1990).

¹⁵ See Shepherd (1997), Heffer (2012).

¹⁶ See Beaton et al (1961).

¹⁷ See Abel-Smith (1964), Houghton (1967).

¹⁸ See Jarvis (2005, pp 144-8), Grimley (2012), Campbell (2014).

¹⁹ The term Black Papers was chosen in order to highlight the contrast between these publications and official government White Papers.

²⁰ See Cox and Dyson (1969a, 1969b).

²¹ See Ramsden (1980, ch 5).

²² Maude (1966 – see also, Gamble (1974, pp 104-5: Ramsden (1996, p 255).

²³ This led Heath to remove Powell from the shadow cabinet; see Schofield (2013).

²⁴ See Maude (1968).

²⁵ See Ramsden (1980, p 276).

²⁶ Though see Raison (1990) and Gilmour and Garnett (1998) for 'dissenting' perspectives.

²⁷ The issue had not been discussed at any length at the conference, but Macleod believed that it always played well with the public and the media.

²⁸ See Green (2002, pp 231-3).

²⁹ See Lowe (1996).

³⁰ England surrendered a two-goal lead, losing 3-2 to their arch rivals West Germany. Stand-in goalkeeper Peter Bonetti was unjustly pilloried at this time for his role in this defeat.

³¹ The Conservatives won 330 seats and a 46.4% share of the popular vote.

³² Joseph presided over a super-ministry the Department of Health and Social Security, which Labour had created as part of its own modernisation agenda in 1968.

³³ Counties were given responsibility for education, social services, transport, fire and police services, while districts were to be responsible for housing, environmental services and local planning.

³⁴ See Sutcliffe-Braithwaite (2012).

³⁵ See Friedman 1962).

³⁶ See Lees (1967).

³⁷ See Lowe (1996, pp 201-3).

³⁸ Macleod was to die in office just three months after having being appointed as Heath's new Chancellor.

³⁹ See Field (1982, pp 38-9).

⁴⁰ See Field and Piachaud (1971), Deacon and Bradshaw (1983).

⁴¹ See Timmins (2001, p 304).

⁴² See Turner (1995).

⁴³ See Timmins (2001, p 304).

⁴⁴ Page (1971) had been dismissed from his post after suggesting, in a number of articles written for *The Spectator* in 1969, that 'large numbers' of claimants were 'obtaining money they do not need, should not have and to which they are not entitled, by processes of deception, fraud and even violence which are making a complete mockery of the whole idea of Supplementary Benefits' (p 64).

[45] In passing, it should be noted that the committee decided not to invite the National Federation of Claimants Unions (NFCU) to assist it with its deliberations after the minutes secretary of the NFCU indicated that it regarded the proposed investigation as 'bullshit' (Fisher, 1973, para, 13 p 5).

[46] See George (1973).

[47] See Lowe (1996).

[48] See Lowe (1996).

[49] See Moore (2014, ch 9).

[50] The Department of Trade and Industry was created by merging the Departments of Technology and the Board of Trade.

[51] See Green (2006, p 105).

[52] See Ramsden (1996, pp 347-8).

[53] This Act was described by the then chair of the 1922 Committee, Sir Harry Legge-Bourke, in a House of Commons debate as 'a socialist bill by ethic and philosophy'; see Seldon (1996, p 7).

[54] See Ramsden (1996, p 367).

[55] The bargaining strength of the miners had been enhanced significantly by the sharp hike in oil prices announced by OPEC in October 1973, following the Yom Kippur war in the Middle East.

[56] See Ramsden (1996, ch 6), Sandbrook (2010, ch 15).

[57] See Campbell (1993), Kavanagh (1996).

[58] Labour secured 301 seats, the Conservatives 297 and the Liberals 14.

[59] The offer was not, however, extended to either the Democratic Unionists or the Vanguard Unionist Progressive Party; see Bogdanor (1996).

[60] Such a slender majority is usually a portent for another contest being called in the near future. However, the fragmentation of oppositional forces 'into five parties and assorted individuals' (Ramsden, 1996, p 433) proved sufficient to see Labour through until 1979 (though it was propped up by the Liberal Party towards the end of its term in office).

Chapter Five

[1] Ralph Harris was Director of the Institute of Economic Affairs. Rhodes Boyson was the head teacher of High Grove comprehensive school in Islington (1967-74) before becoming Conservative MP for Brent North in 1974. Ross McWhirter stood, unsuccessfully, as the Conservative candidate for Edmonton in the 1964 General Election. He went on to establish the Freedom Association in 1975. He was assassinated by the IRA in 1975.

[2] The club had been established by Nicholas Ridley, Jock Bruce-Gardyne and John Biffen.

[3] Lord Coleraine, who had published the influential anti-collectivist text *Return from utopia* in 1950 (Law, 1950), became patron of the group. The Vice Presidents included Richard Body, William Clark and Sir Frederick Corfield. Some younger libertarians acted as officers: David Alexander, Stephen Ayers, Richard Henderson and Anthony and Philip Vander Elst; see Cockett (1995).

[4] See Cockett (1995, p 200).

[5] See Barr (2001).

[6] See Cockett (1995, p 210), Ramsden (1995, pp 416-17).

[7] See Denham and Garnett (2001, pp 238-9).

[8] Sherman was a former Communist and Spanish civil war veteran, who had helped Joseph with some of his speeches during his time in opposition in 1969/70.

[9] Although Heath agreed to the setting up of the CPS, he was sceptical as to whether it would focus, as Joseph had insisted, on the reasons why the social market had brought prosperity to West Germany. Accordingly, he insisted that Adam Ridley of the Conservative Research Department should become a member of the CPS board to oversee its activities.

[10] See Denham and Garnett (1998, ch 4).

[11] See Denham and Garnett (2001, ch 10).

[12] See Welshman (2012). See also Welshman (2013).

[13] See Denham and Garnett (2001, p 255).

[14] The same venue in which Enoch Powell's 'rivers of blood' speech had been delivered in 1968.

[15] See Young (1993, pp 94-5).

[16] See Harris (2013).

[17] Hugh Fraser obtained 19 votes and there were 11 abstentions.

[18] See Campbell (2000).

[19] During a brief meeting with Edward Heath at his Wilton Street flat, Thatcher's offers of a shadow Cabinet post of his choice and the opportunity to lead the party's campaign in the forthcoming European referendum were firmly rebuffed by Heath. In order to avoid damaging media speculation about the reason for the brevity of this meeting, Thatcher decided to remain for a further 15 minutes engaging in polite conversation with Heath's PPS, Tim Kitson, before departing through the press cordon that had formed outside; see Thatcher (2011a, pp 282-3), Aitken (2013, p 179).

[20] See Gilmour and Garnett (1998).

[21] See Bale (2012, p 233).

[22] The term 'Winter of Discontent' was used to describe the series of public sector strikes during the harsh winter of 1978-79 that were called in response to a further round of pay restraint by the Callaghan government; see Sandbrook (2012, chs 30 and 31), Hay (2010), Lipsey (2012).

[23] A discount of 33% was offered to those with a minimum of three years' occupancy and 50% to those who had rented their home for 20 years.

[24] To their neo-liberal critics, the wets were regarded as soft or even spineless. According to Aitken (2013), the term originated from Thatcher herself, who used to scrawl the adjective 'in the margins of memoranda and letters received from Jim Prior during her time as leader of the opposition' (p 307).

[25] The government decided to rely on a broad money supply measure known as M3 (a measure that included all bank account holdings but not those in building societies). M0, in contrast, measured the amount of cash in the economy and M1, a measure used by the Heath government, included some bank account holdings; see Vinen (2009, pp 111-13).

[26] See Wickham Jones (1992), Howe (2006).

[27] This was one of the few occasions in which leading 'wets' such as Walker, Heseltine and Soames (who thought a pay freeze preferable to further expenditure reductions) joined forces with 'tinder box' drys such as John Nott and John Biffen in opposing the Prime Minister (Thatcher, 2011b, pp 148-9).

[28] Hoskyns and Norman Strauss had been responsible for the *Stepping stones* paper in 1977, which had detailed the incremental actions needed to transform British society; see Vinen (2009, pp 90-1); Berlinski (2011), Thatcher (2011a, pp 420-3).

[29] See Moore (2014, pp 640-1).

[30] See Campbell (2003, pp 98-100).

[31] The Chancellor, Geoffrey Howe, had previously announced in 1979 that 100,000 civil service jobs would be lost over the following five years.

[32] Thatcher exacted her 'revenge' on Soames, whom she thought had mishandled the dispute, by subsequently dismissing him from the Cabinet in an acrimonious meeting in which his bitter tirade 'could be heard out of the open window halfway across Horseguards Parade' (Young, 1993, p 221).

[33] See Moore (2014, pp 537-40).

[34] Tebbit served as Conservative member for the constituency of Chingford in Essex from 1974 to 1992, having previously been MP for Epping from 1970-74. His reputation as a 'hardman' was bolstered by his portrayal as a leather-jacketed 'bovver' boy on the satirical ITV programme, *Spitting Image*.

[35] It should be noted that pre-war Conservative attempts to exercise greater control over private industry were not driven by an 'ideological' conversion to public ownership but rather were premised on the merits of the 'rationalisation' of industry, which would result in greater economies of scale. Moreover, the fact that the progressive, post-1945, One Nation Conservative governments accepted that 'utilities' as well as the railways and coal industries should remain under public ownership should not be interpreted as an 'ideological' conversion to the merits of nationalisation. Their default position was that that with some minor exceptions, state involvement in the running of industry was a recipe for inefficiency and poor service. Not surprisingly, therefore, progressive One Nation Conservatives opposed Labour's attempt to nationalise the iron and steel and road haulage Industries. They also supported Tate and Lyle's successful 'Mr Cube' campaign against the proposed nationalisation of the sugar industry in 1950 – 'Tate not State'; see Green (2006, pp 84-5).

[36] Associated British Ports, the National Freight Corporation, British Rail Hotels and British Aerospace were also privatised, though a majority shareholding was retained in the latter case. The British National Oil Corporation was transformed into Britoil prior to eventual privatisation in 1981; see Lawson (1992, ch 18).

[37] See Ridley (1991, p 83).

[38] See Donnison (1982).

[39] See Fowler (1991, ch 10).

[40] See Timmins (2001, pp 381-2).

[41] Housing Benefit was introduced in 1982/83 to amalgamate the various housing allowances that were being provided by local authorities or through the Supplementary Benefits scheme; see Hills (1998).

[42] The 1981 recession had ended, with a return to growth and inflation under control.

[43] The formation of the Social Democratic Party in 1981 by 'disillusioned' former Labour ministers Roy Jenkins, David Owen, Shirley Williams and Bill Rogers (see Crewe and King, 1995; Campbell, 2014) and their subsequent electoral 'alliance' with the Liberal Party posed a serious threat to Labour's status as the main opposition party. Labour's leader at that time, Michael Foot, was regarded as not being sufficiently 'prime ministerial', while the party's left-leaning election manifesto was famously dubbed by Gerald Kauffman as 'the longest suicide note' in political history.

[44] The Liberal party and the Social Democratic party entered into a formal electoral pact (the alliance) in the 1983 General Election.

[45] See Green (2006, ch 3).

[46] See Ball (2011, p 130), Bale (2012).

[47] According to Francis (2012) the Conservative government's commitment to wider share ownership took priority over any perceived need to maximise the receipts from such sales.

[48] See also Glennerster (2007, p 190).

[49] See Fowler (1991, p 207).

[50] See Klein (1995, p 161).

[51] See Harrison (2004).

[52] See Flather (1987) and Welshman (2012).

[53] See Hills (1998, p 127).

[54] Under the leadership of Neil Kinnock, Labour managed to increase both its share of the vote (30.8%) and its number of parliamentary seats (229).

[55] See Lowe (2004), Glennerster (2007).

[56] The passage of the Act took up '370 hours of parliamentary time', which was a 'post-war record' as 'Kenneth Baker and his ministerial colleagues, battered by conflicting pressures from various parts of the educational establishment on the one side and the Prime Minister on the other, were forced to improvise policy as they went along' (Campbell, 2003, p 542).

[57] See Thatcher (2011b).

[58] See Timmins (2001, p 443).

[59] See Timmins (2001, p 448-9).

[60] Moore had lived in the US for several years and was married to an American.

[61] See Timmins (2001).

[62] See Campbell (2003, p 548).

[63] See Lawson, 1992, ch 49.

[64] A British Medical Association campaign poster at this time used the image of a steamroller to depict the government's plans for the NHS.

[65] See Waldegrave (2015).

[66] See Young (1993).

[67] In a memorable resignation speech in the Commons, Howe expressed his frustration when conducting negotiations on European Monetary Union on behalf of Britain. He compared this experience to that of an opening batsman arriving at the crease to face the opening bowling only to discover that your team captain had broken your bat before the match.

[68] See Timmins (2001), Lowe (2005) and Glennerster (2007).

[69] See Park et al (2012, 2014).

[70] See Hennessy (2014).

[71] Though the needs for improvements in education provision were highlighted; see Dorey (1999).

[72] Major conceded that the neo-liberal Conservative policy of privatising some parts of the public sector led people to believe that his party was 'hostile to all of it' (2000, p 246).

[73] See Willman (1994), Lowe (2005).

[74] See Harrop and Scammel (1992).

[75] See Gilmour and Garnett (1998).

[76] See Page (1997).

[77] See Atkinson et al (1998).

[78] No Turning Back Group (1992).

[79] See Deacon (2002).

[80] See Timmins (2001, p 517).

[81] See Ginsburg (2005).

[82] See Malpass (2005).

[83] See Timmins (2001, p 522).

[84] In an attempt to emulate the success of the television programme EastEnders, the BBC launched a new soap opera, *Eldorado*, based on the lives of British and European expatriates living in the fictional town of Los Barcos on the Costa del Sol in Spain. Ratings proved 'disappointing' and the programme was axed by the new Controller of BBC1, Alan Yentob, in July 1993, just 12 months after its much-vaunted launch.

[85] See Major (2000, ch 15).

[86] See Maude, cited in Green (2006, p 45).

[87] Macmillan reissued his influential book, *The middle way*, in 1978 (which had first been published in 1938) to highlight his concerns about the direction of contemporary Conservatism.

Chapter Six

[1] As was noted earlier, Major also attempted, largely unsuccessfully, to nudge the Conservative Party in a compassionate direction.

[2] Hague's 'Fresh Futures' initiative, for example, attempted to increase internal party democracy by providing members with the opportunity to endorse his leadership and to participate more fully in any future such contest. Although many MPs expressed reservations about the greater involvement of grass roots members, it was agreed that members would be able to choose between two leadership candidates following a preliminary contest which would be restricted solely to MPs.

[3] The Texas Governor George W. Bush was one influential Republican who embraced compassionate Conservatism. See Olasky (2000), Ashbee (2003), Norman and Ganesh (2006).

[4] Lilley had previously been regarded as an arch Thatcherite.

[5] See Snowden (2010, p 59).

[6] Lilley's speech was seen as a contributory factor in Hague's decision to axe him from the shadow cabinet in June 1998; see Hayton (2012, p 47).

[7] Shaun Woodward, who had been sacked from Hague's shadow frontbench team because of his refusal to support the party line on Section 28, crossed the floor of the House to join New Labour.

[8] See Dorey (2003).

[9] In these elections, the party won the highest number of seats (36), although turnout was low at just 23%.

[10] See Hayton (2012, p 49).

[11] Labour's share of the vote was 40.7%, which gave it 413 seats and an overall majority of 167.

[12] Portillo returned to the shadow cabinet as Chancellor in February 2000 after winning the Kensington and Chelsea by-election in November 1999.

[13] Cameron and Osborne subsequently helped Duncan Smith prepare for his duels with Tony Blair at Prime Minister's question time. A more openly tolerant approach towards minority groups and non-traditional families formed part of this briefing.

[14] Portillo secured 49 votes compared with 39 for Duncan Smith and 36 for his other leading rival, Kenneth Clarke.

[15] See Snowden (2010, p 88).

[16] This pamphlet developed some of the themes addressed in a number of previous 'blue sky' publications by Conservative modernisers; see Vaisey et al (2001), Streeter (2002), Vaizey (2002).

[17] This was a direct reference to the five giants identified by Beveridge in his report of 1942; see Chapter One.

[18] See Snowdon (2010, p 105).

[19] Duncan Smith had been the subject of adverse media coverage over his decision to continue to use his parliamentary allowance to retain his wife, Betsy, as a paid administrative assistant in the period following his election as Conservative leader, 'a post that afforded him unlimited administrative and clerical support from the Party' (Bale, 2010, p 186). The couple were exonerated of any impropriety following a subsequent investigation; see Snowden (2010, p 114).

[20] Under the new leadership rules introduced in 1997, a vote of confidence in the leader could be triggered if 15% of current MPs (that is, at least 25 MPs in 2003) wrote to the Chairman of the 1922 Committee requesting such a vote.

[21] Duncan Smith had attempted to make a virtue of his lacklustre leadership style by declaring, in what was to prove to be his last leader's speech at the party's annual conference in Blackpool in 2003, that 'the Quiet Man is here to stay and he's turning up the volume'; see Bale (2010, p 187).

[22] During his time as a minister in the Thatcher government, Howard had piloted both the 'poll tax' legislation and the 'Section 28' amendment to the *Local Government Act* through the Commons. He was also widely perceived as a 'hard-line' Home Secretary who believed that 'prison worked'. In a famous assessment of Howard in 1997, fellow MP Anne Widdicombe declared that there was 'something of the night' about him.

[23] Although a number of MPs considered standing for the leadership, Howard was elected unopposed. Howard was perceived as an experienced 'unity' candidate who could provide the effective leadership deemed necessary in the run-up to the next General Election; see Bale (2010), Snowden (2010).

[24] Policy Exchange was founded in 2002 as the result of an initiative by Francis Maude and Archie Norman. Nick Boles became its first Director and Michael Gove its founding chairman.

[25] The speech was drafted by Hilton, Maude and Boles.

[26] See also Cowley and Stuart (2004).

[27] The party whip was subsequently withdrawn from Flight – a decision that left him ineligible to be placed on the party's list of approved candidates; see Bale (2010, pp 249-50).

[28] See Bale (2010), Snowden (2010).

[29] These changes were eventually introduced by the Conservative-led coalition government in 2010.

[30] Though the Labour Party's share of the popular vote fell to just 35.2%.

[31] The Conservatives' share of the vote increased marginally to 32.4%, giving them 198 seats. While the Conservatives enjoyed a 40% lead over Labour in terms of middle-class (ABC1) voters in 1983, this had fallen to 3% by 2001. The small increase in the Conservatives' share of the vote was attributed to a small increase in popularity among working-class (DE) voters; see Snowden (2010, p 79).

[32] Proposals for further reform of the leadership rules were put forward in a document entitled *A 21st century party* (see Bale, 2010). After some four-and-a-half months of deliberation, the proposed changes failed to secure the endorsement of the party's National Convention.

[33] The party's manifesto was seen as reflecting the concerns of Victor Meldrew, a character whose curmudgeonly musings on the state of contemporary society ('I don't believe it') in the hit BBC TV comedy *One Foot in the Grave* seemed to strike a chord with the British public.

[34] Cameron achieved 90 votes in the second round of voting compared with 57 for Davis and 51 for Fox. In the final membership ballot, he secured 198,844 votes (68% of the total votes cast) compared with 134,446 (32%) for Davis.

[35] Davis' conference speech was widely judged to be lacklustre by comparison.

[36] Unlike previous leadership election contests, party members now seemed to be prepared to vote with their head rather than their heart. Post-election inquests from Michael Ashcroft (2005) and Andrew Cooper (2005) of C-Change had drawn attention to the need for the Conservatives to adopt a more modern narrative if the party was to win over floating voters and return to government; see Bale (2009, 2010), Heppell and Hill (2009), Snowden (2010, ch 5).

[37] The earlier and highly effective 'rebrand' undertaken by the US Democrats under Clinton served as a role model for New Labour; see Page (2009).

[38] See Norton (2009).

[39] See Robin (2011).

[40] See Bercow (2002), (Clark and Hunt (2007a, 2007b), Osborne (2009), Reeves (2009), Cameron (2010), D'Ancona (2012), Page (2014).

[41] See Cameron (2009).

[42] See Fielding (2009), Willetts (2009).

[43] See McManus (2010).

[44] See Greenleaf (1983), Williamson (1999), Self (2006), Ball (2013).

[45] See Kirby (2009).

[46] See Haidt (2012).

[47] See Hickson (2010).

[48] See Dorey (2011).

[49] See also Willetts (1992, p 112), Seawright (2005), D'Ancona (2012).

[50] The reviews, which were all to be co-ordinated by Oliver Letwin, examined national and international security (Lord Tom King and Dame Neville-Jones), globalisation and global poverty (Peter Lilley), economic competitiveness (John Redwood), public service improvements (Stephen Dorrell and Lady Perry) and quality of life (John Gummer and Zac Goldsmith).

[51] See Centre for Social Justice, 2007a, 2007b, 2007c, 2007d, 2007e, 2007f, 2007g and 2007h.

[52] See also, Norman, Ussher and Alexander (2007).

[53] Though supporting empirical evidence was also provided.

[54] These were to be delivered by private and third sector (voluntary) agencies.

[55] See Willetts (2002, p 59).

[56] See Norman (2014), Bromwich (2014), see also, Letwin, 208 and Bromwich, 2014, Norman, 2014.

[57] See Cowley and Kavanagh (2010), Laws (2010), Adonis (2013).

[58] According to Dorey et al (2011), 'in terms of personality and beliefs', Howard and Kennedy 'could not have been much further apart' (p 185).

[59] See Marshall and Laws (2004).

[60] The Conservatives had to agree to some Liberal demands such as electoral reform (a referendum on the introduction of the Alternative Vote) and excluding lower-paid workers from income tax. The Conservatives were also seen as making a generous concession to their coalition partners in terms of ministerial appointments.

[61] See Young (2014).

[62] See also Young (2013).

[63] See Hultin (2009).

[64] Teach First, a charitable enterprise founded by Brett Wigdortz in 2002, aims to counter education disadvantage. It provides school based training for 'elite' students in schools with high levels of recorded deprivation. Trainees work towards a PGCE and become Teach First ambassadors on graduation. Some 1400 students were enrolled on this programme in 2014.

[65] Crosby had also advised the party in the 2005 General Election. See p 127 above.

[66] By the end of May 2014, the total caseload for Universal Credit in the four north-west 'pathfinder' and six 'hub' Jobcentre areas stood at just 6,570 individuals, most of whom were young people under 25 with few complex needs. It had been previously estimated that 184,000 claimants would be enrolled on the scheme at around this time; see National Audit Office (2013).

[67] Shiplee had previously delivered the Olympic Park project on time and on budget.

[68] The £2.8 billion scheme was designed to help over two million people over the lifetime of the scheme (June 2011 to March 2016). As with Universal Credit, questions have been raised about both the efficacy (particularly in relation to harder-to-help groups) and cost of the Work Programme during its initial phase. By 2014, for example, just 27% of Jobseekers' Allowance claimants aged 25 and over who had completed the programme had secured employment lasting six months or more – a figure that was markedly less than initial departmental (39%) and contractor (42%) estimates.

[69] This programme provoked considerable media interest when cases came to light, suggesting that some participants had been 'coerced' into participating in this supposedly voluntary scheme because of a fear of losing their benefits (Malik, 2011).

[70] Claimants have voiced concerns about the impersonal and mechanistic approach of these private sector assessors and Jobcentre Plus staff. They have also drawn attention to the lack of transparency, poor official decision making and the complexity of the procedures; see Harrington (2010, 2011, 2012), Litchfield (2013). There have been a large number of appeals relating to Work Capability Assessments, with over a third of these (37%) being upheld; see Department for Work and Pensions (2013b). One of the firms that has been heavily criticised for 'sub-standard' Work Capability Assessments – Atos Healthcare – eventually withdrew from this area of activity in 2014.

[71] In defending the fairness of his proposals, Duncan Smith claimed, for example, that the operation of benefit cap had not (contrary to claims by anti-poverty campaigners) increased the level of homelessness but rather had led to 8,000 claimants moving into paid work – a claim contested by the Office for National Statistics (see Wintour and Butler, 2013).

[72] Though such properties were in short supply in many areas.

[73] See Department for Work and Pensions (2013a).

[74] See Osborne (2011).

[75] See Watson (2012, p 8).

[76] A 'temporary' 50% top rate tax band had been introduced in 2010. The degree to which the Chancellor had fully embraced a progressive Conservative approach to claimants was also highlighted when he sought to distinguish between the 'shirkers' (irresponsible claimants who stay at home all day with the curtains drawn) and the 'strivers' (those who are willing to leave home early in the morning to undertake modestly paid work) in his 2012 autumn statement (5 December 2012).

[77] This is all the more surprising given that these changes formed part of the Conservatives' 2005 manifesto.

[78] These changes were eventually brought about following the passage of the *Health and Social Care Act* in 2012.

[79] See also Page (2011).

[80] The New Labour government had supported such developments. For example, Central Surrey Health, a social enterprise that was established by two health practitioners in 2006 subsequently grew into a 700-strong 'co-owner' organisation providing NHS-branded community, therapeutic and nursing services to around 280,000 residents in central Surrey.

[81] See Timmins (2012).

[82] The National Citizen Service provides an opportunity for all 16- and 17-year-olds in England to take part in a team-based social action project that will benefit their local community. It is envisaged that this scheme will bring together children from diverse backgrounds and aid their personal and social development. The numbers taking part in the scheme have increased steadily since it was first piloted in 2011.

[83] The coalition published its first child poverty strategy in April 2011 (Department for Work and Pensions and Department of Education, 2011) and a second in 2014 (HM Government, 2014). Although the goal of reducing acute financial need was acknowledged in both documents, the need for a more 'holistic' approach to poverty prevention was highlighted.

[84] The remit of the Child Poverty Commission, which was set up under the *Welfare Reform Act* of 2012, was extended to include the broader issue of social mobility (HM Government, 2011; Social Mobility and Child Poverty Commission, 2013).

[85] According to a joint report from Church Action on Poverty, the Trussell Trust and Oxfam, food banks in the UK, of which there were 423 in 2014, received 913,138 applications for a three-day emergency supply of food and support in 2013-14 compared with 346,992 in 2012-13 and 127,697 in 2011-12; see Cooper et al (2014).

[86] See Brewer et al (2011), Poinasmy (2013), Hills (2014).

[87.] See Kwarteng et al (2011, 2012), Scholefield and Frost (2011).

Epilogue

[1] Other points of common agreement include the need to ensure that state welfare does not take such a hold in society that it squeezes out informal, voluntary or private forms of support, and the importance of ensuring that periods of state dependency are minimised whenever possible.

[2] See Le Grand (2003).

Appendix

[1] The Board of Education was renamed the Ministry of Education in 1944.

[2] Sir Walter Womersley was first appointed to this role by Churchill's predecessor Neville Chamberlain.

[3] This was made a Cabinet post on 2 September 1953.

[4] The Ministries of Pensions and Social/National Insurance were merged in 1953.

[5] The name of Department of Education was changed by the Labour government to the Department of Education and Science in 1964.

[6] The Department of Health and Social Security was created by the Heath government in 1970.

[7] The Ministry of Housing and Local Government became part of the Department of the Environment when it was created in October 1970. Subsequently, the housing portfolio became the responsibility of a number of variously titled ministries.

[8] The Department of Education and Science was re-badged as the Department of Education in 1992.

[9] The Department of Education was renamed the Department of Education and Employment in 1995.

[10] A separate Department of Health was created in 1988.

[11] A separate Department of Social Security was created in 1988.

[12] The Department for Work and Pensions was created by New Labour in 2001 following the merger of the Department of Social Security, the employment service and allied policy groups.

[13] Housing is currently the responsibility of the Department for Communities and Local Government, which was established by New Labour in 2006.

References

Abel, D. (2004) 'Benn, Sir Ernest John Pickstone, second baronet (1875-1954)', rev. Marc Brodie, *Oxford Dictionary of National Biography*, Oxford: Oxford University Press (www.oxford.com/view/article/30704, accessed 19 Aug 2011).

Abel-Smith, B. (1964) *Freedom in the welfare state*, London: Fabian Society.

Addison, P. (1977) *The road to 1945*, London: Quartet.

Addison, P. (1992) *Churchill on the home front, 1900-1955*, London: Jonathan Cape.

Adonis, A. (2013) *Five days in May: The coalition and beyond*, London: Biteback.

Aitken, J. (2013) *Margaret Thatcher: Power and personality*, London: Bloomsbury.

Allitt, P. (2009) *The Conservatives*, New Haven, CT: Yale University Press.

Ashbee, K. (2003) 'The US Republicans: lessons for the Conservatives?', in M. Garnett, and P. Lynch (eds) *The Conservatives in crisis*, Manchester: Manchester University Press, pp 29-48.

Ashcroft, M.A. (2005) *Smell the coffee. A wake-up call for the Conservative Party*, London: Michael A. Ashcroft.

Ashcroft, M.A. (2010) *Minority verdict: The Conservative Party, the voters and the 2010 General Election*, London: Biteback.

Atkinson, K., Oerton, S. and Burns, D. (1998) '"Happy families"? Single mothers, the press and the politicians', *Class and Capital*, 64, pp 1-11.

Bale, T. (2009) '"Cometh the hour, cometh the Dave": how far is the Conservative Party's revival down to David Cameron?', *The Political Quarterly*, vol 80, no 2, pp 222-32.

Bale, T. (2010) *The Conservative Party from Thatcher to Cameron*, Cambridge: Polity Press.

Bale, T. (2012) *The Conservatives since 1945*, Oxford: Oxford University Press.

Ball, J. (2013) 'Iain Duncan Smith rapped by watchdog for misusing benefit cap figures', *The Guardian*, 9 May.

Ball, S. (1998) *The Conservative Party since 1945*, Manchester: Manchester University Press.

Ball, S. (2004) 'Davidson, John Colin Campbell, first Viscount Davidson (1889-1970)', *Oxford Dictionary of National Biography*, Oxford: Oxford University Press, (www.oxford.com/view/article/32730, accessed 17 Aug 2011).

Ball, S. (2011) *Dole queues and demons*, Oxford: Bodleian Library.

Ball, S. (2013) *Portrait of a party. The Conservative Party in Britain 1918-1945*, Oxford: Oxford University Press.

Barr, J. (2001) *The Bow Group: A history*, London: Politicos.

Beaton, L., Campbell, A., Fairbairn, D., Howe, G., Hodgson, G., Howell, D., Lemkin, J., Lewis, R. and Raison, T. (1961) *Principles in practice*, London: Conservative Political Centre.

Bercow, J. (2002) 'Tories for social justice', *The Guardian*, 13 December, p 18.

Berlinski, C. (2011) *There is no alternative: Why Margaret Thatcher matters*, New York, NY: Basic Books.

Beveridge, W.H. (1942) *Report of the Committee on Social Insurance and Allied Services* (Beveridge Report), Cmnd 6404, London: HMSO.

Beveridge, W.H. (1944) *Full employment in a free society*, London: George Allen & Unwin.

Blake, R. (1998) The *Conservative Party from Peel to Major*, London: Arrow.

Blond, P. (2010) *Red Tory*, London: Faber and Faber.

Board of Education (1931) *Report of the Consultative Committee on the primary school* (Hadow Report), London: HMSO.

Board of Education (1938) *Report of the Consultative Committee on secondary education with special reference to grammar schools and technical high schools* (Spens Report), London: HMSO.

Bogdanor, V. (1996) 'The fall of Heath and the end of the postwar settlement', in S. Ball and A. Seldon (eds) *The Heath government 1970-74: A reappraisal*, London: Longman, pp 191-214.

Bonham, J. (1954) *The middle class vote*, London: Faber and Faber.

Boothby, R. de V., Loder, J., Macmillan, H. and Stanley, O. (1927) *Industry and the state: A Conservative view*, London: Macmillan.

Boxer, A. (1996) *The Conservative governments 1951-64*, London: Longman.

Boyson, R. (ed) (1970) *Right turn*, London: Churchill Press.

Boyson, R. (1978) *Centre forward: A radical Conservative programme*, London: Temple Smith.

Braine, B. (1948) *Tory democracy*, London: Falcon.

Brewer, M., Browne, J. and Joyce, R. (2011) *Child and working-age poverty 2010-2020*, London: IFS.

Bridgen, P. and Lowe, R. (1998) *Welfare policy under the Conservatives 1951-1964*, London: Public Records Office.

Brittan, S. (1971) *Government and the market economy*, London: IEA.

Bromwich, D. (2014) *The intellectual life of Edmund Burke*, Cambridge, MA: Harvard University Press.

Brooke, S. (1992) *Labour's war: The Labour party during the Second World War*, Oxford: Clarendon.

Brooke, S. (1996) 'The Conservative Party, immigration and national Identity, 1948-1968', in M. Francis and I. Zweiniger-Bargielowska (eds) *The Conservatives and British society, 1880-1990*, Cardiff: University of Wales, pp 147-70.

Bruce, M. (1961) *The coming of the welfare state*, London: Basford.

Bruce-Gardyne, J. (1974) *Whatever happened to the quiet revolution? The story of a brave experiment in government*, London: Charles Knight.

Buchanan, J. (1965) *The inconsistencies of the National Health Service*, London: IEA.

Bulpitt, J. (1986) 'The discipline of the new democracy: Mrs Thatcher's domestic statecraft', *Political Studies*, 34, pp 19-39.

Burke, E. (1969) *Reflections on the revolution in France* (first published, 1790), London: Penguin.

Butler, D. and Stokes, D. (1969) *Political change in Britain*, London: Macmillan.

Butler, R.A. (1971) *The art of the possible*, London: Hamish Hamilton.

Cabinet Office (2010) *The coalition: Our programme for government*, London: Cabinet Office.

Cabinet Office (2013) *The coalition: Together in the national interest. Mid-term review*, London: The Stationery Office.

Cahalane, C. (2011) 'NHS Surrey's decision not to award £500m contract to Central Surrey Health casts doubt over spin outs', *The Guardian*, 30 September.

Calder, A. (1971) *The people's war*, London: Panther.

Cameron, D. (2009) 'The Big Society', Hugo Young Memorial Lecture, London, 10 November.

Cameron, D. (2010) 'Labour are now the reactionaries, we the radicals – as this promise shows', *The Guardian*, 9 April, p 34.

Campbell, J. (1993) *Edward Heath: A biography*, London: Jonathan Cape.

Campbell, J. (2000) *Margaret Thatcher. Volume one: The grocer's daughter*, London: Jonathan Cape.

Campbell, J. (2003) *Margaret Thatcher. Volume two: The iron lady*, London: Jonathan Cape.

Campbell, J. (2004) 'Smith, Frederick Edwin, first Earl of Birkenhead (1872-1930)', *Oxford Dictionary of National Biography*, Oxford: Oxford University Press (www.oxford.com/view/article/36137, accessed 19 Aug 2011).

Campbell, J. (2013) *F.E. Smith: First Earl of Birkenhead*, London: Faber and Faber.

Campbell, J. (2014) *Roy Jenkins*, London: Jonathan Cape.

Cecil, Lord, H. (1912) *Conservatism*, London: Williams & Norgate.

Central Advisory Council for Education (1959) *15 to 18 year olds. Report of the Central Advisory Council for Education (England)* (Crowther Report), London: HMSO.

Central Advisory Council for Education (1963) *Half our future. Report of the Central Advisory Council for Education (England)* (Newsom Report), London: HMSO.

Centre for Social Justice (2007a) *Breakthrough Britain: Overview*, London: Centre for Social Justice.

Centre for Social Justice (2007b) *Breakthrough Britain: Volume:1 Family Breakdown*, London: Centre for Social Justice.

Centre for Social Justice (2007c) *Breakthrough Britain: Volume:2 Economic Dependency and Worklessness*, London: Centre for Social Justice.

Centre for Social Justice (2007d) *Breakthrough Britain: Volume: 3 Educational Failure*, London: Centre for Social Justice.

Centre for Social Justice (2007e) *Breakthrough Britain: Volume: 4 Addictions: Towards Recovery*, London: Centre for Social Justice.

Centre for Social Justice (2007f) *Breakthrough Britain: Volume: 5 Serious Personal Debt*, London: Centre for Social Justice.

Centre for Social Justice (2007g) *Breakthrough Britain: Volume: 6 Third Sector*, London: Centre for Social Justice.

Centre for Social Justice (2007h) *Gambling: Special Report. Gambling addiction in the UK*, London: Centre for Social Justice.

Centre for Social Justice (2009) *Dynamic benefits: Towards welfare that works. A policy report by the CSJ Economic Dependency Working Group*, London: Centre for Social Justice.

Charmley, J. (2008) *A history of Conservative politics since 1830* (2nd edn), Basingstoke: Palgrave Macmillan.

Clark, G. and Hunt, J. (2007a) *Who's progressive now?*, London: Conservative Party.

Clark, G. and Hunt, J. (2007b) 'We Tories can claim to be the truly progressive party', *The Observer*, 16 December, p 18.

Clarke, D. (1947) *The Conservative faith in a modern age*, London: Conservative Political Centre.

Clarke, P. (1996) *Hope and glory*, London: Allen Lane.

Cockett, R. (1995) *Thinking the unthinkable: Think-tanks and the economic counter-revolution 1931-1983*, London: Fontana.

Committee on Higher Education (1963) *Higher Education: Report of the committee appointed by the Prime Minister under the chairmanship of Lord Robbins, 1961-63*, Cmnd 2154, London: The Stationery Office.

Conservative and Unionist Central Office (1947) *The Industrial Charter*, London: Conservative and Unionist Central Office.

Conservative and Unionist Central Office (1949) *The right road for Britain*, London: Conservative and Unionist Central Office.

Conservative and Unionist Central Office, (1950) *This is the road: The Conservative and Unionist Party's policy for the General Election 1950*, London: Conservative and Unionist Central Office.

Conservative Central Office (1976) *The right approach*, London: Conservative Central Office (http://margaretthatcher.org/document/109439).

Conservative Party (2001) *Time for common sense*, Conservative Party General Election manifesto, London: Conservative Party.

Conservative Party (2005) *Are you thinking what we're thinking? It's time for action*, Conservative Party General Election manifesto, London: Conservative Party.

Conservative Party (2010) *Invitation to join the government of Britain*, Conservative Party General Election manifesto, London: Conservative Party.

Conservative Party (2015) *The Conservative Party Manifesto 2015*, London: Conservative Party.

Conservative Policy Unit (2002) *Leadership with a purpose: Better society*, London: Conservative Policy Unit.

Conservative Political Centre (1958) *The Future of the welfare state*. London: Conservative Political Centre.

Conservative Political Centre (1965) *Putting Britain right ahead*, London: Conservative Political Centre.

Cooke, A. (ed) (2009) *Tory policy-making*, Eastbourne: Manor Creative.

Cooke, A. and Parkinson, S. (2009) 'Rab Butler's golden era?', in A. Cooke (ed) *Tory policy-making*, Eastbourne: Manor Creative, pp 27-54.

Cooper, A. (2005) *The case for change*, London: C-Change.

Cooper, N., Purcell, S. and Jackson, R. (2014) *Below the breadline: The relentless rise of food poverty in Britain*, Oxford: Church Action on Poverty/The Trussell Trust and Oxfam.

Cowley, P. and Kavanagh, D. (2010) *The British General Election of 2010*, Basingstoke: Palgrave Macmillan.

Cowley, P. and Stuart, M. (2004) 'The Conservative parliamentary party', in M. Garnett and P. Lynch (eds) *The Conservatives in crisis*, Manchester: Manchester University Press, pp 66-81.

Cox, C.B. and Dyson, A.E. (eds) (1969a) *Black Paper one: Fight for education*, London: The Critical Quarterly Society.

Cox, C.B. and Dyson, A.E. (eds) (1969b) *Black Paper two: The crisis in education*, London: The Critical Quarterly Society.

Crewe, I. and King, A. (1995) *SDP: The birth, life and death of a party*, Oxford: Oxford University Press.

Critchley, J. (1994) *A bag of boiled sweets: An autobiography*, London: Faber & Faber.

Crowson, N.J. (2002) 'Conservative party activists and immigration policy from the late 1940s to the mid-1970s', in S. Ball and I. Holliday (eds) *Mass conservatism: The Conservatives and the public since the 1880s*, London: Cass, pp 163-82.

Dale, I. (ed) (2000) *Conservative Party general election manifestos, 1900-1997*, London: Routledge.

Dale, I. (ed) (2010) *Margaret Thatcher in her own words*, London: Biteback.

D'Ancona, M. (2012) 'Cameron won't let the socialists have fairness all to themselves', *The Sunday Telegraph*, 8th January, p 22.

D'Ancona, M. (2013) *In it together. The inside story of the Coalition Government*, London: Viking.

Davenport-Hines, R. (2013) *An English affair: Sex, class and power in the age of Profumo*, London: HarperPress.

Deacon, A. (2002) *Perspectives on welfare*, Buckingham: Open University Press.

Deacon, A. and Bradshaw, J. (1983) *Reserved for the poor*, Oxford: Blackwell and Martin Robertson.

Deakin, N. (1994) *The politics of welfare*, Hemel Hempstead: Harvester Wheatsheaf.

Denham, A. and Garnett, M. (1998) *British think-tanks and the climate of opinion*, London: UCL.

Denham, A. and Garnett, M. (2001) *Keith Joseph*, London: Acumen.

Department for Work and Pensions (DWP) (2010a) *21st century welfare*, London: The Stationery Office.

Department for Work and Pensions (DWP) (2010b) *Universal Credit: Welfare that works*, London: The Stationery Office.

Department for Work and Pensions (DWP) (2012) *Social justice: Transforming lives*, Cm 8314, London: The Stationery Office.

Department for Work and Pensions (DWP) (2013a) *The single-tier pension: A simple foundation for saving*, Cm 8528, London: The Stationery Office.

Department for Work and Pensions (DWP) (2013b) *Work capability assessments – fairer and more accurate*, Press Release, 30 April 2013, London: DWP.

Department for Work and Pensions and Department for Education (2011) *A new approach to child poverty: Tackling the causes of disadvantage and transforming families' lives*, Cm.8061, London: Stationary Office.

Department of Education (1956) *Technical Education*, Cmnd 9703, London: HMSO.

Department of Education and Science (DES) (1972) *Education: A programme for expansion*, Cmnd 5174, London: HMSO.

Department of Education and Science (DES) (1985) *The development of higher education into the 1990s*, Cmnd 9524, London: HMSO.

Department of Health (DH) (1987) *Promoting better health*, London: HMSO.

Department of Health (DH) (1989) *Working for patients*, Cm 555, London: HMSO.

Department of Health (DH) (1996) *The National Health Service: A service with ambition*, Cm 3425, London: The Stationery Office.

Department of Health and Social Security (DHSS) (1985) *Reform of social security. Volume 1*, Cmnd 9517, London: HMSO.

Department of Health and Social Security (DHSS) (1986) *Primary health care: An agenda for discussion*, Cm 9771, London: HMSO.

Digby, A. (1989) *British social policy: From workhouse to workfare*, London: Faber & Faber.

Donnison, D. (1982) *The politics of poverty*, Oxford: Martin Robertson.

Donoughue, B. and Jones, G.W. (2001) *Herbert Morrison*, London: Phoenix.

Dorey, P. (1999) 'The three Rs – reform, reproach and rancour: education policies under John Major' in P. Dorey (ed), *The Major Premiership: politics and policy under John Major, 1990-97*, Palgrave: Basingstoke, pp 146-64.

Dorey, P. (2003) 'Conservative policy under Hague', in M. Garnett and P. Lynch (eds), *The Conservatives in crisis.* Manchester: Manchester University Press, pp 125-45.

Dorey, P. (2011) *British Conservatism*, London: I.B. Tauris.

Dorey, P., Garnett, M. and Denham, A. (2011) *From crisis to coalition: The Conservative Party, 1997-2010*, Basingstoke: Palgrave Macmillan.

Duncan Smith, I. (2002) 'The renewal of society', in G. Streeter (ed) *There is such a thing as society*, London: Politicos, pp 30-7.

Durant, T., Fox, M., Taylor, C. and Walters, A. (1974) *No more tick: A Conservative solution to inflation*, London: Bow Group.

Dutton, D. (1991) *British politics since 1945: The rise and fall of consensus*, Oxford: Blackwell.

Eccleshall, R., Geoghegan, V., Hay, R. and Wilford, R. (1984) *Political ideologies*, London: Hutchinson.

Ellis, C. (2010) 'Mutualism and the reinvention of civil society: a conservative agenda?', in S. Griffiths and K. Hickson (eds) *British party politics and ideology after New Labour*, Basingstoke: Palgrave Macmillan, pp 138-49.

Enthoven, A. (1985) *Reflections on the management of the NHS*, London: National Provincial Trusts.

Evans, S. (2009) 'The not so odd couple: Margaret Thatcher and One Nation Conservatism', *Contemporary British History*, vol 23, no 1, pp 101-21.

Field, F. (1982) *Poverty and politics: The inside story of the CPAG campaigns in the 1970s*, London: Heinemann.

Field, F. and Piachaud, D. (1971) 'The poverty trap', *New Statesman*, 3 December, pp 772-3.

Fielding, S. (2009) 'Introduction: Cameron's Conservatives', *The Political Quarterly*, vol 80, no 2, pp 168-71.

Finlayson, G. (1994) *Citizen, state and social welfare in Britain, 1830-1990*, Oxford: Clarendon.

Fisher, A. (1974) *Must history repeat itself?*, London: Churchill Press.

Fisher, Sir H. (1973) *Report of the Committee on the Abuse of Social Security Benefits* (Fisher Report), Cmnd 5228, London: HMSO.

Flather, P. (1987) 'Pulling through – conspiracies, counterplots and how the SSRC escaped the axe in 1982', in M. Bulmer (ed) *Social science research and government: Comparative essays on Britain and the United States*, Cambridge: Cambridge University Press.

Fort, A. (2004) *Prof: The life of Frederick Lindemann*, London: Pimlico.

Fowler, N. (1991) *Ministers decide*, London: Chapmans.

Fowler, N. (2008) *A Political suicide*, London: Politicos.

Francis, M. (1996) 'Set the people free? Conservatives and the state, 1920-1960', in M. Francis and I. Zweiniger-Bargielowska (eds) *The Conservatives and British society 1880-1990*, Cardiff: University of Wales Press, pp 58-77.

Francis, M. (2012) '"A crusade to enfranchise the many": Thatcherism and the "property-owning democracy"', *Twentieth Century British History*, vol 23, no 2, pp 275-97.

Fraser, D. (2009) *The evolution of the British welfare state* (4th edn), Basingstoke: Palgrave Macmillan.

Freeden, M. (2003) *Ideology: A very short introduction*, Oxford: Oxford University Press.

Friedman, M. (1962) *Capitalism and freedom*, Chicago, IL: University of Chicago Press.

Friedman, M. and Friedman, R. (1990) *Free to choose*, New York, NY: Harvest.

Gamble, A. (1974) *The Conservative nation*, London: Routledge & Kegan Paul.

Garnett, M. (2005) 'Editor's foreword', in A. Sherman *Paradoxes of power*, Exeter: Imprint Academic, pp 9-17.

Garnett, M. and Hickson, K. (2009) *Conservative thinkers*, Manchester: Manchester University Press.

George, V. (1973) *Social security and society*, London: Routledge & Kegan Paul.

Gilbert, B.B. (1970) *British social policy 1914-1939*, London: Batsford.

Gilmour, I. (1978) *Inside right: A study of Conservatism*, London: Quartet.

Gilmour, I. (1982) *Dancing with dogma: Britain under Thatcherism*, London: Pocket Books.

Gilmour, I. and Garnett, M. (1998) *Whatever happened to the Tories? The Conservatives since 1945*, London: Fourth Estate.

Ginsburg, N. (2005) 'The privatization of council housing', *Critical Social Policy*, vol 25, no 1, pp 115-35.

Glennerster, H. (2007) *British social policy 1945 to the present* (3rd edn), Oxford: Blackwell.

Gove, M. (2013) 'Please sir, I just want to learn more', *Standpoint*, 55, September, 28-31.

Gray, J. (2009) *Gray's anatomy*, London: Allen Lane.

Green, D.G. (1993) *Reinventing civil society: The rediscovery of welfare without politics*, London: IEA Health and Welfare Unit.

Green, E.H.H. (2002) *Ideologies of conservatism*, Oxford: Oxford University Press.

Green, E.H.H. (2006) *Thatcher*, London: Hodder Arnold.

Greenleaf, W.H. (1983) *The British political tradition. Volume Two: The ideological heritage*, London: Routledge.

Grimley, M. (2012) 'Thatcherism, morality and religion', in B. Jackson and R. Saunders (eds) *Making Thatcher's Britain*, Cambridge: Cambridge University Press, pp 78-94.

Haidt, J. (2012) *The Righteous mind*, London: Allen Lane.

Harrington, M. (2010) *An independent review of the Work Capability Assessment*, London: Stationary Office.

Harrington, M. (2011) *An independent review of the Work Capability Assessment – Year Two*, London: Stationary Office.

Harrington, M. (2012) *An independent review of the Work Capability Assessment – Year Three*, London: Stationary Office.

Harris, B. (2004) *The origins of the British welfare state*, Basingstoke: Palgrave Macmillan.

Harris, J. (1997) *William Beveridge: A biography* (rev. edn), Oxford: Clarendon Press.

Harris, R. (2011) *The Conservatives: A history*, London: Bantam.

Harris, R. (2013) *Not for turning. The life of Margaret Thatcher*, London: Bantam.

Harrison, B. (2004) 'Joseph, Keith Sinjbhn, Baron Joseph (1918-1994)', *Oxford Dictionary of National Biography*, Oxford: Oxford University Press (http://oxforddnb.com/view/article/55063, accessed 3 November 2006).

Harrop, M. and Scammel, M. (1992) 'A tabloid war', in D. Butler and D. Kavanagh (eds) *The British General Election of 1992*, Basingstoke: Macmillan, pp 180-210.

Hay, C. (2010) 'Chronicles of a death foretold: the winter of discontent and the construction of the crisis of British Keynesianism', *Parliamentary Affairs*, 63, pp 446-70.

Hay, J.R. (1975) *The origins of the Liberal welfare reforms 1906-14* (rev. edn), London: Macmillan.

Hayek, F.A. (1944) *The road to serfdom*, London: Routledge.

Hayton, R. (2012) *Reconstructing conservatism? The Conservative Party in opposition, 1997-2010*, Manchester: Manchester University Press.

Heffer, S. (2012) 'The role of government and the state of the economy', in Lord Howard of Rising (ed) *Enoch at 100*, London: Biteback.

Hennessy, P. (2014) 'Reflections with Peter Hennessy', BBC Radio 4, (13 August 2014).

Heppell, T. (2014) *The Tories*, London: Bloomsbury.

Heppell, T. and Hill, M. (2009) 'Transcending Thatcherism? Ideology and the Conservative leadership mantle of David Cameron', *The Political Quarterly*, vol 80, no 3, pp 388-99.

Heywood, A. (2007) *Political ideologies: An introduction* (4th edn), Basingstoke: Palgrave Macmillan.

Hickson, K. (ed) (2005) *The political thought of the Conservative party since 1945*, Basingstoke: Palgrave Macmillan.

Hickson, K. (2008) 'Conservatism and the poor: Conservative party attitudes to poverty and inequality since the 1970s', *British Politics*, vol 4, no 3, pp 341-62.

Hickson, K. (2010) 'Thatcherism, poverty and social justice', *The Journal of Poverty and Social Justice*, vol 18, no 2, pp 135-45.

Hills, J. (1998) 'Housing: a decent home within the reach of every family?', in H. Glennerster and J. Le Grand (eds) *The state of welfare* (2nd edn), Oxford: Oxford University Press.

Hills, J. (2014) *Good times, bad times: The welfare myth of them and us*, Bristol: Policy Press.

Hinchingbrooke, Viscount, A. (1943) *Full speed ahead! Essays in Tory reform*, London: Tory Reform Committee.

HM Government (2011) *Opening doors, breaking barriers: A strategy for social mobility*, London: Stationary Office.

HM Government (2014) *Child poverty strategy*, London: Stationary Office.

HM Treasury (1979) *The government's expenditure plans, 1980-81*, London: HMSO.

Hoffman, J.D. (1964) *The Conservative Party in opposition 1945-51*, London: Macgibbon & Kee.

Hogg, Q. (1945) *The left was never right*, London: Faber & Faber.

Hogg, Q. (1947) *The case for Conservatism*, West Drayton: Penguin.

Home office (1959) *Penal Policy in a changing society*, London: HMSO.

Hoskyns, J. and Stauss, N. (1977) *Stepping stones*, www.margaretthatcher.org/document/111771

Houghton, D. (1967) *Paying for the social services*, London: IEA.

Howard, A. (1987) *RAB: The life of R.A. Butler*, London: Jonathan Cape.

Howard of Rising, Lord (ed) (2012) *Enoch at 100*, London: Biteback.

Howe, G. (1961) 'Reform of the social services: Conservatism in the post-welfare state', in L. Beaton, A. Campbell, D. Fairbairn, G. Howe, G. Hodgson, D. Howell, J. Lemkin, R. Lewis and T. Raison (eds) *Principles in practice*, London: Conservative Political Centre, pp 58-73.

Howe, G. (1965a) *In place of Beveridge*, London: Conservative Political Centre.

Howe, G. (1965b) 'The waiting-list society', in Bow Group *The Conservative opportunity: Fifteen Bow Group essays on tomorrow's Toryism*, London: Batsford.

Howe, G. (1990) Resignation statement, 13 November, *Parliamentary Debates*, 180, cols 461-5.

Howe, G. (2006) 'Can 364 economists all be wrong?', in H. Davies (ed) *The Chancellors' tales*, Cambridge: Polity Press, pp 76-112.

Hultin, A. (2009) 'Profit is the key to success in "Swedish schools"', *The Spectator*, 3 October, p 17.

Ishkanian, A. and Szreter, S. (eds), (2012) *The Big Society debate*, Cheltenham: Edward Elgar.

Jacka, K., Cox, C. and Marks, J. (1975) *Rape of Reason: The corruption of the Polytechnic of North London*, London: Churchill Press.

Jackson, B. (2012) 'The think-tank archipelago: Thatcherism and neo-liberalism', in B. Jackson and R. Saunders (eds) *Making Thatcher's Britain*, Cambridge: Cambridge University Press, pp 43-61.

Jarvis, M. (2005) *Conservative governments, morality and social change in affluent Britain, 1957-64*, Manchester: Manchester University Press.

Jefferys, K. (1991) *The Churchill coalition and wartime politics 1940-1945*, Manchester: Manchester University Press.

Jefferys, K. (1997) *Retreat from New Jerusalem: British politics, 1951-64*, Basingstoke: Macmillan.

Jones, H. (2000) '"This is magnificent!" 300,000 houses a year and the Tory revival after 1945', *Contemporary British History*, vol 14, no 1, pp 99-121.

Jones, H. and Kandiah, M. (eds) (1996) *The myth of consensus*, Basingstoke: Macmillan.

Jordan, B. (1973) *Paupers*, London: Routledge & Kegan Paul.

Joseph, K. (1974) Speech to the Edgbaston Conservative Constituency Association, Grand Hotel, Birmingham, 19 October (available from the Margaret Thatcher Foundation at http://margaretthatcher.org/document/101830).

Joseph, K. (1975) *Reversing the trend: a critical re-appraisal of Conservative Economic and Social Policies*, Chichester: Barry Rose.

Kavanagh, D. (1992) 'The postwar consensus', *Twentieth Century British History*, vol 3, no 2, pp 175-90.

Kavanagh, D. (1996) 'The fatal choice: the calling of the February 1974 election', in S. Ball and A. Seldon (eds), *The Heath Government 1970-74 a Reappraisal*, London: Longman, pp 351-70.

Kavanagh, D. and Morris, P. (1994) *Consensus politics from Attlee to Major* (2nd edn), Oxford: Blackwell.

Kavanagh, D. and Seldon, A. (eds) (1994) *The Major effect*, London: Macmillan.

Kincaid, J.C. (1975) *Poverty and equality in Britain* (rev. edn), Harmondsworth: Penguin.

King, P. (2011) *The new politics: Liberal Conservatism or same old Tories?*, Bristol: Policy Press.

Kirkby, J. (2009) 'From broken families to the broken society', *The Political Quarterly*, vol 80, no 2, pp 243-7.

Klein, R. (1995) *The new politics of the NHS* (3rd edn), London: Longman.

Knight, C. (1990) *The making of Tory education policy in post-war Britain, 1950-86*, Brighton: Falmer Press.

Kramnick, I. and Sheerman, B. (1993) *Harold Laski: A life on the left*, London: Hamish Hamilton.

Kwarteng, K., Patel, P., Rabb, D., Skidmore, C. and Truss, L. (2011) *After the coalition*, London: Biteback.

Kwarteng, K., Patel, P., Rabb, D., Skidmore, C. and Truss, L. (2012) *Britannia unchained*, London: Palgrave Macmillan.

Kynaston, D. (2013) *Modernity Britain: Opening the box, 1957-59*, London: Bloomsbury.

Law, R. (1950) *Return from utopia*, London: Faber & Faber.

Laws, D. (2010) *22 days in May: The birth of the Lib Dem-Conservative coalition government*, London: Biteback.

Lawson, N. (1992) *The view from No. 11: Memoirs of a Tory radical*, London: Bantam.

Laybourn, K. (1995) *The foundations of British social policy and the welfare state*, Keele: Keele University Press.

Le Grand, J. (2003) *Motivation, agency and public policy*, Oxford: Oxford University Press.

Leach, R. (2009) *Political ideology in Britain*, Basingstoke: Palgrave Macmillan.

Lee, S. and Beech, M. (eds) (2009) *The Conservatives under David Cameron*, Basingstoke: Palgrave Macmillan.

Lees, D.S. (1961) *Health through choice*, London: IEA.

Lees, D.S. (1967) 'Poor families and fiscal reform', *Lloyds Bank Review*, October, pp 1-15.

Letwin, O. (2008) 'From economic revolution to social revolution', *Soundings*, 40, Winter, pp 112-22.

Lilley, P., Hodgson, P. and Waterson, N. (1973) *Alternative manifesto*, London: Bow Group.

Lipsey, D. (2012) *In the corridors of power*, London: Biteback.

Litchfield, P. (2013) *An independent review of the Work Capability Assessment —year four*, London: Stationary Office.

Lowe, R. (1989) 'Resignation at the Treasury: the Social Services Committee and the failure to reform the welfare state, 1955-57', *Journal of Social Policy*, vol 18, no 4, pp 505-26.

Lowe, R. (1990) 'The second world war, consensus, and the foundation of the welfare state', *Twentieth Century British History*, vol 1, no 2, pp 152-82.

Lowe, R. (1996) 'The social policy of the Heath government', in S. Ball and A. Seldon (eds) *The Heath government 1970-74: A reappraisal*, London: Longman, pp 191-214.

Lowe, R. (2005) *The welfare state in Britain since 1945* (3rd edn), Basingstoke: Palgrave Macmillan.

Lowe, R.A. (2004) 'Education policy', in A. Seldon and K. Hickson (eds) *New Labour, Old Labour: The Wilson and Callaghan governments, 1974-9*, London: Routledge, pp 123-38.

Ludham, S. and Smith, M.J. (1996) *Contemporary British Conservatism*, Basingstoke: Macmillan.

Macleod, I. and Maude, A. (eds) (1950) *One Nation: A Tory approach to social problems*, London: Conservative Political Centre.

McManus, M. (2010) *Tory pride and prejudice: The Conservative Party and homosexual law reform*, London: Biteback.

Macmillan, H. (1933) *Reconstruction: A plea for a national policy*, London: Macmillan.

Macmillan, H. (1938) *The middle way*, London: Macmillan.

Macnicol, J. (1980) *The movement for family allowances, 1918-45: A study in social policy development*, London: Heinemann.

Major, J. (2000) *John Major: The autobiography*, London: HarperCollins.

Malik, S. (2011) 'Young jobless told to work without pay or lose benefits', *The Guardian*, 16 November.

Malpass, P. (2005) *Housing and the welfare state*, Basingstoke: Palgrave Macmillan.

Marsh, S. (2013) 'What were Iain Duncan Smith's welfare reforms really about?', *The Guardian*, 5 September.

Marshall, P. and Laws, D. (eds) (2004) *The Orange Book*, London: Profile Books.

Marwick, A. (2003) *British society since 1945* (4th edn), London: Penguin.

Matthew, H.C.G. (2011) 'Buchan, John, first Baron Tweedsmuir (1875-1940)', *Oxford Dictionary of National Bibliography*, Oxford: Oxford University Press (www.oxfordsnb.com/view/article/32145, accessed 28 May 2014).

Maude, A. (1966) 'Winter of Tory discontent', *The Spectator*, 14 January, 7177, p 39.

Maude, A. (1968) 'The end of consensus politics', *The Spectator*, 10 May, 7298, pp 627-8.

Maude, A. (ed) (1977) *The right approach to the economy*, London: Conservative Central Office (http://margaretthatcher.org/document/112551).

Maude, F. (2005) 'Centre', in K. Hickson (ed) *The Political thought of the Conservative Party since 1945*, Basingstoke: Palgrave Macmillan, pp 51-68.

Maude, F. (2013) 'Foreword', in R. Shorthouse and G. Stagg (eds) *Tory modernisation 2.0*, London: Bright Blue, pp 2-4.

Mead, L. (1986) *Beyond entitlement: The social obligations of citizenship*, New York, NY: Free Press.

Milne, S. (2004) *The enemy within*, (3rd edn), London: Verso.

Ministry of Health (1944) *A National Health Service*, Cmd 6502, London: HMSO.

Ministry of Health (1962) *A ten-year Hospital plan for England and Wales*, Cmnd 1604, London: HMSO.

Ministry of Reconstruction (1944a) *Employment policy*, Cmd 6527, London: HMSO.

Ministry of Reconstruction (1944b) *Social insurance, Part I*, Cmd 6550, London: HMSO.

Ministry of Reconstruction (1944c) *Part II, Workmen's compensation*, Cmd 6551, London: HMSO.

Ministry of Reconstruction (1945) *Housing*, Cmd 6609, London: HMSO.

Minouge, K. (2011) 'Disinterest rates. Review of Norman, J. (2011) *The Big Society*', *Times Literary Supplement*, 14 January, p 5.

Mishra, R. (1977) *Society and social policy*, London: Macmillan.

Montgomerie, T. (2004) *Whatever happened to compassionate Conservatism?*, London: Centre for Social Justice.

Moore, C. (2014) *Margaret Thatcher: The authorized biography. Volume one: Not for turning*, London: Allen Lane.

Murray, C. (1980) *Losing ground*, New York, NY: Basic Books.

National Audit Office (2013) Report by the Comptroller and Auditor General, *Universal Credit: Early Progress*, HC.621, Session 2013-14, 5 September 2013, London: Stationary Office.

No Turning Back Group (1993) *Who benefits? Reinventing social security*, London: No Turning Back Group.

Norman, J. (2010) *The Big Society*, Buckingham: University of Buckingham Press.

Norman, J. (2014) *Edmund Burke: The visionary who invented modern politics*, London: William Collins.

Norman, J. and Ganesh, J. (2006) *Compassionate Conservatism*, London: Policy Exchange.

Norman, J., Ussher, K. and Alexander, D. (2007) *From here to fraternity: Perspectives on social responsibility*, London: CentreForum.

Norton, P. (ed) (1996a) *The Conservative Party*, Hemel Hempstead: Prentice Hall/Harvester Wheatsheaf.

Norton, P. (1996b) 'History of the party III: Heath, Thatcher and Major', in P. Norton (ed) *The Conservative Party*, Hemel Hempstead: Prentice Hall/Harvester Wheatsheaf, pp 52-82.

Norton, Lord, P. (2009) 'David Cameron and Tory success: Architect or by-stander' in S. Lee and M. Beech (eds), *The Conservatives under David Cameron*, Basingstoke: Palgrave Macmillan, pp 31-43.

Oakeshott, M. (1962) *Rationalism in politics and other essays*, London: Methuen.

O'Hara, K. (2011) *Conservatism*, London: Reaktion Books.

Olasky, M. (2000) *Compassionate Conservatism*, New York, NY: Free Press.

One Nation Group (1959) *The responsible society*, London: Conservative Political Centre.

Osborne, G. (2009) 'I'm with the progressives', *The Guardian*, 7 May.

Osborne, G. (2011) 'We've ensured tax cheats have no place to hide', *The Observer*, 28 August.

O'Sullivan, J. and Hodgson, P. (1971) *Goodbye to nationalization*, London: Churchill Press.

O'Sullivan, N. (1999) 'Conservatism', in R. Eatwell and A. Wright (eds) *Contemporary political ideologies* (2nd edn), London: Pinter, pp 51-79.

Page, R. (1971) *The benefits racket*, London: Tom Stacey.

Page, R.M. (1997) 'Young single mothers', in H. Jones (ed) *Towards a classless society*, London: Routledge, pp 151-78.

Page, R.M. (2007) *Revisiting the welfare state*, Buckingham: Open University Press/McGraw-Hill.

Page, R.M. (2009) 'With love from me to you. The new Democrats, new Labour and the politics of welfare reform', *Journal of Poverty and Social Justice*, vol 17, no 2, pp 149-58.

Page, R.M. (2010a) 'David Cameron's modern Conservative approach to poverty and social justice: towards one nation or two?', *Journal of Poverty and Social Justice*, vol 18, no 2, pp 147-60.

Page, R.M. (2010b) 'The changing face of social administration', *Social Policy & Administration*, vol 44, no 3, pp 326-42.

Page, R.M. (2011) 'The emerging blue (and orange) health strategy: continuity or change?', in S. Lee and M. Beech (eds) *The Cameron-Clegg government*, Basingstoke: Palgrave Macmillan, pp 89-104.

Page, R.M. (2014) '"Progressive" turns in post-1945 Conservative social policy', *Political Studies Review*, vol 12, no 1, pp 17-28.

Park, A., Clery, E., Curtice, J., Phillips, M. and Utting, D. (eds) (2012) *British Social Attitudes 28*, London: Sage Publications.

Park, A., Bryson, C., Clery, E., Curtice, J. and Phillips, M. (eds) (2014) *British Social Attitudes 30*, London: Sage Publications.

Peacock, A. and Wiseman, J. (1964) *Education for democrats: A study of the financing of education in a free society*, London: IEA.

Pimlott, B. (1988) 'The myth of consensus', in L.M. Smith (ed), *The making of Britain: Echoes of greatness*, Basingstoke: Macmillan, pp 129-41.

Pinker, R.A. (2003) 'The Conservative tradition of social welfare', in P. Alcock, A. Erskine and M. May (eds) *The Student's companion to social policy*, Oxford: Blackwell, pp 78-84.

Pitchford, M. (2011) *The Conservative party and the extreme right 1945-75*, Manchester: Manchester University Press.

Poinasmy, R. (2013) *The True Cost of Austerity and Inequality: UK Case Study*, Oxford: Oxfam.

Powell, E. and Maude, A. (eds) (1954) *Change is our ally*, London: Conservative Political Centre.

Prest, A.R. (1960) *Financing university education: A study of university fees and loans to students in Great Britain*, London: IEA.

Raison, T. (1990) *Tories and the welfare state*, Basingstoke: Macmillan.

Ramsden, J. (1980) *The making of Conservative Party policy: The Conservative Research Department since 1929*, London: Longman.

Ramsden, J. (1995) *The age of Churchill and Eden, 1940-1957*, London: Longman.

Ramsden, J. (1996) *The winds of change: Macmillan to Heath, 1957-1975*, London: Longman.

Reeves, R. (2009) 'It's hard to believe, but the Tories really are progressives', *The Observer*, 2 August, p 23

Ridley, N. (1991) *My style of government*, London: Hutchinson.

Ritschel, D. (1995) 'Macmillan', in V. George and R. Page (eds), *Modern thinkers on welfare*, Hemel Hempstead, Prentice Hall/Harvester Wheatsheaf, pp 51-68.

Robin, C. (2011) *The reactionary mind*, Oxford: Oxford University Press.

Roth, A. (1972) *Heath and the Heathmen*, London: Routledge & Kegan Paul.

Sandbrook, D. (2005) *Never had it so good*, London: Little Brown.

Sandbrook, D. (2010) *State of emergency. The way we were: Britain, 1970-1974*, London: Allen Lane.

Sandbrook, D. (2012) *Seasons in the sun: The battle for Britain, 1974-79*, London: Allen Lane.

Schofield, C. (2013) *Enoch Powell and the making of postcolonial Britain*, Cambridge: Cambridge University Press.

Scholefield, A. and Frost, G. (2011) *Too 'nice' to be Tories? How the modernisers have damaged the Conservative Party*, London: Social Affairs Unit.

Scruton, R. (2001) *The meaning of Conservatism* (3rd edn), Basingstoke: Palgrave Macmillan.

Scruton, R. (2013) 'Postmodern Tories', *Prospect*, March, pp 34-6.

Scruton, R. (2014) *How to be a conservative*, London: Bloomsbury.

Seawright, D. (2005) 'One Nation', in K. Hickson (ed) *The political thought of the Conservative Party since 1945*, Basingstoke: Palgrave Macmillan, pp 69-90.

Seawright, D. (2010) *The British Conservative Party and One Nation politics*, London: Continuum.

Seebohm, F. (1968) *Report of the Committee on Local Authority and Allied Personal Social Services* (Seebohm Report), Cmnd 3703, London: HMSO.

Selbourne, D. (2013) 'Into the new blue void', *New Statesman*, 29 March-11 April, pp 29-33.

Seldon, A. (1994) 'Consensus: a debate too long?', *Parliamentary Affairs*, vol 47, no 4, pp 501-14.

Seldon, A. (1996) 'The Heath government in history', in S. Ball and A. Seldon (eds) *The Heath government 1970-74: A reappraisal*, London: Longman, pp 1-19.

Seldon, A.F. (1957) *Pensions in a free society*, London: IEA.

Seldon, A.F (1967a) *Universal or selective benefits*, London: IEA.

Seldon, A.F (1967b) *Taxation and welfare*, London: IEA.

Seldon, A.F (1969) *After the NHS*, London: IEA.

Self, R.C. (2006) *Neville Chamberlain: A biography*, Aldershot: Ashgate.

Sewill, B. (2009) 'Policy-making for Heath', in A. Cooke (ed) *Tory policy-making*, Eastbourne: Manor Creative, pp 55-7.

Sheard, S. (2013) *The passionate economist*, Bristol: Policy Press.

Shepherd, R. (1997) *Enoch Powell*, London: Pimlico.

Sherman, A. (2005) *Paradoxes of power*, Exeter: Imprint Academic.

Shore, P. (1952) *The real nature of conservatism*, London: Labour Party.

Skidelsky, R. (2014) 'It is indefensible for Osborne to cut the welfare state as if it were the cause of the crisis', *New Statesman*, 12-18 December, p.21

Snowdon, P. (2010) *Back from the brink*, London: HarperPress.

Social Mobility and Child Poverty Commission (2013) *Social mobility and child poverty in Great Britain*, London: Social Mobility and Child Poverty Commission.

Steadman Jones, D. (2012) *Masters of the universe: Hayek, Friedman and the birth of neoliberal politics*, Princeton, NJ: Princeton University Press.

Stewart, J. (1999) *The battle for health. A political history of the Socialist Medical Association, 1930-51*, Aldershot: Ashgate.

Streeter, G. (ed) (2002) *There is such a thing as society*, London: Politicos.

Sullivan, M. (1996) *The development of the British welfare state*, Hemel Hempstead: Prentice-Hall.

Sutcliffe-Braithwaite, F. (2012) 'Neo-liberalism and morality in the making of Thatcherite social policy', *The Historical Journal*, vol 55, no 2, pp 497-520.

Taylor, R. (1996) 'The Heath government and industrial relations: myth and reality', in S. Ball and A. Seldon (eds) *The Heath government 1970-74: A reappraisal*, London: Longman, pp 161-90.

Temple, W. (1942) *Christianity and the social order*, London: Penguin.

Thane, P. (1982) *The foundations of the welfare state*, London: Longman.

Thatcher, M. (2011a) *The path to power*, London: Harper.

Thatcher, M. (2011b) *The Downing Street years*, London: Harper.

Thorpe, A. (2009) *Parties at war*, Oxford: Oxford University Press.

Thorpe, D.R. (2004) *Eden: The life and times of Anthony Eden first Earl of Avon, 1897-1977*, London: Pimlico.

Thorpe, D.R. (2007) *Alec Douglas-Home*, London: Politicos.

Thorpe, D.R. (2010) *Supermac: The life of Harold Macmillan*, London: Chattus and Windus.

Timmins, N. (2001) *The five giants* (rev. edn), London: HarperCollins.

Timmins, N. (2012) *Never again? The story of the Health and Social Care Act 2012*, London: Institute for Government/Kings Fund.

Torrance, D. (2010) *Noel Skelton and the property-owning democracy*, London: Biteback.

Tory Reform Committee (1943) *Forward by the right*, London: Tory Reform Committee.

Tory Reform Committee (1944) *One year's work*, London: Tory Reform Committee.

Toye, R. (2013) *The roar of the lion*, Oxford: Oxford University Press.

Turner, J. (1995) 'A land fit for Tories to live in: the political ecology of the British Conservative Party, 1944-94', *Contemporary European History*, vol 4, no 2, pp 189-208.

Vaisey, E. (ed) (2002) *The blue book on health*, London: Politicos.

Vaisey, E., Boles, N. and Gove, M. (eds) (2001) *A blue tomorrow*, London: Politicos.

Vincent, A. (1992) *Modern political ideologies*, Oxford: Blackwell.

Vinen, R. (2009) *Thatcher's Britain*, London: Simon & Schuster.

Waldegrave, W. (2015) *A different kind of weather: A memoir*, London: Constable.

Walsha, R. (2000) 'The One Nation Group: a Tory approach to backbench politics and organisation, 1950-55', *Twentieth Century British History*, vol 11, no 2, pp 183-214.

Walsha, R. (2003) 'The One Nation Group and One Nation Conservatism, 1950-2002', *Contemporary British History*, vol 17, no 2, pp 69-120.

Watson, R. (2012) 'Jimmy Carr tax arrangements "morally wrong", says Cameron', *The Times*, 21 June, p 8.

Webster, C. (1988) *The health services since the war, volume 1: Problems of health care. The National Health Service before 1957*, London: HMSO.

Webster, C. (2002) *The National Health Service* (2nd edn), Oxford: Oxford University Press.

Welshman, J. (2012) *From transmitted deprivation to social exclusion: Policy, poverty and parenting*, Bristol: Policy Press.

Welshman, J. (2013) *Underclass: A history of the excluded since 1880*, London: Bloomsbury Academic.

West, E.G. (1965) *Education and the state*, London: IEA.

White, R.J. (ed) (1950) *The Conservative tradition*, London: Nicholas Kaye.

Wickham Jones, M. (1992) 'Monetaism and its critics: the university economists' protest of 1981', *The Political Quarterly*, 63, pp 171-85.

Willetts, D. (1992) *Modern Conservatism*, London: Penguin.

Willetts, D. (2002) 'The new contours of British politics', in G. Streeter (ed) *There is such a thing as society*, London: Politicos, pp 52-9.

Willetts, D. (2009) 'The meaning of Margaret', *Prospect*, May, pp 32-6.

Williamson, P. (1999) *Stanley Baldwin*, Cambridge: Cambridge University Press.

Willman, J. (1994) 'The civil service', in D. Kavanagh and A. Seldon (eds) *The Major effect*, London: Macmillan, pp 64-92.

Wintour, P. and Butler, P. (2013) 'Iain Duncan Smith defends use of statistics over benefits cap', *The Guardian*, 15 July.

Wood, J. (ed) (1965) *A nation not afraid: The thinking of Enoch Powell*, London: Batsford.

Worsthorne, P. (1978) 'Too much freedom', in M. Cowling, M (ed) *Conservative essays*, London: Cassell, pp 141-54.

Young, H. (1993) *One of us* (rev. edn), London: Pan.

Young, T. (2013) 'The best leader Labour never had', *The Spectator*, 15 June, pp 14-15.

Young, T. (2014) *Prisoner of the Blob: Why most education experts are wrong about nearly everything*, London: Civitas.

Ziegler, P. (2011) *Edward Heath*, London: HarperPress.

Zweiniger-Bargielowska, I. (2000) *Austerity in Britain: Rationing, controls and consumption 1939-1955*, Oxford: Oxford University Press.

Index

Note: Page numbers followed by '*n*' suffix refer to notes.